W9-AEL-914

Cyprus

Vassos Karageorghis

Cyprus

FROM THE STONE AGE
TO THE ROMANS

WITH 137 ILLUSTRATIONS

THAMES AND HUDSON

Ancient Peoples and Places
GENERAL EDITOR: GLYN DANIEL

Any copy of this book issued by the publisher as a paperback is sold
subject to the condition that it shall not, by way of trade or otherwise,
be lent, resold, hired out or otherwise circulated without the
publisher's prior consent in any form of binding or cover other than
that in which it is published, and without a similar condition including
these words being imposed on a subsequent purchaser.

© 1982 Thames and Hudson Ltd, London

First published in the USA in 1982 by Thames and Hudson Inc.,
500 Fifth Avenue, New York, New York 10110

Library of Congress Catalog Card Number 81–86679

All rights reserved. No part of this publication may be reproduced or
transmitted in any form or by any means, electronic or mechanical,
including photocopy, recording or any other information storage and retrieval
system, without permission in writing from the publisher.

Printed in Great Britain by BAS Printers Limited,
Over Wallop, Hampshire.
Bound in Great Britain

Contents

Preface

Interest in Cypriot art and archaeology has increased considerably during recent years for a number of reasons. Intensive excavations have led to a great increase in the number of publications on Cyprus; interest among a wider public has been aroused by numerous exhibitions of ancient Cypriot art in various European countries and in the USA, organized by the Department of Antiquities since independence; and new trends in archaeological studies, which link Cyprus with both the Aegean and the Near East, have drawn a large number of younger scholars to seek research subjects related to Cyprus.

Following the character of the 'Ancient Peoples and Places' series, more attention is given in this book to the archaeology than to the history of Cyprus, since most of the island's past is illustrated only by material remains. There has been little change in our knowledge of historical periods, but a very important contribution is the collection made by K. Hadjiioannou of Greek literary and epigraphical sources which refer to Cyprus. The present volume is an attempt to synthesize the results of both the earlier and the more recent work on the whole timespan from the Neolithic to the Roman periods, and to describe the latest excavations and new aspects of research.

The excavations of the Swedish Cyprus Expedition in the early 1930s revolutionized theories concerning the archaeology and history of Cyprus. The *SCE* excavation reports and the synthesis volumes presented a copious new source of information about ancient Cyprus. Since the island's independence in 1960 there has been an additional boost to archaeological research in Cyprus, both from the Department of Antiquities and foreign missions. The prehistoric period has received most attention, many of the problems which were unanswered after the Swedish excavations since having been solved. The Neolithic and Chalcolithic periods are now illustrated by excavation results from several sites, and improved scientific dating methods have raised considerably the chronology of the initial phases of the Cypriot Neolithic. Though the Early Bronze Age has not received much attention in recent years, research in the Middle and Late Bronze Ages has opened new horizons for their study and has emphasized particularly the interrelations between Cyprus and other countries of the Near East on the one hand, and the Aegean on the other. In fact we now know far more about the archaeology of Late Bronze Age Cyprus than any other period of the island's prehistory. It is unfortunate, however, that inscriptions in Cypro-Minoan still retain their secrets, despite numerous efforts to decipher them. Considerable light has also been thrown on the 'Dark Ages' of the 11th and 10th centuries BC, mainly as a result of recent excavations at Alaas and Palaepaphos. In addition, the impact of the Phoenicians on Cyprus is now far better understood, as a result of the extensive excavations at Kition, their main centre. The necropolis of Salamis initiated a new era in 'Homeric studies', and the splendour of the 'royal' tombs has had an impact on archaeology and the history of art reaching far beyond the limits of Cyprus.

Though much material has been accumulated to illustrate the Classical and Hellenistic periods, there have been no excavations of settlements dating from these periods, which hinders further study. It was hoped that excavations at Salamis and Soloi, which began in the 1960s, would have filled this gap in our knowledge, but their discontinuation in 1974, as a result of the invasion of Cyprus and the subsequent occupation of her northern territories, makes any further research there impossible.

Salamis, Kourion, Palaepaphos and Nea Paphos have amplified our understanding of the Roman period, and their public buildings, statues and inscriptions have provided considerable evidence for Roman art, architecture and institutions in Cyprus.

The final publication of excavation reports has been prompt in many cases, but other sites have been discussed only in preliminary reports. In dealing with the various archaeological periods the reader is usually referred to recent publications, where references to the earlier literature are found.

The author hopes that this synthesis will prove of some help to those young scholars who, no doubt, will soon take the study of ancient Cyprus further in their own research, both in the field and in the library.

Acknowledgments

This book owes a great deal to a large number of people, too numerous to be thanked by name. First of all to all archaeologists, both Cypriot and foreign, who are currently excavating in Cyprus and who have promptly supplied information and illustrations relating to their excavations. A number of colleagues discussed with the writer particular topics of the archaeology of Cyprus and offered advice and advance information in fields of their own research, mainly with regard to the prehistoric periods. We mention in particular Dr A. le Brun, Dr E. Peltenburg, Dr Stuart Swiny and Dr Ian Todd. Professor J. N. Coldstream and Professor Anthony Snodgrass discussed and advised on matters concerning the Early Iron Age. Dr Carolyn Elliott read the text and made a provisional editing; she also discussed with the writer various topics and offered valuable advice. Dr Sylvia Törkvist kindly prepared the index at very short notice.

Colleagues in the Department of Antiquities and the Cyprus Museum offered their collaboration and assistance. We are particularly indebted to members of the technical staff of the Department of Antiquities for most of the photographs (Xenophon Michael) and drawings (Elias Markou and Chrysilios Polykarpou). Yiannis Hadjisavvas offered valuable technical assistance during the preparation of the text and illustrations.

Last but not least our thanks go to Professor Glyn Daniel, General Editor of this series, who first suggested a volume on Cyprus and invited the present author to write it.

Chronology

The chronology of Cypriot prehistory is rapidly changing in the light of new excavations and further C14 dating and calibration of the results. It is too early yet, however, to have a consensus, and we therefore give below the main trends. It should be stated that the lack of excavations for certain periods with absolute dating makes some of these dates arbitrary to a large extent. Although most of the earliest calibrated C14 dates fall within the second half of the 7th millennium BC, the beginning of the Cypriot culture sequence must be earlier because the Khirokitia culture appears fully developed. For the Neolithic and Chalcolithic periods the apparent discrepancy between the C14 dates published by P. Dikaios in *SCE* IV.IA and those in Table A below is due to the calibration of Dikaios' materials.

Table A

Neolithic I (Khirokitia)		7000/6800–6000 BC
Lacuna in C14 dates between aceramic Khirokitia and Sotira culture		
Neolithic II (Sotira)		4500–3900/3800 BC*
Chalcolithic	I–III	3900/3800–2900/2500 BC
Early Bronze Age	I	2500–2075 BC
(or Early Cypriot)	II	2075–2000 BC
	III	2000–1900 BC
Middle Bronze Age	I	1900–1800 BC
(or Middle Cypriot)	II	1800–1725 BC
	III	1725–1650 BC
Late Bronze Age	IA	1650–1575 BC
(or Late Cypriot)	IB	1575–1475 BC
	IIA	1475–1400 BC
	IIB	1400–1325 BC
	IIC	1325–1225 BC
	IIIA	1225–1190 BC
	IIIB	1190–1150 BC
	IIIC	1150–1050 BC
Geometric	I	1050–950 BC
(or Cypro-Geometric)	II	950–850 BC
	III	850–750 BC
Archaic	I	750–600 BC
(or Cypro-Archaic)	II	600–475 BC
Classical	I	475–400 BC
(or Cypro-Classical)	II	400–325 BC
Hellenistic	I	325–150 BC
	II	150–50 BC
Roman	I	50 BC–AD 150
	II	AD 150–AD 250
	III	From about AD 250

* Differences are due to marked regional variations.

(*Note*: The dates for the Bronze Age have mainly been suggested by R. S. Merrillees, in *Report of the Department of Antiquities*, Cyprus 1977, 33ff. For the Iron Age we follow Gjerstad's dates (*Swedish Cyprus Expedition* vol. IV: 2), with the exception of the initial date for the Cypro-Archaic I period, which most scholars now agree to have been *c.* 750 B C.)

Table B

Early Bronze Age	I A	3200/2900–2850/2750 B C
(or Early Cypriot)	I B	2850/2750–2700/2600 B C
	I C	2700/2600–2400/2300 B C
Early Bronze Age	II	2400/2300–2250/2150 B C
(or Early Cypriot)	III	2250/2150–1900/1800 B C

(*Note*: The above dates are suggested by E. Gjerstad in *Report of the Department of Antiquities* 1980, 15f. He considers the 'Philia Culture' as the initial date of the Early Cypriot period, while others, including R. S. Merrillees and S. Swiny, consider it as part of the Chalcolithic period, beginning *c.* 2500 B C.)

1
Geographical introduction

An island the size of Cyprus could well have been condemned to eternal oblivion and isolation had it not been for her privileged geographical position in the East Mediterranean, in approximately the centre of the 'civilized' ancient world and on the threshold between the Orient and the Occident. At the dawn of her prehistory, before man could cross the seas with fairly large boats, her only connections were with her immediate neighbours: the southern coast of Asia Minor to the north, and the Syro-Palestinian coast to the east. On clear days the coast of Cyprus is visible from both these regions and a sea-crossing in small rafts would have been possible, if dangerous. For more than four millennia, from the beginning of the Neolithic period to the Middle Bronze Age (c. 7000–1650 BC), it is less a question of trade or cultural relations with neighbouring countries, than of settlers who came to seek their fortunes on the 'green island' which they could see from their own coasts, and who were moved by curiosity and the hope that nature would provide a better living across the sea. Thus, in the first millennia of her settlement, the island had received successive waves of immigrants who formed the core of the Cypriot people, the *Eteocypriots*.

From the Bronze Age onwards – when it was technically possible to cross the Mediterranean from the Aegean to the coast of Syria and Palestine, and from southern Anatolia to the Nile Delta – Cyprus found herself in the midst of 'international' trade routes, with all the ensuing beneficial and adverse consequences. With the rise of empires and powerful nations, whose aim was to expand their territory or increase their political power and wealth by controlling 'international' trade in the East Mediterranean, Cyprus became a bone of contention between foreign powers attracted by her unique strategic position. When her rich copper ore resources began to be exploited her importance increased even more, as she now served a dual role: a direct source of wealth and ideal centre for trade in time of peace, and a key strategic position in time of war. Although methods have changed during the five millennia which have elapsed since the Bronze Age, the basic character of relations between Cyprus and the rest of the world has remained the same. Empires, great powers and groups of nations still aim to expand their political and economic power, and the Mediterranean countries have never lost their attraction for those whose ambition is to dominate. Copper may have lost its importance in modern times, and the oil of the Middle East may have replaced it as the key commodity for exploitation in peace time and as a source of strength in war; but Cyprus' destiny remains unchanged: in the midst of international antagonism and rivalries she plays her own vital role in every development in the East Mediterranean and beyond. It is significant, therefore, that her importance in history is out of all proportion to her size.

With an area of 3584 sq. miles Cyprus is the third-largest island in the Mediterranean after Sicily and Sardinia, and is slightly larger than Crete. Her maximum length, east-west, is 138 miles and her maximum width, north-south, 60 miles. Her coastline offers good natural harbours, and did so even more in antiquity when inlets and river mouths which have since silted up served as waterways. Towns such as Enkomi, Kition and Hala Sultan Tekké must have had inner harbours through the navigable mouths of rivers, lakes and marshes, all of which have disappeared today. The proximity of the mainland encouraged maritime connections with all her neighbours: the distance from the northern coast to the southern coast of Asia Minor is 43 miles; from Cape Andreas to Latakia on the Syrian coast 76 miles; from Larnaca to Port Said in Egypt 264 miles, and to Piraeus 500 miles. Maritime communications were also encouraged by stable winds during summer, and favourable currents in the East Mediterranean and around the coast of Cyprus.

Yet the Cypriots themselves have always been a mainly agricultural people, and in this pursuit they were favoured by the land and the climate. The main geophysical features of Cyprus are two mountain ranges and a large plain. The Kyrenia range, formed of hard limestone, runs parallel to the northern coast for about 60 miles and rises from sea-level to a maximum height of slightly over 1000 m. Between its northern slopes and the sea runs a narrow but very fertile plain, about 60 miles long and 3 miles wide, comprising undulating terrain which is well irrigated by perennial springs and abundant rainfall. The mountains form a barrier against the humidity which reaches the coast from Asia Minor. It is on this protected narrow plain that some of the richest villages of Cyprus are situated today, including Lapethos and the nearby Karavas with its *Kefalovryso*, or perennial spring. Conditions must have been the same throughout antiquity, since this area was densely populated from earliest times. The southern slopes of the Kyrenia range often contrast with those of the north, with their rocky, barren hillocks forming a fringe along the northern edge of the central plain. There is one notable exception, the perennial spring of Kythrea, which still irrigates the plain round it, and in late antiquity provided water even for Salamis on the east coast.

The first impression one has when flying over Cyprus is the mountainous nature of the landscape. In fact most of the central and western areas are occupied by the Troodos mountain range – a pre-Campanian volcanic and plutonic complex, with sedimentary deposits of limestone, gypsum, chalks and marls surrounding it. Its highest point rises 1950 m above sea level, and it rarely falls below 700 m. The highest peaks are covered with snow for about three months every winter. Today it is covered with pine forests which constitute an important economic resource. In antiquity they provided timber for smelting copper ores and for shipbuilding. But the most important resources of this mountainous area, both in antiquity and in modern

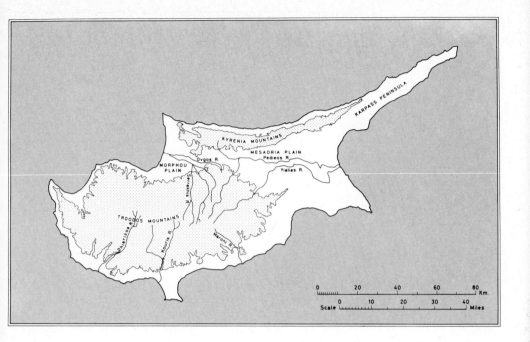

1 Geographical map of Cyprus.

times, are the copper mines scattered along its north and northeast slopes. Mention should also be made of the Amiandos mines, rich in short-fibred asbestos. The information provided by Eratosthenes that there were silver mines in Cyprus may not be correct. Melting snow and abundant rainfall supply the various rivers which cut deep into the massif and form numerous valleys which extend as far as the southern and northwestern coasts. Though these rivers are today dry during the summer season, rainfall may have been heavier in antiquity, and extensive forests would have increased precipitation. Today the rivers carry down to the sea valuable vegetal soil (*terra rossa*) after the torrential rains, particularly in autumn.

A large and fertile plain lies between the two mountain ranges. It extends westwards from Nicosia to Morphou Bay and eastwards to the Bay of Salamis, being about 57 miles long and from 12 to 25 miles wide. The easterly plain is known as the Mesaoria ('between the mountains') and is larger than that of Morphou, though less well irrigated and less fertile. The ferric soil of the Morphou plain, irrigated by perennial springs and by the Serakhis and Ovgos rivers, provides most of the fruit and vegetables of Cyprus. The Mesaoria plain is drained by the Pedieos and the Yialias rivers and today produces most of the island's corn. In antiquity it must have been covered with forests as, in contrast to the Morphou plain, very few settlements have been traced there. Strabo (*Geographica* XIV. 6. 5) attributes to Eratosthenes the statement that the plains of Cyprus were once so covered with thick forests that no one could settle there. We may imagine most of the Mesaoria plain, particularly in its eastern part, as an uncultivated, marshy forest with only a few settlements on elevated plateaus.

1

Arable and well-irrigated land attracted prehistoric settlers who built their homes mainly on low hill slopes and among the pastures between the plain and the highlands, thus leaving arable land for cultivation and avoiding winter floods. The river valleys, especially in the Morphou plain and along the south coast, must have been particularly thickly populated in early prehistoric times. Several other factors, however, contributed to the development of various areas, especially during the Late Bronze Age. This saw the rise of flourishing harbour towns mainly along the east and south coasts of the island, engaged in trade with Egypt and the Near East.

One important economic resource which is rarely mentioned is the salt industry which must have flourished in antiquity. The salt-lakes of Limassol and Larnaca would have been exploited from very early times. That of Larnaca may have been an important source of income for the Late Bronze Age towns which flourished in the vicinity.

Wild animals, some of which were already domesticated in the Neolithic period, abounded in the woods and forests of Cyprus. We know that the mouflon (*Ovis orientalis*), Persian fallow deer (*Dama mesopotamica*) and the wild pig (*Sus scrofa*) were present on the island from the Neolithic, having been introduced during the initial settlement of Cyprus in the 7th millennium B C.

Communications within the island were fairly well developed, especially from the Bronze Age onwards, when semi-refined copper and ingots were transported from the mines to the 'industrial' centres where they were worked, and to the harbour towns. Through the Kyrenia mountain range, three well-defined passes (near Vasilia, above Kyrenia and above Lefkoniko) connect the northern coast with the central plain. It would have been easy to communicate from one end of the central plain to the other, over the plateaus and the high rocky lands rather than through the marshy forests bordering the rivers. The only isolated part of the country was the Paphos district, for there the Troodos mountains extend in places to the northern and southern sea-shore. In Chalcolithic times, when communication with other parts of the island was not imperative, the valleys of the numerous rivers flowing down from the Troodos massif were thickly populated. The abundance of steatite and igneous rocks in this region may have been one of the reasons for this development. Later, however, and particularly during the Bronze Age, when communication with the rest of the island, especially with the mining areas, was an absolute necessity, settlement in the Paphos district declined, except for the fertile plain along the western and southwestern coasts.

Though there may have been no drastic climatological changes in the East Mediterranean since ancient times, Cyprus must have seen certain modifications which influenced its general ambience. The indiscriminate cutting down of trees for metallurgical purposes and for shipbuilding transformed the plains into dry lands, whereas in antiquity they would have been green and cooler in the summer. Sea breezes, however, still make the climate pleasant, even in midsummer. This favours the cultivation of vegetables and fruit and also the production of cereals, particularly when there is adequate irrigation. Periods of drought, however, are not uncommon, and these may seriously disturb the island's economy even when they last for only one year. In the same way, torrential rains and hail, particularly in autumn, cause considerable damage to crops. Cyprus lies within a seismic belt which is shaken at quite frequent intervals, though the sea protects her from violent earthquakes such as those which devastate large areas in Asia Minor and the Balkans. These may have been the cause for the destruction or abandonment of cities in antiquity, as archaeological evidence often suggests.

2

The earliest settlements

The Neolithic period

Prehistorians have often been puzzled by the relatively late appearance of human settlement on the island of Cyprus, which is not far from flourishing Palaeolithic settlements in Anatolia to the north and in Syria and Palestine to the east. The earliest record of human occupation in Cyprus, according to calibrations of C14 dates, is *c.* 7000–6500 BC. The relative isolation of Cyprus may partly explain this phenomenon. Though it is not improbable that a pre-Neolithic culture may one day be discovered through the investigation of cave and rock-shelter sites, it should be stated that such an early inhabitation would be extremely limited, as archaeological surveys of a considerable part of Cyprus have so far produced negative results. Attempts to identify flints in the Kyrenia District near the north coast as Palaeolithic have failed;[1] the suggestion that a large, non-pottery-using Neolithic settlement, situated on and around a conical hill in the proximity of the village of Kataliondas near the northeastern slopes of the Troodos mountains, may be earlier than *c.* 7000 BC remains hypothetical, since no excavation has yet been carried out there.[2] It more probably represents a cultural variant that is no earlier than the other known aceramic settlements. It was inhabited by a community which did not have an agriculturally based economy, but which pursued hunting and industrial activities.

The discovery of a Neolithic phase in Cyprus was made in the 1920s by E. Gjerstad, but it was a full decade later (1936–9, 1946) that large-scale, systematic investigations began under the direction of P. Dikaios. This partly accounts for the various chronological problems related to this period which still remain unsolved. Complications in the application of C14 methods have rendered their solution even more difficult. With the revival of interest in this period in Cyprus, that has led to extensive excavations being undertaken during recent years in various parts of the island, there is reason to believe that the remaining problems will soon be overcome.

Neolithic I

2 The largest Neolithic settlement excavated so far is that of Khirokitia,[3] situated about 4 miles from the south coast, on a hill near a bend of the south bank of the Maroni river. The date initially given to the earliest remains of Khirokitia by its excavator, Porphyrios Dikaios, was *c.* 4000 BC, but analysis and C14 calibration has revealed *c.* 7000 BC as the date of what is known as Neolithic I.[4] This aceramic phase is also

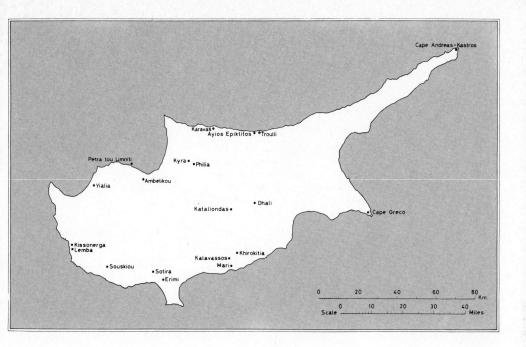

Cape Andreas-Kastros

Karavas•
Ayios Epiktitos • •Troulli

Petra tou Limniti•
Kyra • •Philia

•Yialia
•Ambelikou

Kataliondas •
• Dhali
•Cape Greco

•Kissonerga
•Lemba
• Khirokitia
Kalavassos•
Mari•

• Souskiou
• Sotira
•Erimi

| 0 | 20 | 40 | 60 | 80 Km. |
Scale | 0 | 10 | 20 | 30 | 40 Miles |

2 Neolithic and Chalcolithic sites in Cyprus.

represented by other settlements, of which the following are the best known: Cape Andreas-*Kastros*, at the very end of the promontory which points towards Syria and southern Anatolia; Cape Greco, on the southeastern tip of the promontory which points to the Lebanon; Troulli, an outcrop of land on the north coast, to the east of Kyrenia; Petra tou Limniti, a small offshore island near the northwest coast; and Kalavassos-*Tenta*, on a hillock not far from Khirokitia. There are a few other sites, on or near the coast or near major rivers in the central and southern parts of the island. The common characteristic of most of these locations is that they are conspicuous landmarks; many are situated on the coast near sheltered anchorages, or in valleys near the banks of rivers which are easily accessible from the coast. There is arable land and an adequate water supply in their vicinity, except in a few cases, such as Kataliondas where the economy of the settlement was based not on mixed farming, but on hunting and 'industrial' activity, or Cape Andreas-*Kastros* where the main occupation of the inhabitants was fishing. The location of these aceramic settlements will be of crucial importance when we discuss the possible origin of these early Neolithic settlers.

Of the above-mentioned settlements, that of Khirokitia is still the best known and by far the most representative for the study of architecture, art and the social structure of Neolithic I.

KHIROKITIA

Arable land and perennial springs in the immediate vicinity of this settlement, plus the defensive qualities of the hill, may have been the principal attractions for early settlers. Though only a small portion of the hill has been excavated so far, a magnetometer survey of the area

3 General view of the largest *tholos* so far uncovered at Khirokitia (excavated by the Cyprus Department of Antiquities, 1936–46). Its two rectangular piers supported a type of attic or *sende*. A semicircular wall around the exterior provided a sheltered corridor for storage etc.

has shown that almost all the hill was occupied. The recently renewed excavations at this site, directed by A. Le Brun, will no doubt throw more light on the extent and importance of this settlement, of which about sixty houses have now been uncovered.[5]

Dwellings consist normally of one circular hut (*tholos*) whose walls stand on solidly built foundations of river boulders laid in several courses, with a superstructure of *pisé* or unbaked mudbrick, or light materials for the upper part of the dome. The walls of some of the newly excavated houses consist of one or two circles of stones around an inner circle of *pisé* with a mud-facing. This form of architecture recalls much earlier prototypes of the Natufian culture in the Levant and persisted in Cyprus at a time when neighbouring countries had adopted dwellings of rectangular plan. Insularity and conservatism may account for this phenomenon.

The buildings at Khirokitia have a diameter of between 3–4 or 7–8 m. There is no preconceived layout, but the houses occupy all available open spaces, with narrow passageways winding through the various sections of the settlement. The largest hut (Tholos Ia) has an inner diameter of about 6 m. Unlike other smaller structures it had an attic, obviously reached by a ladder, which provided extra space for sleeping or for storing goods, a feature which is not uncommon in the folk architecture of modern Cyprus (*sende*). Round the east, west and north sides of this house there was a roofed passage which provided space for various domestic purposes; the south side was left open for the summer sea breezes and the winter sun. Three smaller tholoi belong to the same building complex; this was obviously the house of the most prominent and perhaps one of the largest families of Khirokitia. Two

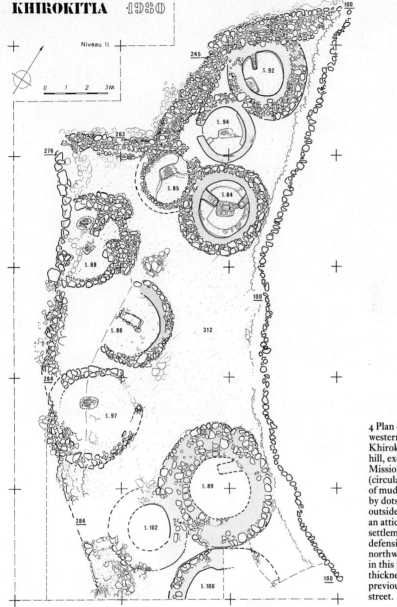

KHIROKITIA 1980

Niveau II

245

S. 92

S. 94

263

276

S. 85

S. 84

S. 88

S. 86

312

284

S. 97

S. 89

284

S. 102

S. 100

100
0

100

100

100

0   1   2   3 M

4 Plan of the north-
westernmost part of
Khirokitia, at the top of the
hill, excavated by the French
Mission. Several *tholoi*
(circular structures) are built
of mudbrick inside (indicated
by dots) and of rubble
outside. Some have piers for
an attic. This part of the
settlement is confined by a
defensive wall of which the
northwestern angle is shown
in this plan. Its maximum
thickness is *c.* 1 m and was
previously thought to be a
street.

other groups of huts, of two and four structures respectively, have been   4
distinguished in the recently excavated sector of the settlement. Each
hut served a specific purpose, such as living place, workshop or kitchen.

The main characteristics of the interior of a tholos are a flat floor of
beaten earth, a hearth, platforms built against the walls for sleeping,
and a central post to support the domed roof.

5 Aerial view of the Neolithic settlement at Kalavassos-*Tenta*. The site is located on a hillock in the Vasilikos river valley. The settlement had a defensive wall and ditch of which parts have been uncovered on the southern slopes of the hillock (top right).

6 Kalavassos-*Tenta*. The inner surfaces of the walls of the tholoi were plastered. On one such surface a wall-painting with a red pigment was found representing the upper part of a human figure with uplifted arms, and traces of at least a second figure. This composition, though crudely rendered, is the earliest wall-painting found so far in Cyprus.

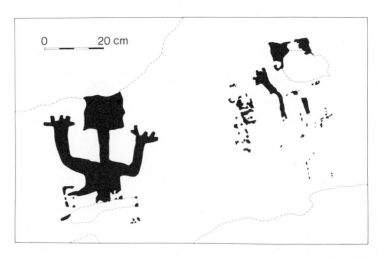

0   20 cm

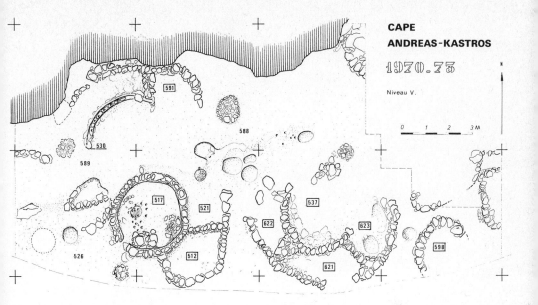

CAPE ANDREAS-KASTROS

1970-73

Niveau V.

7 Plan of the area of Cape Andreas-*Kastros* excavated by the French Mission (1970–3). The tholoi are constructed of rubble and are more or less circular in plan, but often their plan is dictated by the uneven surface of the ground.

KALAVASSOS-TENTA

Recent excavations by Ian Todd at the aceramic settlement of *Tenta*, south of the village of Kalavassos near the south coast and not far from Khirokitia, have revealed an important complex of huts on a hilltop and its slopes.[6] They are of circular or elliptical shape, with one or two rectangular piers to support an upper storey. The inner faces of the walls are plastered. One such plastered wall bears clear traces of red pigment, forming what looks like a crudely rendered human figure with uplifted arms. Further traces of paint on the same wall suggest a composite scene. Doorways and windows are clearly defined. Mudbrick is used extensively, and where there are double walls, the outer one might be of mudbrick and the inner one of stones. One particular hut is encircled by two concentric walls, recalling the features round the large Tholos Ia of Khirokitia. There must have been more than one phase of this aceramic period at *Tenta*, for below the wall foundations of hut 17 are clear remains of an earlier mudbrick structure. The huts at Cape Andreas-*Kastros* are also circular, but their construction is more modest than that of Khirokitia and Kalavassos-*Tenta*.

5, 6

7, 8

SECURITY AND SUBSISTENCE

Khirokitia was from the very beginning fortified with a massive wall, about 1 m thick, which has now largely been uncovered. It crossed the settlement obliquely from the top of the hill down to the river. When it was first discovered it was identified by the excavator as a street, but recent excavations have shown another portion of this wall at the northernmost part of the settlement, which turns to form the western limits of the inhabited area, outside of which there are no structures. It is true, however, that at some point houses were built even outside this fortification wall, probably as a result of population growth at a time

8 General view of Cape Andreas-*Kastros* at the easternmost part of the Karpass peninsula. The Neolithic settlement was built on the southern slope of a hill and was thus protected from the north winds; at the same time its location offered protection for the community of fishermen who inhabited it.

when such a venture was not discouraged for security reasons, though a second defensive wall was later constructed to include these tholoi as well.

There is a similar defensive wall round the lower slopes of the Kalavassos-*Tenta* settlement, but only small portions of it have been uncovered. As at Khirokitia, extra-mural structures appear at a later stage.

The settlements at Cape Andreas-*Kastros* and Troulli were well defended by the very nature of their locations.

The economy of Khirokitia was based on farming. Apart from carbonized grains found on the floors of houses, there is also evidence

9 Two flint arrowheads: *left*, from Khirokitia, with a tang for hafting, L. 6.7 cm; *centre*, from Karavas, L. 4.5 cm; *right*, curved flint sickle blade from Khirokitia, L. 7.7 cm. Cyprus Museum, Nicosia.

from flint sickle blades, querns and grinders, that corn was harvested   9
and ground into flour. The diet of the Khirokitians was supplemented
with meat; wild animals were hunted (a few flint arrowheads have been
found), but some may already have been domesticated, such as sheep,
goats and pigs. Fallow deer was hunted. Einkorn, emmer, hulled barley
and small quantities of lentils, beans and peas have been found during
recent excavations;[7] since olive trees are indigenous to Cyprus their
fruit may have been exploited as well.

Kalavassos-*Tenta* reflects a similar economy. The inhabitants
cultivated cereals, including two varieties of corn, lentils and probably
barley. The fauna of *Tenta* does not differ from that of Khirokitia.

At Cape Andreas-*Kastros*, excavated by A. Le Brun, fish and shell-
fish formed part of the basic diet. Fish bones and sea-shells as well as
fishing implements were found on the house floors.[8]

In spite of its primitive architecture, the Neolithic I community was
well organized and the settlements firmly and permanently established.

BURIAL RITES
The only 'religious' practices which may be noted during this period
are burial rites. The veneration by the living for the dead may
ultimately have been inspired by fear. Each corpse was buried in a   10
shallow pit, either inside the habitation beneath a floor or just outside.

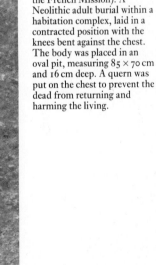

10 Khirokitia (excavated by
the French Mission). A
Neolithic adult burial within a
habitation complex, laid in a
contracted position with the
knees bent against the chest.
The body was placed in an
oval pit, measuring 85 × 70 cm
and 16 cm deep. A quern was
put on the chest to prevent the
dead from returning and
harming the living.

11 Head of a human figure in unbaked clay, from Khirokitia. There is an obvious effort to render the facial characteristics in a naturalistic manner, unlike the crude idols of andesite. The hair at the back of the head is rendered by vertical wavy lines in relief. H. 10.5 cm. Neolithic I period. Cyprus Museum, Nicosia.

It was laid in a contracted position, with the knees bent against the chest. Single burials were common at first, but in the later periods double burials, often of a woman and child, became frequent. A large stone, usually a quern, was placed on the chest of the deceased. Gifts were frequently offered to the dead: necklaces, pins and pendants for women and other offerings for men or children. Stone bowls were also placed with the corpse after having been ceremoniously broken. Infantile mortality was very high, as attested by the large percentage of infant burials.

It has been suggested that burial rites at Khirokitia have their origins in the Levant,[9] as for example the mainly single inhumations, the placing of deliberately broken stone bowls in the grave, the laying of stones over the dead body and so on. Some other practices from the Levant, such as the separation of the skull and its public display, may be echoed at Khirokitia by the wedging of the head with lumps of *pisé* or pebbles, and in one case (Tholos XV, grave IV), the separation of the skull. It should also be added that the skull was usually left uncovered by the grave fill and libations were probably poured by the living in honour of the dead. These similarities between burial customs in the Levant and at Khirokitia may be supplemented by others, for example, the display of stone figurines – in one case the unbaked clay protome (or bust) of a woman with a hole in the base for fixing on a stand or shaft, and artificial head moulding. This evidence may support the suggestion that the earliest inhabitants of Neolithic I came from the northern Levant which, as mentioned above, is visible from the easternmost

11

coast of Cyprus on a clear day.[10] The location of some of the earliest settlements, such as Cape Andreas-*Kastros* and Cape Greco, may provide corroborating evidence. Anthropological studies have not given an explicit answer to the problem of cultural origins, and have indicated only that they belong to a short-headed race.

The general characteristics of the burial customs at Khirokitia may also be observed at Kalavassos-*Tenta* and at Cape Andreas-*Kastros*, and this helps to argue for the cultural homogeneity of early Neolithic Cyprus.

The colonization hypothesis is also supported by other aspects of Neolithic I.[11] The occurrence in small quantities of obsidian blades from Çiftlik in central Anatolia, as well as carnelian, 'greenstone' and the use of dentalium, mother-of-pearl and so on, for ornaments, would suggest that these early settlers brought with them these uncommon raw materials which gradually became more rare and finally disappeared, since the colonists did not maintain relations with the mainland after they had settled in Cyprus. These relations with the Levant do not, of course, exclude entirely the possibility that some colonists may also have come from the even closer coast of southern Anatolia. Whatever the facts, these early settlers crossed the straits in boats or on rafts, bringing with them their belongings and perhaps also animals for breeding, such as the fallow deer, wild goat, wild sheep and wild pig. Cattle, which were raised in Anatolia as well as in Crete, were not introduced into Cyprus until the Early Bronze Age.

ART AND ARTEFACTS

The characteristic art of the early inhabitants of Khirokitia includes stone bowls made of grey-green igneous rocks from river beds, and human and animal figures of the same material. We have already noted the human head of unbaked clay which was probably associated with the cult of the dead. Other stone idols are less naturalistically rendered. They are schematized, and often violin-shaped. Grooves indicate the legs, and occasionally facial characteristics are shown by incised lines or depressions, or are carved in relief; their sex is not indicated. Animal protomes may have served as heads of sceptres. A complete quadruped has been found on the surface at Mari near Kalavassos.[12] Small, grooved conical stones have been found at Khirokitia and have been interpreted as models of round houses (tholoi) offered to the dead, but it has also been suggested that they were gaming pieces. The stone bowls are often elegant, decorated with grooved or relief patterns. They have thin walls, polished surfaces and carefully rendered spouts and

12

12 Bowl of grey andesite from Khirokitia. It is roughly rectangular, with an open spout. The exterior is decorated with dots in relief arranged in the form of a cross and with parallel chevrons on either side of the spout. It was repaired in antiquity.
L. 30.5 cm. Neolithic I period. Cyprus Museum, Nicosia.

13 Hemispherical bowl of baked clay from Khirokitia, decorated in the 'combed' technique, with wavy bands both inside and out. Diam. 32.5 cm. Neolithic II period. Cyprus Museum, Nicosia.

small, perforated handles by which they were hung on string. Sometimes they copy wooden prototypes, and have large, often angular, horizontal loop handles. There must also have been receptacles of leather and basketry. Attempts to make clay vessels have been observed at Khirokitia, but there is not enough evidence for an early 'ceramic' phase. The technique of making pottery was known in the contemporary Levant, and perhaps the colonists brought with them some elementary knowledge which was subsequently 'lost in transmission'.[13]

The flint industry was significantly inferior to that of neighbouring countries. There are no javelin points, although a few arrowheads have been brought to light in recent excavations, and there are also sickle blades. Maceheads of polished stone served as weapons. Bone was used for needles and awls, but river boulders were the basic material for tools such as pounders, grinders and querns. Spindle whorls and needles show that weaving, perhaps of wool, was practised. Necklaces of carnelian and dentalium beads, and pendants of 'greenstone' and sea-shells were worn as ornaments.

A cultural trait of some importance, resulting in deliberate cranial deformation, was common at Khirokitia. More than half the skulls from the site showed traces of occipital flattening achieved by binding the infant to a cradle-board while lying on its back. Skeletal evidence suggests that this custom was still practised in the Bronze Age.[14]

Neolithic II

It is unfortunate that no settlement in Cyprus with continuous occupation from the beginning to the end of the Neolithic has yet been excavated. The early phase of Khirokitia (Neolithic I) lasted for about one thousand years, and then the site was abandoned *c.* 6000 BC to be occupied again by new settlers 1500 years later. The Neolithic I culture at Khirokitia, Kalavassos-*Tenta*, Cape Andreas-*Kastros* and elsewhere did not end as the result of destruction, but rather of a natural decline due to socio-economic factors.

C14 dating has made necessary a reconsideration of the sequence established by Dikaios between the lower (Neolithic I) and the upper

(Neolithic II) settlement levels of Khirokitia. The settlers who occupied the upper strata of this site (and also of Sotira-*Teppes*) used a type of pottery known as Combed Ware, and the earliest C14 (calibrated) date proposed for this ceramic phase is *c.* 4500 BC. In order to bridge the gap, Dikaios suggested an intermediate period, Neolithic Ib, which would immediately follow the end of Neolithic Ia at Khirokitia (*c.* 6000 BC) and would last for some 300 years, using the chronology corresponding to calibrated C14 dates. This phase was observed by Dikaios at Troulli,[15] a headland site on the northern coast, where the lower occupation layers, comparable to the earliest level at Khirokitia, are aceramic. The upper layer at Troulli, which supposedly followed the lower layer without a break, produced pottery with red painted patterns on a white ground, known as Red-on-White ware. The excavator classified this as a predecessor of the Combed Ware of the upper levels at Khirokitia, and consequently a candidate for a Neolithic Ib phase that would partly fill the gap between Neolithic I and II. The same kind of pottery has been found at ceramic sites in northern Cyprus, such as Ayios Epiktitos-*Vrysi*, the earliest date of which, according to the excavator, is 3875 ± 145, which, when calibrated, is *c.* 4660 BC. The majority of sites associated with this pottery have an average date of *c.* 4300 BC.

At another ceramic site, Philia-*Drakos* A in the Ovgos valley in northwestern Cyprus, Red-on-White pottery has also been found, but there the excavator proposes an even earlier ceramic phase with Dark-Faced Burnished ware, but if this is accepted, the upper limits of Philia-*Drakos* A2, with the first Red-on-White pottery, cannot be earlier than the beginning of the 5th millennium BC. The site of Dhali-*Agridhi*, on the southern banks of the Yialias river, has produced pottery which is comparable to the earliest pottery of Philia-*Drakos* A and is dated by C14 to 4465 ± 310 (*c.* 5310 BC), together with Philia-*Drakos* A1. If the date is correct then this is the only Neolithic site in Cyprus so far excavated which could partly fill the gap between aceramic Neolithic I and ceramic Neolithic II.

It was hoped that the site of Kalavassos-*Tenta*, where pottery appears in the upper levels, would have provided an uninterrupted sequence, but this pottery is not yet associated with any architectural remains. Thus, in spite of the evidence from the preliminary report of the Dhali-*Agridhi* excavations,[16] the problematic gap of 1500 or 1000 years between Neolithic I and II still exists, representing a decline or, as has often been suggested, a break in the occupation of Cyprus.

At Dhali-*Agridhi* there is evidence for a population practising a mixed economy: cultivating the well-irrigated land in the Yialias river valley and also herding sheep and goats, breeding pigs and hunting wild boar and deer.

Neolithic II is marked by the arrival of a new wave of settlers to the island, who established themselves initially near the coast at sites which provided naturally defended positions such as Ayios Epiktitos-*Vrysi*, or inland at sites around which they built defensive walls, such as Philia-*Drakos* A. Soon, however, the initial precautions for defence were discontinued and these Neolithic II settlements developed peacefully until their final abandonment *c.* 3800 BC.

ARCHITECTURAL DISCOVERIES

Ayios Epiktitos-Vrysi

Ayios Epiktitos-*Vrysi*, excavated by E. J. Peltenburg, is situated on a narrow headland on the northern coast, east of Kyrenia,[17] with good arable land stretching behind it in the fertile and well-irrigated plain which extends from the foot of the Kyrenia mountain range to the sea. In the initial phase, dwellings of this settlement were wooden and not very substantial, but in the second phase they had stone foundations with *pisé* superstructures. Many are irregular in plan owing to the uneven surface of the ground, but others are rectangular with rounded corners. They are partly subterranean, with walls built inside hollows cut out of the rock to provide sunken floors. The interiors of the one-roomed houses are frequently divided into smaller units by wooden beams, of the kind also used for the often sloping roof and for bracing walls. The walls are thin and plastered on their inner face. Some are preserved to a height of 3 m, the reason being that in later phases the floors were raised and the earlier walls used as foundations for new houses. The floors of mud or clay were equipped with benches against the walls, and circular, off-centre platform hearths. In one house two stone pillars were found, 52 and 58 cm in height respectively, which were originally clothed in fibrous plaiting. One of them is phallic in appearance and may have had a cultic purpose. There are several housing blocks in the settlement, separated by winding passages.

The settlement of Ayios Epiktitos-*Vrysi* was fortified in its initial stages by a V-shaped ditch, 7 m wide at the top, 1.3 m at the bottom and 4 m deep. It runs across the headland as a barrier separating the promontory settlement from the mainland. Soon after it was dug, however, this defensive ditch must have become unnecessary, for the settlement expanded beyond it as the population grew. The rebuilding of houses was frequent and as a result the original sunken floors had risen above ground level by the time the settlement was abandoned.

The inhabitants were mainly farmers, and the remains of wheat, barley, lentils, grapes and olives have been found. There is also evidence for the pasturing of caprids, domestication of pigs and the collection of sea-shells. There are signs of considerable industrial activity on house floors and occasionally outside them. The painted pottery of Vrysi is of particular interest. Bold motifs in dark red or brown are painted on a white surface: at first these included circles, strokes and points, but ripples were used in the later phases. Shapes include large spouted bowls as well as large bottles. Bowls of the latter phase are decorated with thick, reserved circles and horizontal vertical rows of festoons. Combed Ware is very rare, even in the late phase. It seems that this ware was fashionable only in southern Cyprus, for very little appeared in the north, though the rippling of Red-on-White ware betrays the same stylistic trends. There may be no chronological difference between the two.

Philia-Drakos

At Philia-*Drakos* A, excavated by T. Watkins, the stratigraphy had been badly disturbed by erosion.[18] Architectural remains consist of

houses of various shapes, mainly rectangular with rounded corners, built of stone and *pisé*. The roofs were of canes and mud, supported by a central post. The site was fortified, at least on its southern and western boundaries, by a wall and a ditch 2 m wide and 1.5 m deep. Large subterranean shafts, channels and chambers have been found at Philia, the purpose of which is not yet clear. After the initial period of settlement the defensive wall became superfluous, as at Ayios Epiktitos-*Vrysi*, and collapsed into the ditch. It was replaced by another wall in a later phase. The inhabitants were farmers, herdsmen and hunters. No burials within the houses have been found, but a chamber-tomb was discovered within the area of the settlement. The skeletal remains were poor and there were no grave goods.

14 General view of the excavated remains at the Neolithic site of Ayios Epiktitos-*Vrysi* (excavated by a British Mission, 1969–74). The plans of the houses are irregular, dictated by the uneven terrain. Walls are preserved to a considerable height (over 3 m), and were often strengthened by wooden beams. There were narrow winding streets through the settlement.

Sotira-*Teppes*

Sotira-*Teppes*, excavated by P. Dikaios, is the most important of the Neolithic II settlements.[19] It has given its name to this culture, characterized by a remarkable uniformity despite difficulties of communication between sites.

The pottery here, found also in the upper layers of Khirokitia and throughout this period in southern Cyprus, is Combed Ware. Forty-seven houses have been uncovered at the site, which occupied at first the top and later the slopes of a prominent hill. Two phases have been recognized, the first dated by C14 to 3455 ± 110 (*c.* 4350 BC) and the second to 3145 ± 130 (*c.* 3900 BC). Sotira, like Ayios Epiktitos-*Vrysi*, Philia-*Drakos* A and Kalavassos A, was abandoned at the beginning of the 4th millennium BC after an earthquake. The houses are closely packed, and vary considerably in shape: circular, oval, subrectangular, horseshoe-shaped and irregular, recalling those of Ayios Epiktitos-*Vrysi*. They are constructed of stone with mudbrick superstructures. They had central poles to support the roof, a hearth, and benches as sleeping places on the floor. There were partitions in some houses to define working areas. Querns and rubbing stones found on the floors bear witness to the agricultural nature of the community, but there is also evidence for the pasturing of caprids and the domestication of pigs. Stone bowls, so common in Neolithic I, are absent at Sotira-*Teppes*. The settlement was probably encircled by a large peripheral wall of uncertain function, which the excavator concluded could not have been used for defensive purposes. At the foot of the southeastern slope of the hill is a separate cemetery. The dead were buried without any grave-goods in a contracted position with a large stone laid over the body. The extra-mural burials again contrast with those of Khirokitia. There is a remarkable uniformity between the culture of Sotira-*Teppes* and that of Ayios Epiktitos-*Vrysi*, in spite of differences in the pottery.

Kalavassos A

At Kalavassos A, excavated by P. Dikaios, architecture is atypical, with subterranean pits.[20] A central post supported a light superstructure. The excavator has suggested that this style of architecture is connected with that of the Beersheba culture of southern Palestine. Though the houses of Sotira-*Teppes* are much more solid and advanced, there is no reason to suggest that it is later in date than Kalavassos A. They may both derive from the same cultural region where two different architectural tendencies were prevalent, or it may be that both ceramic Khirokitia and Kalavassos A postdate the earthquake that destroyed Sotira. One may go even further and suggest that the light constructions at Kalavassos A and the squatter occupation among the tholoi at Khirokitia, and possibly also at Kalavassos-*Tenta*, were a precaution against seismic activity. The earthquake which destroyed Sotira-*Teppes* may also have been responsible for the abandonment of settlements in northern Cyprus.

The inhabitants of Kalavassos A were farmers, like those of Sotira-*Teppes*. They lacked the artistic skill of the Khirokitians in the carving of stone idols and vases, but they produced high-quality Combed Ware pottery.

The Neolithic period in Cyprus may not be as eventful as later periods, but no one can deny its vitality. Moreover, the three thousand years which elapsed from the earliest Neolithic I settlements to the end of Neolithic II saw the arrival of people from neighbouring countries who were to form the core of the population of Cyprus. These are formative years, which constitute the background for the cultural flowering of the Bronze Age.

The Chalcolithic I–II period

Unlike the transition from Neolithic I to Neolithic II, when there is a gap in the cultural sequence, the transition from the end of the

15 Andesite polished axe-head or chisel within a bone sheath, from Kalavassos site A. L. 17 cm. Cyprus Museum, Nicosia.

16 Idol of grey andesite, from Khirokitia. It has a rectangular flat body, but there is an attempt to render the legs and the details of the head. It shows an advanced style, if compared with some of the very crude idols of the early Neolithic period. Ht 19 cm. Neolithic II period. Cyprus Museum, Nicosia.

Neolithic to the beginning of the Chalcolithic is characterized by cultural continuity, the one succeeding the other after a well-defined cultural change. Even though this transition was marked by violent earthquake destruction, the succeeding period still has roots in the Late Neolithic. In fact, there is even a suggestion that a group of newcomers brought the Chalcolithic culture with them to Cyprus before 3500 BC. Their origin is not certain, but there are indications that the island had relations with Tarsus, as painted Chalcolithic I sherds were found there in an Early Bronze II level.

The settlement pattern also changes in the Chalcolithic. The western part of the island, including the mountains, the central plain and the Karpass peninsula, were uninhabited during the Neolithic period, but now the west was populated and some of the best-known Chalcolithic settlements flourished there. Although it is probable that new settlers came to the island, the old stock lingered on, maintaining for a while certain Neolithic traditions such as Combed Ware.

ERIMI-BAMBOULA

The first Chalcolithic I site to be excavated was Erimi-*Bamboula*, near the south coast on the east bank of the Kouris river, where round huts with stone foundations were uncovered.[22] It seems that fear of seismic disturbances, like that which destroyed Sotira-*Teppes*, was over. The huts have sunken floors, as at Kalavassos A and Chalcolithic Kalavassos B, but they have stone foundations with superstructures of light wattle

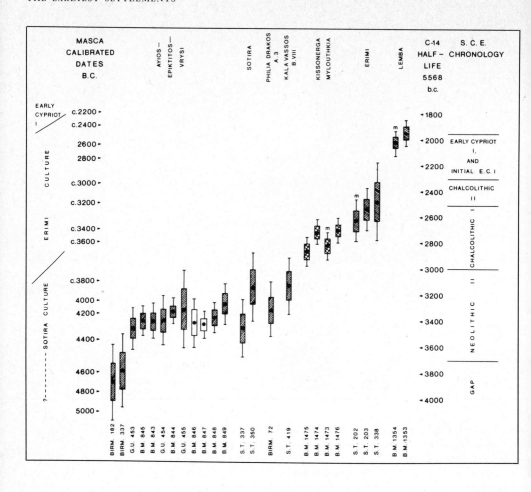

| MASCA CALIBRATED DATES B.C. | AVIOS – EPIKTITOS – VRYSI | SOTIRA | PHILIA DRAKOS A.3 KALA VASSOS B VIII | KISSONERGA MYLOUTHKIA | ERIMI | LEMBA | C-14 HALF – LIFE 5568 b.c. | S. C. E. CHRONOLOGY |

17 Radiocarbon dates of Sotira and Erimi culture sites, with *MASCA* calibrated dates, and the *Swedish Cyprus Expedition* IV:1A chronology, established before the need for calibration was known (After E. J. Peltenburg, in *RDAC* 1979, 73, Table 1).

and daub; roofs were supported by central posts. There was a hearth on the floor inside and occasionally outside the dwelling. The burial customs attested at Sotira-*Teppes*, where there is a separate cemetery, are not encountered at Erimi-*Bamboula*, where the dead were buried in a contracted position inside or just outside the habitation, as at Khirokitia and other Neolithic sites. In one case the antlers of a fallow deer, and other animal bones, were associated with a burial. Rich gifts are also known from the Chalcolithic I cemetery at Souskiou-*Vathyrkakas* near Palaepaphos, to be described below. The pottery of Erimi is Red Lustrous, probably following a Neolithic II tradition, and also Red-on-White with geometric and other abstract or floral motifs. Erimi contained the first copper object, a chisel, but there is no contemporary evidence for copper-mining or metallurgical activities in Cyprus. There are many newly discovered Chalcolithic sites on either side of the Kyrenia mountain range, and more have been found along the west and southwest coasts. Of particular density and importance are the Chalcolithic I settlements near the village of Lemba on the west coast, north of Paphos.[23]

17

Lemba-Lakkous

At Lemba-*Lakkous*, Areas I and II, excavated by E. Peltenburg, several houses have been uncovered. They are circular, in the tradition of Erimi architecture, with stone foundations; they had conical roofs, probably of mud and reeds. The maximum diameter is 8.5 m. They are scattered irregularly on slight terraces and were used as habitations, kitchens and workshops. Outdoor shelters supported on wooden posts were used for storage jars. One, a roughly D-shaped hut, was divided into two compartments by a pebble-lined groove which obviously supported a partition screen. One compartment, in which the limestone figurine of a nude female goddess dated to the Chalcolithic I period was discovered, also had a thick plaster floor and may be regarded as a sacred area. On the floors of other houses various stone and bone tools, as well as the first copper chisel found at Lemba-*Lakkous*, were discovered. Bones of pigs, sheep, goats and deer were also found.

18

19

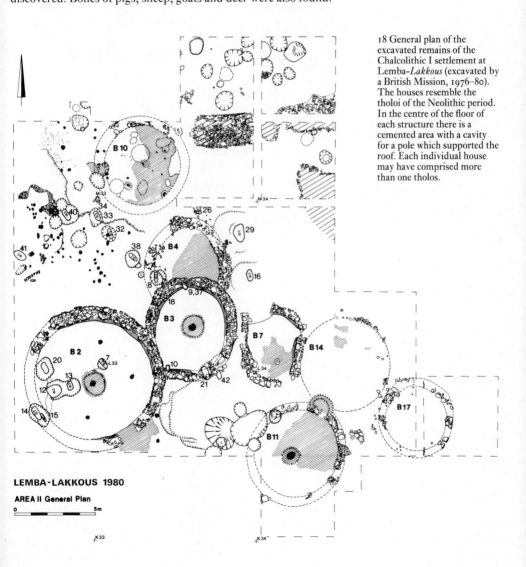

18 General plan of the excavated remains of the Chalcolithic I settlement at Lemba-*Lakkous* (excavated by a British Mission, 1976–80). The houses resemble the tholoi of the Neolithic period. In the centre of the floor of each structure there is a cemented area with a cavity for a pole which supported the roof. Each individual house may have comprised more than one tholos.

LEMBA-LAKKOUS 1980

AREA II General Plan

0   5m

19 Limestone figurine of a nude woman, found in building 1 at Lemba-*Lakkous*. The breasts and genitals are distinctly shown by grooves. The figure has a long neck and simplified facial characteristics. It may represent the divinity of fertility which is known from terracotta figurines. This is the largest Chalcolithic limestone figurine found so far in regular excavations. Ht 36 cm. Cyprus Museum, Nicosia.

Twenty pit-graves covered with limestone slabs were excavated beneath the floor of one particular building which must have been of special significance. The burials are slightly earlier than the occupation of the houses which must be assigned to the Chalcolithic II period. They contained skeletons of children, laid on their right sides in a contracted position. Holes through the floors were probably meant to allow for the pouring of libations in honour of the dead, recalling a custom at Khirokitia. There were no burial gifts. The cemetery for adults may be located elsewhere.

OTHER SITES

Among other Chalcolithic sites, those near the neighbouring modern village of Kissonerga have produced rich ceramic material and steatite figurines of cruciform type, both male and female. At the site of Kissonerga-*Mylouthkia* no architectural remains have been found; several large cavities of irregular shape, up to 16 m long and 1.5 m deep, have been excavated; they contained mainly pottery, stone bowls, small stone and bone tools, animal bones, figurines in steatite and terracotta, carbonized cereals and lentils. A copper fish-hook, the earliest from Cyprus, was also discovered. The Kissonerga sites have also produced fragmentary painted clay figurines. Rich ceramic material has been discovered at Lemba-*Lakkous* which resembles that of Erimi-*Bamboula* in the initial stages, but which changes to types found at the Ambelikou Chalcolithic II period settlement. Calibrated C14 dates for the initial stages at Kissonerga-*Mylouthkia* are *c.* 3500 BC, which means that this site is earlier than Lemba-*Lakkous*. The pottery is mainly Glossy Burnished ware, and the prevailing shape is the shallow bowl with straight flaring sides.

At Kissonerga-*Mosphilia* there is Red Monochrome Painted and Red-on-White pottery with bold patterns such as multiple festoons decorating hemispherical bowls. Scanty architectural remains have so far been uncovered. They may constitute the earliest traces of human occupation in this area.

The best evidence for burial customs of the Chalcolithic period comes from the cemetery of Souskiou-*Vathyrkakas*.[24] The site is

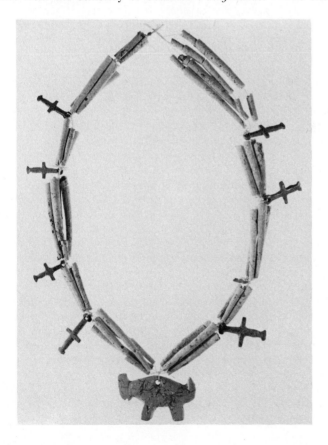

20 Necklace from a tomb (excavated by the Cyprus Department of Antiquities) at the Chalcolithic I cemetery of Souskiou-*Vathyrkakas*. It consists of dentalia and small steatite cruciform pendants in human form as well as a larger animal pendant. L. 35.5 cm. Cyprus Museum, Nicosia.

situated *c.* 1.5 km southwest of Souskiou, and *c.* 2 km northeast of Kouklia (Palaepaphos), near the edge of a rocky plateau close to a ravine which leads down into the Dhiarizos river valley. The associated settlement lies some distance from the cemetery. The graves have nearly all been looted, but three tombs were excavated by the Department of Antiquities. They are deep bottle-shaped shafts, back-filled with soil after burial and sealed with a large stone slab. These shaft graves – about 2 m deep, 1.2–1.5 m in diameter at the bottom, and 75–90 cm at the elliptical entrance (stomion) – recall the only chamber-tomb at Philia-*Drakos* A, as well as the pit-graves at Lemba-*Lakkous*, though the latter are very modest compared with the well-executed shafts of Souskiou. Up to three skeletons were found in the same tomb. The dead were laid in a contracted position, with a large number of gifts including pottery, steatite figurines, necklaces of dentalium beads and steatite pendants. A stone phallus was found by looters on the surface in the area of the cemetery.

20

Art and religion

Our knowledge of religious beliefs during the Early Chalcolithic has been enriched by recent discoveries. The Lemba-*Lakkous* limestone figurine of a nude female goddess,[25] and the slightly larger limestone statuette of a similar type from Cyprus (now in a private collection in Switzerland), suggest the existence of cult statues in sacred places. They were imitated in steatite[26] to be offered as gifts to the dead or worn as pendants, and were perhaps intended as copies of a religious symbol which was uniformly and widely accepted, in the same way that crosses are worn by Christians today. A steatite idol from Yialia in the Paphos District shows a human figure wearing such a cruciform pendant. Steatite, or more correctly picrolite,[27] is indigenous to southwestern Cyprus and provides an excellent material for the development of 'minor sculpture' in the Chalcolithic centres. It has a grey-green surface which can be highly polished. These cruciform statuettes, *c.* 10–12 cm in height (the pendants are much smaller), have facial characteristics rendered in relief. The legs are separated by a groove, and the figures are usually shown seated, with outstretched arms. Occasionally their gender is indicated. There are also double figurines (male and female) in a cross-shaped arrangement, and there is one example of a small figurine standing on the head of another, recalling similar renditions in marble from the Cyclades. Other objects in steatite include pendants in the form of quadrupeds, and also a steatite bowl from Souskiou. The two large, limestone figures mentioned above demonstrate the boldness and dexterity of Chalcolithic sculptors. They are 36 and 39 cm in height respectively. They display affinities both with the Cycladic figurines of the Aegean and also with nude female figurines from the Asiatic mainland, though one should not exclude the possibility that they are the fruit of an internal development, with roots in an earlier cultural stage of Cyprus.

21

Clay models of a nude female divinity with tattooed breasts have also been found on Chalcolithic sites. One example, now in the Louvre,[28] represents the divinity seated, with a large bowl on her outstretched legs, pressing her breasts with both hands, probably in a ritual gesture.

21 Cruciform figurine of grey-green steatite from Lemba-*Lakkous*. The breasts are clearly indicated. Ht 5.8 cm. Cyprus Museum, Nicosia.

A unique hollow terracotta figure, 36 cm high, represents a nude male seated on a low stool.[29] He has both arms bent up, with the elbows on the knees and the head between the hands. The mouth is half open. There is a perforation at the top of the head, through which water was probably poured. This flowed through the prominent tubular penis. The attitude of this grotesque figure recalls that of a much smaller terracotta figure from Roumania, known as 'The Thinker'.

Discoveries such as that of a phallus at Souskiou (recalling that of Ayios Epiktitos-*Vrysi*), of twin statuettes of steatite (male and female) in a cross-shaped arrangement, and of nude female figures such as the Lemba-*Lakkous* goddess, illustrate that the prehistoric religion of Cyprus, which started with the veneration of the dead in the Neolithic period, had now apparently developed into the veneration of life through the worship of a divinity (male and female?) of fertility. This was to dominate the Cypriot pantheon for many centuries afterwards.

The ceramic industry

Considerable progress was made in the ceramic industry during the Chalcolithic. Though Red Lustrous pottery, which appeared already in the Neolithic II period, was still produced, the pottery style *par excellence* during Chalcolithic I was Red-on-White ware. Bold, abstract, geometric and vegetal motifs were applied in red or brown paint on the white-slipped surface of vases. Shapes include large pithoi with straight or convex sides, jugs or bottles with a pointed base, composite jugs, pyxides with lids, mastoid bowls, stemmed bowls and askoi (zoomorphic or bird-shaped vessels for pouring). Of particular importance is an askos with a body of a quadruped and a human face (a centaur?) recalling similar monsters of the same period from the Balkan region.[30] There are uniform stylistic tendencies apparent in various centres such as Erimi-*Bamboula*, Souskiou-*Vathyrkakas* and Lemba-*Lakkous*; bowls are often decorated with geometric patterns arranged

22

23

24

22 Large pithos from the Chalcolithic I settlement of Erimi (excavated by the Cyprus Department of Antiquities, 1933, 1935). It is decorated with elaborate geometric motifs in red paint on a white background. Ht 53 cm. Cyprus Museum, Nicosia.

23 (*Left*) Composite vase consisting of three intercommunicating bottles. Their surface is decorated with geometric motifs in red paint on a white background. From the Chalcolithic I cemetery at Souskiou-*Vathyrkakas* (near Palaepaphos).

24 (*Below*) Zoomorphic vase. Its neck is in the shape of a human face, the rest of the body represents a quadruped with a pointed tail. The body surface is decorated with geometric patterns in the Red-on-White technique. Similar monsters, which recall the much later centaurs of Greek mythology, are also known from the Balkan region and date to the same (Chalcolithic) period. From the Chalcolithic I cemetery of Souskiou-*Vathyrkakas*. L. 22 cm; ht 13.5 cm. Hadjiprodromou Collection, Famagusta.

in narrow bands applied vertically, horizontally or obliquely on the exterior, leaving large reserved spaces which make the decoration more prominent. There is an infinite variety of motifs, including latticed triangles, lozenges, chequers and meanders, all very delicately applied. Here we see the initial flowering of a strong tradition of painted decoration which was to develop spectacularly over the next three millennia of the island's history. The vases have handles and spouts, lugs and knobs.

Even if one excludes the possibility of an external influence on the development of the cruciform figurines and the zoomorphic and bird-shaped vases, it should be noted that these appear in Cyprus at the same time as the first copper objects: a chisel at Erimi, a chisel and a blade fragment at Lemba, a spiral ornament at Souskiou and a fish-hook at   25 Kissonerga-*Mylouthkia*, though it would be wrong to assume that these copper objects were imported. Considering the sudden increase of population in western Cyprus, one might cautiously hypothesize some connection with the Balkans or the Aegean which encouraged the development of new cultural ideas.

25 Copper hook, the earliest metal object from Cyprus. From Kissonerga-*Mylouthkia*. Chalcolithic I period. L. 1.13 cm.

The end of the Chalcolithic

Because of the gap between the end of the Chalcolithic I period at Erimi-*Bamboula* c. 2500 BC (Dikaios' C14 dating) and the beginning of the Early Bronze Age c. 2300 BC, a Chalcolithic II and III period had to be postulated. The site which provides some evidence for the first of these is Ambelikou, near the northwestern coast.[31] A limited excavation there brought to light a circular hut associated with Monochrome pottery (Red Lustrous and Red-and-Black Lustrous). The Red-on-White pottery which flourished during the Chalcolithic I period deteriorated in quality and diminished considerably in quantity. A settlement site at Philia, referred to as Philia site B, has produced pottery similar to that of Ambelikou-*Ayios Georghios*, along with a few specimens of a new fabric known as Black-Slip-and-Combed ware. this also appears at the settlement site of Kyra-*Alonia* and the cemetery of Kyra-*Kaminia*. Because of the above ceramic interrelations, Dikaios proposed that the Ambelikou-*Ayios Georghios* material should be dated to around 2500 BC (Chalcolithic II) and that the other two sites which produced Monochrome wares and Black-Slip-and-Combed ware immediately followed Ambelikou. The same Black-Slip-and-Combed ware also appears at Tarsus during Early Bronze II, and this provides a useful chronological datum for the beginning of the Early Bronze Age.

3

The Early Bronze Age

The transition from the end of the Chalcolithic period to the beginning of the Early Bronze Age is not in the least easy to distinguish, either chronologically or culturally, nor does it cover the island homogeneously. Although the systematic study of the Early Bronze Age (or Early Cypriot as it is usually known) began more than half a century ago, archaeologists have confined themselves almost exclusively to the excavation of cemeteries, either because of the rich tomb-gifts which they frequently yield or because these cemeteries, often lying on hill slopes, are exposed to looting or destruction by levelling operations. The rescue excavation of tombs constitutes more than fifty per cent of the field activity of the Department of Antiquities every year. Thus our knowledge of the Early Bronze Age relies almost entirely on the evidence of tomb material, although this is incomplete and occasionally deceptive.

As early as 1926 Einar Gjerstad proposed that the Early Bronze Age culture of Cyprus had its origins in Anatolia.[1] He based his arguments on the resemblance of Early Bronze Age pottery types (Red Polished ware) with those of Anatolia. This view, arrived at well before the Neolithic and Chalcolithic periods in Cyprus had been distinguished, still forms the basis of modern theory and has been further strengthened by a fresh study of the problem by the same scholar fifty-five years later.[2]

Excavations at several sites in the Ovgos river valley in northwestern Cyprus, near Morphou and Ambelikou, have brought ceramic material to light which is new to the island. This is 'Philia ware', from the site which has since been assigned to the 'Philia Culture'[3] or, more satisfactorily, to Chalcolithic III.[4] Unfortunately these researches, made during the Second World War, were of a restricted character and were never followed up.[5] The Philia ceramic assemblage is mostly dominated by Red Polished ware, though other types are present. Jugs with flat bases and cut-away necks are the most characteristic shapes, but there are also goblets in the shape of cut-away necks, bottles, amphoriskoi and some other vessels. The surface is usually plain polished, but occasionally it is decorated with engraved linear patterns such as parallel chevrons, zigzag lines, herring-bone motifs and parallel lines. Other fabrics found together with Red Polished Philia ware are Red-on-White, with painted decoration in red on a whitish surface, and the Black-Slip-and-Combed ware. The latter is usually represented by small bowls which have a red undercoat and a black surface; part of the black paint is combed off before it dries, to expose the red undercoat.

26

27

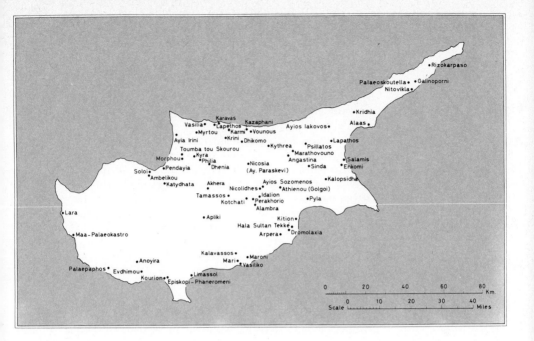

26 Bronze Age sites in Cyprus.

This pottery is also known at Tarsus in Cilicia.[6] A fourth fabric is Black Slip Painted ware, which is decorated with red or with red and white bands, though there are variants. A recent study, by Gjerstad, of the material found by Dikaios in 1942 in a stratigraphic excavation at Ambelikou-*Ayios Georghios*, is most revealing.[7] The so-called Philia ware of Chalcolithic III date is found side by side with ceramic types of the Chalcolithic II period. He proposes that these new ceramic types were introduced by foreign immigrants who mingled with a local native population that continued for a while to produce its own Chalcolithic wares. The closest parallels for the newly imported wares are in southwestern Anatolia, on the Konya plain and in Cilicia. Gjerstad has thus reconfirmed his 1926 theory that Anatolians introduced these wares and were therefore the driving force behind the Early Bronze Age in Cyprus.

The stratigraphy at Ambelikou-*Ayios Georghios* suggests not only the peaceful coexistence of the foreign immigrants with the Chalcolithic II population of that region, but also that this site may have been the first to be settled by the new immigrants in Early Cypriot IA. They then spread to Kyra-*Alonia* and to Philia in Early Cypriot IB. The tombs at the latter site contained numbers of metal adzes, knives, pins and ear-rings, apart from pottery, which suggests that the newcomers brought with them advanced metallurgical techniques.[8] It is true that copper objects were already known in Chalcolithic I, but these may either have been imports or made of native copper, and there is still insufficient evidence to speak of extensive metallurgical activity in this period.

The immigrants did not settle in all the Chalcolithic II sites of the Morphou region, but spread to Vasilia to the north and to Dhenia and Ayia Paraskevi to the east. There are two other sites not far from the southwestern coast, near the villages of Anoyira and Sotira, which produced pottery of the 'Philia Culture'.[9] Are we to suppose that the immigrants of the Morphou region later crossed the Troodos mountains and spread to the south, or is it possible that some of them settled directly along the southwestern coast? The absence of 'Philia Culture' pottery at the main Chalcolithic centres of Erimi-*Bamboula* and Lemba-*Lakkous* may discount such a possibility, but further investigations in this area might, for example, reveal that the problem is one of chronology. C14 analysis has shown that the Chalcolithic sites near Lemba-*Lakkous* survived until a late date, possibly after the Early Bronze Age I was introduced into northern Cyprus.[10] A recent archaeological survey has brought to light a settlement pattern which helps fill the gap between the end of the Chalcolithic I and the beginning of the Early Cypriot period in the southern part of the island. The earliest Bronze Age settlements which have been traced lie close to the southern end of a route which crossed the Troodos mountains via the Amiandos pass. This might explain how the 'Philia Culture' penetrated to the south.[11]

Gjerstad, trying to support his theory for a peaceful symbiosis between native Cypriots and Anatolian immigrants, suggests that metal weapons found at Ayia Paraskevi and in the tombs of Vasilia – though some authorities believe these tombs are later – may date to the Early Cypriot IC period. This was the stage when the foreign and local people had become a united population prepared to defend the sources of their wealth against the inhabitants of Cyprus who did not have access to copper mines. The same phenomenon is certainly evident in later periods, when rivalry between the eastern and western regions for control of the copper mines caused the formation of a fortified line dividing the northern part of the island. One should not exclude the possibility, however, that such weapons, known to the Anatolians prior to their immigration to Cyprus, were prestige possessions of the male population. But Gjerstad's suggestion is attractive and may explain the small number of sites with Philia ware that have been found so far in the east.[12] A few Red Polished IC and II pottery fragments have been found at Kalopsidha in eastern Cyprus,[13] but these may be imports traded from the west. In the course of such trade, no doubt, the east was introduced to the Early Bronze Age during the Early Cypriot III period.

This view of the sequence of events in the initial stages of the Early Bronze Age, based on the foreign character of the 'Philia Culture', is by no means universally accepted. James Stewart, the excavator of a number of Early Bronze Age sites in Cyprus (Vasilia, Ayia Paraskevi, Vounous), and several others, has suggested that the 'Philia Culture' is a regional phenomenon and that the Early Bronze Age begins with Vounous. At this cemetery, in the southern foothills of the Kyrenia coastal plain near Bellapais, the development of Red Polished ware from its earliest phase can be traced. According to Stewart this ware is a development of the Chalcolithic Red Polished ware,[14] but his theory has many weaknesses and few supporters. It does not account for the fact that there are many new shapes of Red Polished ware in the 'Philia Culture' which is too widespread to be a localized variant of the Morphou region. Nevertheless, the debt of the Early Cypriot I culture to the Chalcolithic period, at least in the initial transition stages, should be considered. In the beginning there may have been a limited number of immigrants, and the process of settlement was perhaps gradual. It is also possible that in some areas – especially at Vasilia – elements of the 'Philia Culture' persisted longer, side by side with the later phases of Early Cypriot II and III.[15]

It is unfortunate that excavation of this crucial phase in the island's prehistory has been so limited and that no settlement site has been extensively explored.

Suggested chronology

The calibrated date for the introduction to Cyprus of the Early Bronze Age culture (Early Cypriot IA) is *c.* 3000/2900 BC, according to Gjerstad's high dating. Other chronological schemes envisage the start of the 'Philia Culture' in *c.* 2500 BC. This date coincides with the end of Early Bronze Age II in Anatolia. Whether the immigrants who came to Cyprus constitute the invading elements which destroyed the Early Bronze Age II Tarsus in Cilicia, or whether they are refugees from the latter region, is not very clear. It should be borne in mind that Cyprus had connections with Tarsus even *before* the Early Bronze Age II catastrophe.[16]

The calibrated dates recently put forward by Gjerstad for the whole of the Early Bronze Age are as follows (though these, since they are very high, are not universally accepted):[17]

27 Red Polished ware jug with a beak-shaped spout and a flat base. A projection near the rim opposite the spout served as a handle. The neck and shoulder are decorated with linear patterns incised after firing. The influence of Anatolian pottery is apparent. From the Early Bronze Age I cemetery of Philia, Tomb 1. Ht 30 cm. Cyprus Museum, Nicosia.

Period IA 3000/2900–2850/2750 BC
       IB 2850/2750–2700/2600 BC
       IC 2700/2600–2400/2300 BC
       II 2400/2300–2250/2150 BC
      III 2250/2150–1900/1800 BC

A lower system of dating has been proposed by R. S. Merrillees:[18]

I   2300–2075 BC
II   2075–2000 BC
III   2000–1900 BC

R. S. Merrillees and S. Swiny now consider the 'Philia Culture' as part of the Chalcolithic period, beginning c. 2500 BC. E. J. Peltenburg proposes 2500/2300 as the end of the Chalcolithic period.[19]

Tomb architecture

Wealthy tomb-gifts reflect a prospering community. However, there are serious problems connected with the funerary architecture of the Early Cypriot I period. At Vounous Cemetery A, the first burial chambers of humble dimensions with small entrance passages (dromoi) obviously evolved from the Chalcolithic III ('Philia Culture') examples at Ayia Paraskevi, Philia-*Vasiliko* or Sotira-*Kaminoudhia*, which, in essence if not in shape, are linked to the earlier Chalcolithic I 'bottle-shaped' pits without dromoi at Souskiou-*Vathyrkakas*.

Some scholars have argued,[20] primarily on the ceramic evidence, that the monumental chamber tombs at Vasilia, 3 to 5 m long, are of 'Philia Culture'-Early Cypriot I date. If so, they are a sudden development both in size and shape, without recorded antecedent in Cyprus. It is unlikely that the chamber tomb was introduced by Anatolians, since the type is unknown in that area. The closest parallels are to be found in the Palestinian Middle Bronze Age,[21] and a reappraisal of this controversial cemetery is necessary.

The necropolis at Vounous is one of the most fully excavated in Cyprus.[22] Its chamber tombs were initially small rock-cut chambers, with a short dromos leading to the chamber through a stomion which was sealed with a stone slab. The dead bodies (at the beginning there were one or two interments in each chamber) were accompanied by gifts such as food, weapons, ornaments and particularly pottery. The material from these tombs ranges chronologically from Early Cypriot II (Gjerstad's chronology) to the Early Cypriot III period, the dating criteria being mainly pottery styles.

The Early Cypriot II period, as defined at Vounous A, is short in duration, with pottery types developing from Early Cypriot I. Red Polished wares continue to predominate; the shapes develop forcefully, though they lack the elegant simplicity of Early Cypriot I. The small jug with a beak-shaped mouth is the commonest form and now has a stump-type base. There are also small and medium-size bowls, the latter decorated round their rim with plastic figures such as birds and 28 animal protomes. Large bowls, supported by a high cylindrical stem, have their rim decorated with animal figures in the round or with small bowls. These vases are frequently identified as ritual vessels, but there may be instances when the potter simply wished to produce extraordinary and elaborately decorated vessels for his rich clients. Incised decoration is now much more complex than on vases of the Early Cypriot I period. This consists of linear and geometric motifs engraved on the polished red surface of the vase, and is often

supplemented by relief ornamentation, such as bull-heads and snakes, in the form of wavy bands or figures in the round. The interiors of the bowls and the rim exteriors are blackened by a special firing process, resulting in a pleasing bichromy. The bull and snake may be associated with the divinities of fertility and death respectively, but the frequent occurrence of the bull as a decorative motif may well be due to the introduction of cattle to replace the pig, less suited to a partly arable economy. The long association of the bull with ritual in Anatolia is of course well known. In general the ceramic industry bears witness to highly skillful and imaginative potters who surpassed the imported models of the earlier periods.

28 Deep bowl of Red Polished ware, with a blackened surface around the rim. The handle is shaped like that of a dagger. The rim is decorated with three bull-heads and one ram-head, two spoon-like projections and one bird protome. Most of the exterior is decorated with incised abstract patterns. Early Bronze Age II period. From Vounous, Tomb 160, chamber B, no. 12. Cyprus Museum, Nicosia.

Trade and daily life

Foreign relations began during this period, though perhaps on a modest scale, as is shown by a Plain White ware jug from Syria found in an Early Cypriot II tomb at Vounous A.

The final phase of the Early Bronze Age (Early Cypriot III) is better known than Early Cypriot I and II, though information again derives solely from tombs, particularly those at Vounous B, Lapethos and Limassol. During this period the Bronze Age culture spread throughout the island. At first the valleys along the northern and southern slopes of the Kyrenia mountains were the most thickly populated, though the fringes of the central plain also had their clusters of settlements. No doubt the flourishing economy caused a population increase and expansion was necessary. The economy continued to be

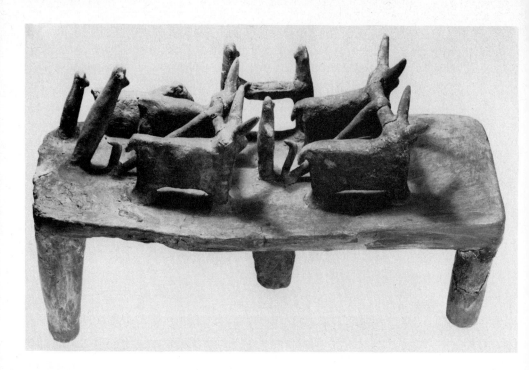

29 Clay model representing a ploughing scene. It consists of a table resting on five legs on top of which are two pairs of oxen drawing a plough; there are also four human figures, two behind the ploughs and two holding a trough(?) with grain. End of the Early Bronze Age. From a tomb in the cemetery of Vounous, special series 1. Ht 19 cm; L. 41 cm. Cyprus Museum, Nicosia.

basically agricultural, encouraging the preference for irrigated arable land. The clay model of a ploughing scene from Vounous shows that a wooden elbow plough, probably equipped with a metal ploughshare, was used. Increasing numbers of settlements near copper-mining areas, however, such as Ambelikou, indicate the increasing economic importance of metallurgy. Hunting must have continued to be a favourite sport, illustrated by the frequent occurrence of stags on vases.

We may assume that agriculture, hunting and metallurgy were major preoccupations. The horse had been introduced to Cyprus, probably from Anatolia, as shown by a skeleton found in a tomb at Lapethos. This must have facilitated considerably both transport and agriculture. In their leisure time, Cypriots enjoyed the game of *Senet*, if the interpretation as a gaming board of a Red Polished tablet with rows of shallow depressions belonging to a private collection is correct. This Egyptian game was played on boards which had three rows of ten squares, but in Cyprus they were usually of limestone and were known already at the beginning of the Early Bronze Age, as recently discovered at Sotira-*Kaminoudhia*.

Commercial relations with the outside world increased in this period. An Early Minoan III–Middle Minoan Ia jar from Lapethos and a few dagger blades of Early Minoan III–Middle Minoan I types from Vounous and Lapethos were imported from Crete, and faience beads were imported from Egypt. There is no evidence yet of Cypriot exports in these lands, but perhaps these were of a perishable character or simply of copper.

In spite of the fact that no settlements of this period have so far been excavated, architecture is illustrated by a house excavated at Alambra, in the central part of Cyprus near the eastern foothills of the Troodos mountains.[23] The development from the Chalcolithic house type is marked: now there are two four-sided rooms in an L-shaped arrangement with a pen for animals within an enclosure. The walls have rubble foundations and a superstructure of mudbrick; the roof was flat.

Certain aspects of daily life may be ascertained from decorative motifs on vases or from *genre* clay models. These belong to the very end of Early Cypriot III and perhaps show Egyptian influence. We have already mentioned the ploughing scene from Vounous; other representations show women grinding corn, making bread, or human figures riding animals, pouring liquids and so on. Spindle whorls are plentiful in tombs. These, and bronze toggle-pins, suggest the kind of clothes that were worn. In fact, impressions and even some remains of woven cloth have survived. Hair-ornaments in gold and silver, though rare, appear side by side with others in bronze. Women also wore necklaces of paste beads.

Pottery-making continued to be a major activity, probably of the female population. Regional styles appear on the northern and southern coasts as well as at the tip of the Karpass peninsula, but there is also a kind of *koene* of Red Polished ware vases. The jugs have rounded or nippled bases and there is an infinite variety of other forms. Apart from the richness of the engraved, relief and plastic decoration on the vases, one should mention the exuberant character of their shapes. They are often composite, and show extraordinary potting-skill. The combination of functional vase-forms with plastic figures, for example the composite bowl with a high vertical handle in the form of a perforated, plank-shaped human figure, appears to us astonishingly 'contemporary'. Zoomorphic and bird-shaped askoi complete a ceramic repertoire rich in imagination and humour.

30

30 Zoomorphic vase of Red Polished III ware representing a quadruped with a long neck. A small bowl is modelled on the neck behind the head. The whole surface is covered with incised linear patterns. The potter's sense of humour is apparent. Ht 14 cm. Cyprus Museum, Nicosia, A472.

31 Clay model of a sanctuary consisting of an open-air enclosure containing human and animal figures rendered in the round. Opposite the gate, against the wall, are three human figures in relief holding snakes and wearing bull-masks. There are groups of human figures, including one kneeling in front of the figures in relief. Oxen stand on either side of the gate. Another human figure is climbing up the wall near the gate to see what is going on inside; perhaps the ritual was of a mystic character. This is an important religious document dating to the very end of the Early Bronze Age. From Vounous, Tomb 22, no. 26. Ht 8 cm; diam. 37 cm. Cyprus Museum, Nicosia.

Apart from the Red Polished wares which still predominate, there are small vessels in Black Polished ware, decorated with deep, broad incisions often filled with lime (a similar phenomenon appears in the decoration of Red Polished engraved vases) so as to accentuate the engraved decoration against its dark background.

Metallurgy

During the Early Cypriot I period the communities of western Cyprus enjoyed a thriving economy, due mainly to the new dynamism and metallurgical skills introduced by the newcomers. It is not known where copper was mined during this early period or where it was smelted. But there is no doubt that the majority of metal objects found in the tombs of this period were made in Cyprus, even though we may discount some of them as imports. Although we have no evidence for mining or smelting in the Early Cypriot,[24] it must have existed, for the Middle Cypriot industrial complex at Ambelikou probably mirrors an earlier tradition. This site, near the copper mines, produced crucibles associated with stone and terracotta moulds for casting axes. A large variety of metal objects such as daggers, knives, axes, chisels, tweezers and razors, occur in tombs. For the first time there is evidence for tin-bronze (in Vounous cemetery) which implies the importation of tin from abroad, perhaps from Mesopotamia or Asia Minor.[25]

Religious life

A rich religious life is evident in the communities of the Early Cypriot III period, and particularly at Vounous where, it has been suggested, there may even have been a major religious centre. Apart from the frequent occurrence of religious symbols on vases (bull-heads and snakes) there are models of open-air sanctuaries in which libations or animals are being offered to the divinities of fertility and death. The well-known model of an open-air sanctuary found in a tomb at Vounous is perhaps the most precious document for the prehistoric religion of Cyprus which has survived. It consists of a circular enclosure within which several human figures attend a religious ritual. The centre of worship is a triad probably of *xoana* (or cultic portrayals) shown in relief against the wall opposite the entrance. They wear bull-masks and hold snakes in their hands, the symbols of fertility and death respectively. One person is kneeling in front of these *xoana*, while others are seated on benches to either side. There is a figure seated on a throne, obviously the high priest or the chief of the community. Bulls

31

32 Clay model of a sanctuary in Red Polished ware, from a tomb at Kotchati. It consists of a rectangular panel with three poles in relief topped by bull-heads, and two horned projections between the poles. On the flat rectangular 'floor' stands a female human figure about to pour libations into a jar. This model may be an abbreviated version of the Vounous sanctuary model. End of the Early Bronze Age. Ht 19 cm. Cyprus Museum, Nicosia, no. 1970/V–28/1.

49

33 Terracotta figurine of Red Polished III ware representing a seated woman holding an infant. Probably detached from the rim decoration of a large bowl. She has tattooed breasts and may be connected with a fertility scene. Ht 12.2 cm. Cyprus Museum, Nicosia, no. 1970/VI–26/6.

34 Plank-shaped idol of Red Polished III ware. The body is rectangular, without any indication of arms or legs; there are two long necks topped by flat heads with large pierced ears and a prominent nose. The front surface is decorated with incised linear patterns. From a tomb in the cemetery of Dhenia, west of Nicosia. Ht 30 cm. Cyprus Museum, Nicosia, no. 1943/IV–13/4.

for sacrifice stand on either side of the entrance, as well as human figures holding infants, which are also, according to some suggestions, destined for sacrifice. Another person is trying to see what is going on within the enclosure by climbing the wall, an eloquent detail showing the mystic character of the ritual which could be attended only by initiated persons. Two other models of sanctuaries have been found in a tomb at Kotchati in central Cyprus. They are somewhat abbreviated versions of the Vounous model, with the three *xoana* topped by bull-heads fixed against a panel. There is a human figure in front of the *xoana* near a large jar, clearly in the act of pouring libations.[26] The fact that similar sanctuary models have been found in northern and central Cyprus illustrates the homogeneity of religious beliefs based on the veneration of the divinities of life and death. Human figurines, mainly associated with fertility, are found round the shoulder of large bowls: a group of human figures assisting in childbirth, a wedded couple in bed, women with their tattooed breasts showing prominently,[27] or holding infants. There are also plank-shaped clay idols elaborately decorated with engraved patterns. They represent women and may perhaps imitate life-size wooden *xoana* which the artist could see in the sanctuaries.[28]

Cyprus at the crossroads

About one thousand years after the end of the Chalcolithic period, Cyprus found herself in contact with her more sophisticated neighbours in the Near East and the Aegean, where social and

35 Composite bowl of Red
Polished III ware. It consists
of four hemispherical bowls
which have a common handle
in the form of a long plank-
shaped figurine; it terminates
in a female figure holding an
infant in her arms. Ht 46 cm.
From Vounous, Tomb 48, no.
2. Cyprus Museum, Nicosia.
(The bowls are restored.)

technological developments had started much earlier. Trade relations
began with neighbouring countries and new cultural ideas were
introduced. The rich religious life and outstanding artistic creations
bear witness to an advanced culture and an air of confidence. This
development was due mainly to the exploitation of the copper mines,
which were to become the major economic resource of the island, but
which were also to cause friction between the two rival regions of east
and west, which vied for their control. Though there is no evidence for
armed conflict during the Early Bronze Age, the occurrence of so many
weapons in tombs, mainly at Vounous and Lapethos, indicates that the
danger of war between the rival communities was always present. In the
central part of the island are some fortified refuges, but conditions as a
whole remained peaceful, and this explains the unified cultural
development throughout Cyprus.

4

The Middle Bronze Age

The Middle Bronze Age, or Middle Cypriot, is of short duration, and the early part can be linked to the end of the Early Bronze Age from which it follows on in unbroken sequence. The later part heralds the Late Bronze Age and differs substantially from the early part.[1] The beginning of the Middle Cypriot period is difficult to define in absolute chronological terms, since it is not characterized by any major cultural innovations. Scholars usually define it by the appearance of a specific type of pottery known as White Painted II (White Painted I had already appeared at Vounous at the very end of Early Cypriot III). The absolute dates of this period of transition, from the end of Early Cypriot III to the beginning of the Middle Cypriot, are provided by the Early Minoan III or Middle Minoan Ia spouted jar found in a tomb at Lapethos, which is dated to the end of Early Cypriot III, and a Middle

36 Minoan II Kamares cup found in a Middle Cypriot I tomb at Karmi.[2] The chronology of the end of the Middle Cypriot period is based on evidence from Egypt and Palestine, where Cypriot imports have been found dating to the very beginning of the Late Cypriot period. The generally accepted dates for the Middle Cypriot period range from $c.$ 1900 to $c.$ 1600 BC.[3] The period is arbitrarily divided into three phases, I–III, each lasting about one hundred years.

Settlements

Compared with the Early Cypriot, this period is one of cultural decline in the north, though it also heralds the bold political, social, cultural and economic ventures of the Late Cypriot period. The Middle Cypriot is well documented because, unlike its predecessor, we now have for the first time evidence from excavated settlements with their adjoining cemeteries, as at Kalopsidha, Episkopi-*Phaneromeni* and Alambra. The island was widely inhabited except for the mountainous areas.

The pattern of settlement at the beginning of the Middle Cypriot is marked by considerable changes.[4] The Early Cypriot centre of Vounous gradually declined and Lapethos became the most important of all the settlements of northern Cyprus, probably also functioning as a port for the copper trade. The plateau between the western end of the Kyrenia mountain range and the Aloupos river valley to the south also supported many settlements. Scattered among them, however, are several forts which indicate that conditions were not peaceful, or that an imminent danger obliged the inhabitants to defend themselves by

36 Middle Minoan II (Kamares style) skyphos, found in a tomb of the Middle Bronze Age at Karmi, Kyrenia District (excavated by an Australian Mission, 1962). Several Middle Minoan vases and bronzes have been found at sites along the northern coast of Cyprus. Ht 9 cm. Cyprus Museum, Nicosia.

building places of refuge. The thick walls and bastions of the fortress of Krini, on the south side of the Kyrenia mountain range, stand even today to a height of 2 m. There is another fort near Dhikomo and others north of the Aloupos river valley in the Karpashia forest. The character and location of these fortresses, quite far from the sea and behind the mountains, suggest that they were places of refuge rather than defences against an external enemy. The danger was internal, the result of traditional enmity and antagonism between the east and west of the island. This was already evident at the beginning of the Early Bronze Age when the west controlled the copper mines and the east the good arable land. Eastern Cyprus, which was sparsely inhabited during the later part of Early Cypriot III, now developed rapidly, especially the northern edge of the Mesaoria plain, from Nicosia in the west to Trikomo in the east, which now boasted centres such as Kythrea, Marathovouno, Psillatos and Lapathos. The Karpass peninsula is also to be noted, with centres such as Galinoporni and Rizokarpaso. Kalopsidha, east of the Bay of Salamis, became a very important centre and may be considered the 'capital' of east Cyprus, as Lapethos was for the west. Fortresses occur also in the centre of the island, two in the area of Ayios Sozomenos in the vicinity of two large Middle Cypriot settlements, and at Nitovikla in the Karpass, where a fortress of Anatolian or Syro-Palestinian type was built at the end of the Middle Cypriot.

The Nitovikla fort was constructed on a low hill near the coast. It is a rectangular building, with a strong screen wall round an open courtyard onto which several rooms opened. The flat roofs were reached by wooden ladders and thus served as platforms for the soldiers. There was a cistern in the courtyard to supply water.

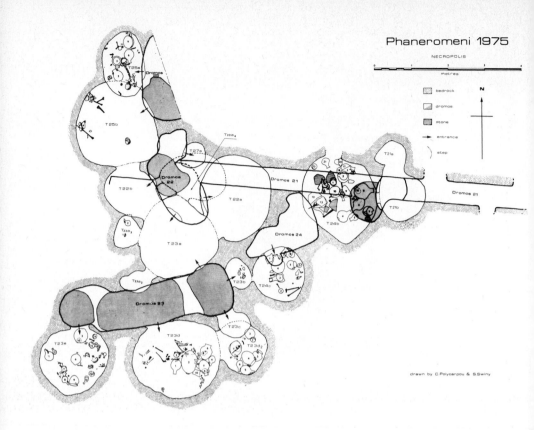

37 Plan of the tombs
excavated at the necropolis of
Episkopi-*Phaneromeni*. The
cemetery lies a short distance
from the settlement. It dates
to the very end of the Early
Bronze Age and the Middle
Bronze Age. The tombs are
chambers, often with a
common dromos.

The south coast of the island was not thickly populated in the
Larnaca District, but in the Limassol area population seems to have
been dense, contrary to previous views. Apart from the settlement at
Episkopi-*Phaneromeni*, near the mouth of the Kouris river, other
settlements and cemeteries have been traced in the course of a recent
surface survey.[5] In fact, the gap in this region from Early Cypriot I
down to the Late Cypriot period has now been filled.[6] Of note,
however, is the complete lack of fortified settlements in the south,
which suggests that the upheavals affecting the northern half of the
island were not witnessed in the south, which continued to prosper as it
approached the Late Bronze Age.

Fortifications, houses and cemeteries

Though the fortifications indicate tensions between the two northern
regions of the island, the situation is not one of war, and there is clear
evidence of trade between the two. Considerable wealth is demonstrated by the tombs of Lapethos, where large quantities of vases as well
as bronzes were placed as tomb-gifts, but particularly daggers,
indicating that the male population had to be ready for any eventuality.

Military architecture of the final phase of the Middle Cypriot has
been mentioned briefly. Domestic architecture is represented by the
Middle Cypriot and Late Cypriot IA settlement at Episkopi-
37 *Phaneromeni*. The cemetery, whose unusually long dromoi contain up
to eight rock-cut chamber tombs, lies a short distance to the southwest.

The earlier habitations consist of large, multi-roomed structures which unfortunately are poorly preserved. More is known about the later settlement, also consisting of multi-roomed structures, here divided by a street. The rooms are rectangular with rubble foundations supporting flat-roofed mudbrick and *pisé* superstructures. There is evidence that at least one of the two houses had a second storey. Although looted and then burnt, the houses show evidence for a well-organized, self-sufficient agrarian community.

At Alambra-*Moutes* a settlement and an adjoining looted cemetery have recently been excavated.[7] Houses with large rectangular rooms and unusually well-preserved walls have so far been uncovered. One such room, with very thick walls, measures 7.5 × 6 m. The settlement has been tentatively dated to the Middle Cypriot I period.

At Kalopsidha a house forming part of the Middle Cypriot III town complex was excavated by Gjerstad. It is adjoined by a second house on the east side, and a street that runs along its south side. There are ten rooms, eight of them rectangular, arranged along three sides of an open courtyard. The size of the whole building is *c.* 15 × 12 m. The walls are of the same construction as at Episkopi-*Phaneromeni*. The roof was flat and there is no evidence for a second storey.

On the floors of the houses are the signs of considerable industrial activity. Lime plaster bins were found in many rooms at Episkopi-*Phaneromeni*, together with a multitude of lithic artefacts, pounders, querns and the like. At Kalopsidha and Episkopi bones found on the floors of the rooms indicate the presence of red deer, sheep, goats,

38 Aerial view of the remains at Episkopi-*Phaneromeni* (excavated by an American mission, 1975–7). Two complexes of houses have been uncovered, consisting of a number of rooms; the two houses were separated by a street. The settlement dates to the very end of the Middle Bronze Age and the beginning of the Late Bronze Age.

39

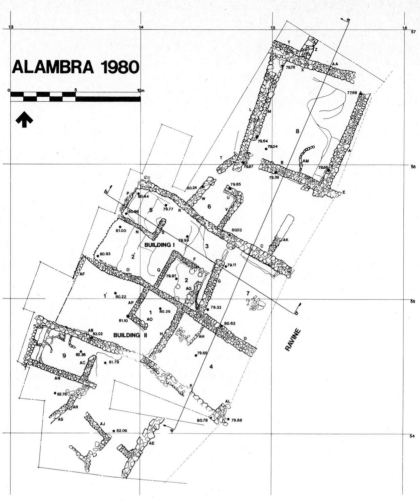

ALAMBRA 1980

BUILDING I

BUILDING II

RAVINE

39 Plan of the excavated remains of the Middle Bronze Age settlement at Alambra, south of Nicosia (excavated by an American Mission, 1976–80). The houses consist of spacious rooms with massive walls.

donkeys, cows and horses. We know that the horse was introduced to the island towards the end of Early Cypriot III or the beginning of Middle Cypriot I, and it must have revolutionized the transport of people and goods.

Funerary architecture continued Early Cypriot traditions. The dead were buried seated or in a crouched position and were supplied with food, weapons, tools and jewelry. In the northern half of the island, during the later part of the Middle Cypriot period, the chambers have a long, narrow stepped dromos, perhaps influenced by practices in the Near East. There are, however, some clear innovations: at Palaeo-skoutella, in the Karpass, low tumuli appear above the tombs, which may be a sign of Syro-Palestinian influence. In some cases there are sacrificial pits below the tumuli. At *Palaealona*, near Karmi on the northern foothills of the Kyrenia mountains, an important cemetery was excavated. One rock-cut tomb showed, on the northern side-wall of its dromos, a flat, crude relief of a human figure about 1 m in height. This is the earliest funerary relief on the island and probably reflects Egyptian influence.[8] Above the lintel of the entrance to the chamber the façade is carved to imitate the doorway of a building.

40 Shallow-hemispherical bowl of Red and Black Polished ware with two opposed rectangular perforated horizontal lug handles. The surface is decorated with finely incised linear patterns in a style which is particular to the northeastern part of the island. Middle Bronze Age. Ht 7 cm; diam. 18 cm. From Kridhia, Famagusta District. Hadjiprodromou Collection, Famagusta.

Ceramics

Anxiety and tension among the population is echoed in the vast variety of pottery styles and regional developments. During the early part of the period in the north,[9] White Painted II ware, represented by vases decorated with geometric motifs in thick red lustrous paint, perpetuates some of the vitality of Early Cypriot III pottery. White Painted II ware was first introduced at Lapethos. Already at the beginning of the Middle Cypriot the distinct separation between the east and west dominates also the cultural and artistic fields. The White Painted pottery of Kalopsidha, the 'capital' of the east, is linear, while that of Lapethos, the capital of the west, is geometric. During the middle and late phases of the period various decorative styles of White Painted ware that seem to be degenerate forms of the earlier style appear. Though the White Painted technique predominates, there are several others, such as the Red-on-Red or Red-on-Black which are characteristic of the Karpass peninsula; the debased, matt version of

41

41 Jug of Red-on-Black ware, decorated with linear patterns on a black surface. This ware is very common in the eastern part of Cyprus, and particularly in the Karpass peninsula, during the Middle Bronze Age. Ht 26 cm. Cyprus Museum, Nicosia, Inv. no. A960.

Red Polished, often covered with thin grooves carelessly rendered with a multiple hard brush; and the Black Slip and the Red Slip. There is an infinite variety of forms, the most characteristic of which are the composite jugs and bowls and the zoomorphic or bird-shaped askoi. White Painted pottery is decorated with geometric motifs over the whole surface of the vase: latticed chequers, latticed triangles, solid diamonds and groups of parallel or wavy lines, all of which are framed within rectangular panels or horizontal zones, in groupings usually poorly suited to the surface of the vase they decorate. The potter, moreover, loads his vases with string-hole projections (small lugs with holes for hanging-cords) and other accessories. Often he tries to give an anthropomorphic character to the neck and mouth by rendering facial characteristics such as ears, eyes and mouth, or putting breasts or even short arms on the shoulder. The elegance of the Early Cypriot pottery is lost, though occasionally there are some successful and pleasing specimens, such as the double flask in the Pierides Foundation Museum. This piece combines two flasks as if they were two human figures.

In the south, on the other hand, there is an unbroken tradition of monochrome pottery commencing in Chalcolithic III and only passing with the appearance of Late Cypriot painted wares. Here, incision or relief decoration are preferred, and the vitality and skill of the southern potters are second to none. The elaborate incised decoration and exuberant shapes of Red Polished I South Coast ware may be contrasted with the fine sobriety of the more functional Red Polished III mottled jars, multiple jugs and skillets.

42 Jug of White Painted III ware. The body is decorated all over with geometric patterns in black paint on a white surface. From the necropolis of Dhenia, Nicosia District. Ht 25 cm. Cyprus Museum, Nicosia, CS 992/6.

Religion

Religious ideas continue the traditions of the Early Cypriot period. A clay model of a sanctuary from Kalopsidha is almost a replica of the Early Cypriot III models from Kotchati, illustrating not only continuity but also homogeneity of religious beliefs throughout the island.[10] The idea of fertility persists and is symbolized by numerous plank-shaped idols, mainly female figures holding infants. They are found in tombs, perhaps as companions to interred men. These idols are more naturalistic than those of Early Cypriot III. Their facial characteristics are rendered more naturalistically and carefully, and for the first time they are provided with arms and legs. They are painted either in the Red Polished or White Painted technique. Apart from the female figures there are occasionally male figures with large pierced ears, probably for the suspension of clay or copper ear-rings.[11] A plank-shaped figure from Ayia Paraskevi, with White Painted decoration, has a long flat beard and quite distinct arms and legs.[12] Other plank-shaped male figures have grotesque faces.[13]

Very often there are groups of terracotta human figures, continuing the Early Bronze Age ceramic tradition in which such groups appear round the rim of large bowls. One of the most characteristic is a group in Red Polished ware, now in the Louvre, with seven human figures in front of a large trough. Their facial characteristics are carefully modelled; they wear head-dresses and rows of necklaces. Five are washing or grinding, one holds a vase and the other an infant. They are

43 Boat-shaped pyxis decorated with geometric patterns in the White Painted ware technique. On the shoulder at either end is a protome of a horse and a rider, an indication that the horse had already been introduced to the island. From the cemetery of Vounous, Tomb 64, no. 138. Ht 23.5 cm; L. 39.5 cm. Cyprus Museum, Nicosia.

59

perhaps engaged in preparing bread for the deceased. The group possibly forms part of the decoration of a vase, as mentioned above.

Trade relations

During Middle Cypriot II, foreign relations developed rapidly, especially with Syria, Palestine and Egypt. Middle Cypriot pottery is often found at such sites as Megiddo and Ras Shamra. Copper continued to be the main export. Indeed, Cyprus (*Alashiya*) is mentioned in the Mari tablets of the 17th century BC as a copper-producing country. A clay model of a ship, dated to the beginning of the Middle Cypriot and now in the Louvre,[14] illustrates the vitality of Cypriot harbours where this export trade flourished.

The end of Middle Cypriot III is marked by dramatic changes.[15] Lapethos loses her importance, as does Kalopsidha, and their place was taken by the harbour town of Enkomi which served her for long as a port for trade with the Levant. Hala Sultan Tekké, another harbour town, also increased in importance. No doubt this new pattern was the result of growing trade relations. Cypriot pottery, found in large quantities along the Syro-Palestinian coast, even appears in Cilicia. Though two new fabrics, the Tell el-Yahudiya and the Bichrome Wheelmade wares, made their appearance in the island *c.* 1600 BC, they may have been imported in the first instance in the course of trade. The latter ware, however, as we shall see below, was produced in Cyprus in the 16th century BC, perhaps by immigrant potters from the Syrian coast.

Cultural differences between east and west Cyprus and the south persisted, though they were rendered less marked by trading links between the regions – the east needing copper and the west corn. This may explain why pottery from the northern regions was frequently taken across country. The old enmities persisted, however, and it was only during the Late Cypriot period that complete cultural uniformity was achieved in the island.

5

The Late Bronze Age

Late Cypriot I–II

At the dawn of the Late Bronze Age (or Late Cypriot), *c.* 1650/1550 BC, Cyprus was experiencing much the same political conditions which prevailed at the end of Middle Cypriot III.[1] A fortress built at the northernmost part of Enkomi was destroyed soon after its construction in Late Cypriot IA, but was quickly rebuilt. By the end of Late Cypriot IA part of it was used for copper-smelting. The fortress at Nitovikla, destroyed at the end of Middle Cypriot III, was rebuilt in Late Cypriot IA in order to defend the area against sea raids from Syria or Asia Minor. The fortress at Nicolidhes was also reconstructed at this time and destroyed by the end of Late Cypriot IA.

The reason for this apparent state of emergency at the beginning of Late Cypriot IA may have been the antagonism already mentioned between western and eastern Cyprus over the control of the copper mines in the west and the arable land in the east. The necessity for territorial expansion would have become even more acute with the population increase, especially in urban centres. Other fortresses and refuges were destroyed at this time and there is also evidence for

44

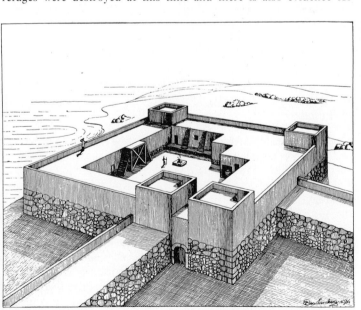

44 Reconstructed sketch of the fortress at Nitovikla, in the Karpass peninsula. It was built at the end of the Middle Bronze Age and was restored at the beginning of the Late Bronze Age. This is a period of unrest in the island. (After E. Sjöqvist, *Reports on excavations in Cyprus* (1940), 92, fig. 37.)

destruction at Kalopsidha and Episkopi-*Phaneromeni*. Were these destructions due to the activities of the Asiatic Hyksos or did they result from the internal strife which gave the west domination over eastern Cyprus? At about the same period, in Late Cypriot IA and B, mass burials were made in tombs at Pendayia, Myrtou-*Stephania* and Ayios Iakovos in the northern part of the island. It is not improbable, however, that these burials resulted from an epidemic.

During the early part of Late Cypriot I, the political life of Cyprus was influenced by internal strife, but during Late Cypriot II it was partly determined by external factors. Antagonism and war often characterized relations between the island's powerful neighbours, namely the Hittites, Ugaritans and Egyptians, and the expansion of the Mycenaeans in the East Mediterranean was also in evidence.

The coastal harbour towns, established *c*. 1600 BC, such as Enkomi, Maroni, Hala Sultan Tekké, Morphou and Ayia Irini were becoming cosmopolitan industrial centres by the beginning of Late Cypriot II. External relations were peaceful and trade with the outside world unhindered.[2] Similar conditions must have prevailed within the island, allowing smooth distribution of copper ore to the 'factories' in the harbour towns. Whether there was one central authority which administered the distribution of copper ore throughout the island, or whether each individual town made its own arrangements, is difficult to ascertain. The inscribed tablets may one day tell us more, but they still retain their secrets.

With the expulsion of the Hyksos from Egypt and the establishment of the 18th Dynasty, a new era begins in the East Mediterranean *c*. 1555 (under the rule of Amosis), which favoured the growth of the urban centres of the eastern and southern coasts of Cyprus. These had already been established several decades earlier: Enkomi, Hala Sultan Tekké and Maroni, at the expense of the old centres of the north such as Dhenia and Lapethos which declined rapidly.[3] The antagonism between east and west gave way to an increasing homogeneity in the island. Along with the harbour towns of the coast, which were connected with the copper industry, rural centres developed in the hinterland whose agriculture supported the harbour towns, and which shared in the general prosperity. The areas near the copper mines were not neglected; on the contrary, they acquired new importance with the increase in metallurgical production and trade.[4] Preliminary smelting was carried out in the mining areas where there were ample wood supplies. Townships like Katydhata, Akhera and Kalavassos must have had an important role to play in the dispatch of copper ore. Trade in copper would have been carried out through harbour towns such as Enkomi and Hala Sultan Tekké, each of which must have had their own workshops for the final smelting processes. But the two major centres of the northwestern coast, Morphou and Ayia Irini, which were not far from the copper mines, must have also contributed considerably. It is not clear what sort of agreements or arrangements existed between the harbour towns in order to safeguard the continuous and smooth dispatch of ore from the distant mining areas. Routes were doubtless guarded, and this may explain the growth of certain inland settlements such as Nicosia and Ayios Sozomenos. A settlement such as Athienou (north of Larnaca) where a sanctuary connected with metallurgy was built in Late Cypriot II, must have been on the route which supplied ore to Kition.[5] It is tempting to suggest that several cities either worked entirely independently or collaborated with one another. An inscription on the temple at Medinet Habu of the time of Ramesses III (1194–1162 BC) mentions enemy towns, some of which have been identified, rather uncertainly, as Salamis, Kition, Marion (?), Soloi and Idalion. The fact that the material culture of Cyprus reflected by the ceramic industry developed in a homogeneous manner may be indicative of a unified country, with the various cities enjoying frequent and friendly trade relations.

The Cypro–Minoan script

The growth of large urban centres, especially along the eastern and southern coasts of Cyprus, the development of trade and industry and the new era in the cultural and social life which began in Late Cypriot I, necessitated a script for administrative and other purposes.[6] The earliest inscribed document is a fragment of a baked clay tablet with engraved signs in horizontal rows. It was found at Enkomi and is dated by the excavator to *c.* 1500 BC. This script has been compared with Linear A of Crete, though some scholars deny that it shows any Aegean influence. Sir Arthur Evans labelled it Cypro-Minoan.[7] The majority of scholars, however, emphasize the Aegean character not only of the script, but also of its development during the 1st millennium BC to what is known as the Cypriot syllabary, though both its form and structure were modified to suit the Greek language.

45

Very few documents survive in the earliest form of Cypro-Minoan. Apart from the Enkomi tablet referred to above, there are only a clay loomweight and a cylinder seal from the same site, and a vase from Katydhata with an inscribed handle. The script was firmly established from the 14th century BC onwards. Nevertheless, even if the Aegean parentage is correct, Near Eastern influence and local adaptations are not impossible. The cushion-like form of the 13th-century BC tablets, and the fact that they were intentionally baked after engraving, brings them closer to Near Eastern documents than to those of the Aegean. Furthermore, later tablets were engraved in a style which recalls the cuneiform script. If the Cretan origin of Cypro-Minoan is accepted, we are faced with the problem of how this script reached Cyprus, since relations between the two islands were not all that close around 1500 BC. A suggestion has been made that the Cypriots borrowed this script from Cretans living in Syria, for example at Ugarit, where they met as merchants from the end of Middle Cypriot III onwards.

Several attempts have been made to decipher Cypro-Minoan but have all failed, and the language, or languages, of the texts that have come to light remains unknown. It cannot be Greek, since the inflow of Achaean colonists to Cyprus from the Aegean began much later than *c.* 1500 BC. One theory is that it may be Hurrian, but the few objects discovered in Cyprus which might be labelled 'Hurrian' do not justify such an assertion. Certainly some foreign elements were present among the population of Cyprus during this period,[8] as is shown by the Bichrome Wheelmade pottery style which was made locally but in a

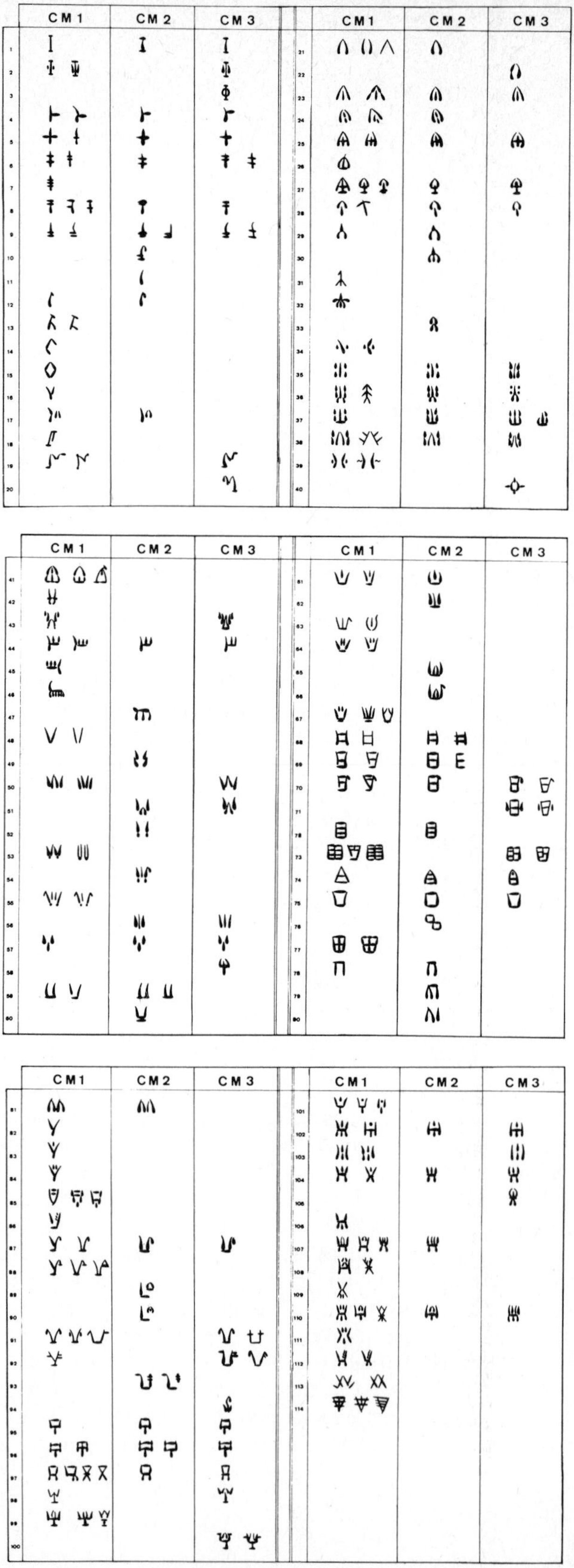

45 Tables showing the three classes of Cypro-Minoan script (Cypro-Minoan 1, 2 and 3). This script was introduced to Cyprus *c.* 1500 BC. It is still undeciphered. (After Emilia Masson, *Cyprominoica* (*SIMA* XXXI:2), Göteborg, 1974, figs 2–4.)

46 Cylinder of baked clay from Enkomi with signs engraved before firing on its curved surface, in 27 lines. This is the only complete long text discovered so far in the Cypro-Minoan script. Other documents are represented by fragments of cushion-shaped tablets. The fact that the language of these documents is still unknown constitutes the main difficulty for their decipherment. 13th century BC. L. 5.2 cm; diam. 4 cm. Cyprus Museum, Nicosia, (French Excavations) no. 1619.

foreign (Syrian ?) tradition. In addition, Red Lustrous Wheelmade pottery, whose characteristic fusiform jugs and arm-shaped vessels appear for the first time during Late Cypriot I, may have close Anatolian affinities.

Although so few documents inscribed in Cypro-Minoan have so far been found, they appear on a variety of inscribed objects, unlike the Aegean examples where the script is confined mainly to palace archives. The script is known in the main urban centres throughout Cyprus, though tablets with long texts have been found only at Enkomi. The occurrence of bone styli at Kition and Palaepaphos, and the discovery of inscribed clay balls of unknown use at Kition and Hala Sultan Tekké, testify to the wide diffusion of the script. It also appears engraved after firing or painted on vases, or engraved on bronze or clay votive objects, ivory objects, seals, weights and so on. Noteworthy is a bronze votive kidney with a few engraved signs from the holy-of-holies in Temple 2 at Kition, recalling the inscribed clay votive livers of the Near East which were used for teaching divination to apprentices.[9] This may mean that Cypro-Minoan was widespread among the island's population.

The development of the firmly established script may be followed from the 14th century BC onwards. This is the so-called 'Cypro-Minoan 1' script, which appears on a variety of objects and continues down to the 11th century BC with a predominance in the 12th century BC. There are about eighty signs in the Cypro-Minoan 1 script. Specialists working on the classification of the signs and their decipherment confirm that the script and the language it represents are the same throughout the island, indicating linguistic uniformity.

Towards the end of the 13th century BC, 'Cypro-Minoan 2' appears, represented by large tablets from Enkomi. They are rectangular, either cushion-shaped or in the form of a cylinder, and are baked in a furnace. The script is divided into vertical columns in the Near Eastern fashion.

46

47 Impression of a cylinder
seal from Idalion. The
engraved composition consists
of a procession of human
figures holding vases. The
style betrays obvious
influences from the Aegean.
L. 1.5 cm. Cyprus Museum,
Nicosia, no. 69.

The average size of the tablets is 22×19 cm, to judge from the
dimensions of the four fragmentary ones discovered at Enkomi so far.
They are thought to be literary or religious texts, probably in verse.
This new script consists of sixty signs and may represent a different
language from Cypro-Minoan 1.

There is even a 'Cypro-Minoan 3' script, on a tablet found at Ugarit
on which, in the Ugaritic fashion, a list of Semitic proper names
appears. Though Madame E. Masson has been able to decipher twenty
out of the total of twenty-five names on this tablet, the language itself is
still unknown.

One problem concerning Cypro-Minoan is that it remained in use in
the 12th century BC when the ruling classes of Enkomi and elsewhere
must have been Mycenaeans, whom one would expect to have
introduced their own Linear B script. The only explanation is that the
Mycenaeans were using local scribes.

Other objects, perhaps connected with administrative functions
such as the authentication of documents and the endorsement of
contracts, are the seals which appear during Late Cypriot II.[10] The
Cypriot seal-engraver, basing his iconography on that of the Near East
as well as the Aegean, produced a style of his own of which some very
fine examples have survived. The usual form is the cylinder seal of
steatite, haematite, lapis lazuli or paste and, very rarely, gold, but there
are also other shapes such as prisms and conoid stamp seals. The latter
become very common during Late Cypriot III. A number of Cypriot
cylinder seals have been found in the Aegean and the Near East. Of
particular note are the fine cylinder seals of lapis lazuli discovered in the
Mycenaean palace at Thebes in Boeotia.

47

Cyprus in the texts – Alashiya
Although Cypro-Minoan documents are still silent on the history of the
island during the Late Cypriot period, the name of Cyprus, *Alashiya* or

Asy, is often mentioned in Near Eastern texts.[11] It appears, in association with copper, on the tablets from Alalakh and Mari of the 18th and 17th centuries BC respectively. It would be interesting to know whether reference to Cyprus is made in the texts of the 3rd millennium BC found recently at Ebla (Tell Mardikh) in Syria. References to Alashiya are particularly frequent from the 14th century BC. It should be said here that although some scholars still deny or are sceptical about the identification of Alashiya with Cyprus, the vast majority accept it, especially since it has been shown that the name was used for the *island* of Alashiya, for which Cyprus is the only possibility.[12]

In the course of a correspondence, dating to the second quarter of the 14th century BC, between Pharaoh Akhenaton of Egypt and the king of Alashiya, the king refers to the Pharaoh as his 'brother'. Cyprus, therefore, is an ally of Egypt, and in this capacity the king of Alashiya advises the Pharaoh not to conclude a treaty with the Hittites who were enemies of Alashiya. In several letters the king of Alashiya promises to send copper ingots, probably as a tribute to the Pharaoh for keeping the peace in the East Mediterranean. Other gifts include oil, wood, horses and ivory. Cyprus did not produce ivory, of course, but they may have been current commodities in the large industrial towns of the island, where ivory-working was not unknown. In return, the king of Alashiya requests gifts such as a bedstead of ebony inlaid with gold, a gold chariot, two horses, silver and good oil.

In another letter, the king of Alashiya informs the Pharaoh that the latter's envoy had to stay for three years in Alashiya because the god Nergal killed all the men in his land and there was nobody to produce copper. It has been suggested that this may refer to a plague which devastated the Near East after an earthquake in the middle of the 14th century BC, and that this phenomenon may be associated with the

48 Head of a sceptre in blue faience with white inlay, in the shape of an Egyptian open papyriform capital, from the Late Cypriot site of Hala Sultan Tekké. It probably had an ivory shaft. At the top is a cartouche of Pharaoh Horemheb, but the object was found on a floor of a later period (Late Cypriot IIIA:1). Ht 3.7 cm. Cyprus Museum, Nicosia no. N1188 (Swedish Excavations).

destruction at Enkomi of between *c*. 1375 and 1350 BC. Others, however, associate this destruction to the Lukki who attacked Alashiya annually, as we know from the same sources. In one instance the Lukki are reported to have attacked Egypt also, accompanied by people from Alashiya. Some of the latter were captured and the king of Alashiya asked the Pharaoh to return them. The names of the captives seem to be Hurrian and Semitic, a fact which supports the theory that a small part of the population of Cyprus during this period may have been foreign.

Relations with Egypt are evident to some extent from the archaeological evidence. Several Egyptian objects with cartouches of Pharaohs have been discovered in Cyprus. A faience sceptre head found in a 12th-century BC context at Hala Sultan Tekké is decorated at the top with the cartouche of Horemheb (1348–1320 BC).[13] The same site has also produced a wine jar stamped with the cartouche of Pharaoh Seti I who reigned at the end of the 14th century BC (*c*. 1312–1300 BC). From Palaepaphos-*Skales* comes a large commemorative scarab of Amenophis III (1402–1364 BC) with his cartouche in hieroglyphs which mentions his exploits in lion-hunting.[14] The scarab was found in a tomb of the 11th century BC. It seems that relations with Egypt ceased after Ugarit became a vassal of the Hittites, for trade between the two was carried out via Ugarit.

In the Hittite tablets Cyprus is referred to as part of the Hittite empire from *c*. 1400 to *c*. 1200 BC, and as a place to which Hittite kings sent prisoners and adversaries in the 14th and 13th centuries BC.[15] According to the Hittites, King Shuppiluliuma II fought a naval battle in about 1190 against Alashiya, in which he destroyed the enemy ships in the middle of the sea. He then landed and completely vanquished a great number of enemies who came against him in large numbers. He ordered the Alashiyans to pay him tribute: silver, copper, but also women and children whom he took to his capital, Hattusha. It is interesting to note that recent excavations at Hattusha have brought to light for the first time a fragment of a Cypriot (?) oxhide copper ingot.[16]

It is not easy to determine the accuracy of the statements in the Hittite documents and to know how much is boastful assertion, at least with regard to the early part of this period. The claim that Cyprus formed part of the Hittite empire cannot be substantiated by archaeological evidence, though one gold Hittite seal was found at Tamassos[17] and two other seals with Hittite connections have been found recently at Hala Sultan Tekké. There is also some Anatolian pottery at Hala Sultan Tekké,[18] Kition, Kazaphani and Ayios Iakovos.[19] However, the correspondence between the king of Alashiya and his allies, the Pharaoh of Egypt and the king of Ugarit, would suggest that Alashiya was independent.

References to Alashiya and her Near Eastern neighbours also appear in tablets dating to the end of the 13th and the beginning of the 12th century BC, and refer to the disturbances caused in the East Mediterranean at the very end of Late Cypriot II by the Sea Peoples.

Architecture

We have already briefly described the fortress at Nitovikla as an example of Middle Cypriot III military architecture. Many fortresses were built or reconstructed during Late Cypriot I, and the fortress of Enkomi is a case in point. It was built in the northern part of the town, on the inside of the later city wall. It is rectangular in plan and measures 34×12 m and has massive external walls enclosing a number of rooms. Its southwest gate was protected by a rectangular tower projecting from the main building. Staircases from the interior of the rooms led to an upper storey and the roof.

Kition,[20] on the southeast coast of Cyprus, was founded in Late Cypriot II *c.* 1300 BC, and was fortified with a mudbrick wall resting on rubble foundations. This wall follows the edge of the low plateau on which the town was built, at least at its northernmost part, for the area surrounding the plateau was swampy. This explains the irregular course of the wall in the Late Cypriot III period. Two rectangular bastions built against the side of the plateau, and therefore against the mudbrick wall, have been uncovered at the northernmost part of the town. One of them measures 18×5 m and is preserved to a height of about 2.5 m. The lower courses, up to the present preserved height at least, are built of ashlar blocks, and the superstructure would have been of mudbrick. In antiquity the three sides of these bastions were no doubt washed by the waters of the marshes, as they still are today in winter when the water level is high. This swamp must have played a useful role in the fortification of the town. The rectangular bastions were retained even after the catastrophe which befell the site at the end of Late Cypriot IIC; only their damaged mudbrick superstructures were rebuilt.

Sacred architecture is represented by several examples from the Late Cypriot II period.[21] Of particular interest is the sanctuary of Ayios Iakovos which follows Early Bronze Age traditions. It consists of a large circular area which was probably encircled by a wooden fence. A low screen wall divided the sanctuary into two sections which communicated with one another through a lateral entrance. The inner area enclosed a large and a small altar which were probably dedicated to the divinities worshipped in the sanctuary (perhaps a mother goddess and her young consort). On the floor of the courtyard lay a bath-tub-shaped terracotta basin full of ashes and burnt bones. All the votive offerings were found on the floor around this basin.

At Myrtou-*Pigadhes* the Late Cypriot II sanctuary consists of a western and an eastern part, each of which has rooms opening onto a courtyard with benches.

At Kition two small sanctuaries of Near Eastern type were built in Area II at the northernmost part of the town (sanctuaries 2 and 3). There was a 'sacred garden' between them, enclosed along its south side by a boundary wall. The sanctuaries consist of a rectangular courtyard with a lateral entrance to the east, which leads through a lateral opening to a narrow holy-of-holies along the western part of the sanctuary. This holy-of-holies must have been roofed and it is here that cult objects were kept. There was a hearth-altar in the courtyard. The larger of the two sanctuaries had a portico on the north and south sides of the courtyard, with wooden pillars supporting the roof.

The domestic architecture of the Late Cypriot II period is represented by houses and workshops at Enkomi, Kition and Apliki.[22]

The houses at Enkomi usually consist of a rectangular courtyard with rooms on three sides. Bathrooms with cemented floors have been found there and at Kition, and clay bath-tubs at Enkomi. At the latter there are even lavatories with a well-constructed drainage system.

Workshops for copper-smelting were found at Kition. Their large rooms were probably unroofed to enable the smoke to blow away. On the workshop floors were small furnaces, channels and wells. Fragments of crucibles and tuyères were found on the floors, mixed with ashes and copper slag.

The development of funerary architecture is well illustrated from the Late Cypriot I period onwards. The standard tomb type is the chamber tomb with a dromos and a stomion sealed with a slab, rubble or mudbricks. There are, however, some interesting innovations. Three small 'tholoi' or circular type tombs have been found at Enkomi.[23] Tomb 21, excavated by the Swedish Cyprus Expedition, dates to the Late Cypriot IA period, and the other two, excavated by the French Mission, to a somewhat later period.

Tomb 21 has a small chamber, roughly circular in plan, and a short pit dromos. The chamber measures 2.38×2.26 m in diameter and 2.43 m in height. Its vaulted walls are built of rubble and a stone slab covers the top of the vault. The floor is cut into the bedrock. The tomb was free standing and may have been covered by an earth tumulus. The second tomb, found at locus 1432, has a rectangular chamber the interior measurements of which are 2.5×2.7 m. It is preserved to its entire height of 2 m, with courses of slabs forming the top. It has a short pit dromos. The excavators date this tomb to the 15th or 14th century BC. The third tomb, found at locus 1336 near tomb 1432, has been dated to c. 1400 BC by the ceramic material it contained. The ground plan of the chamber is approximately oval. The long axis measures 3.2 m and the short 2.5 m. It has a short pit dromos, 80×80 cm. The lower two courses of the vaulted walls are constructed of stone blocks on which rest nine other courses of furnace-baked bricks.

It has been suggested that these 'tholoi' derive from Aegean funerary architecture. But the fact that at least one is of early date, when Aegean influences were not so strong, may exclude this hypothesis. The other two tombs, though dated to a later period, were perhaps used for a considerable length of time, and their construction may be even earlier than their associated material remains. In any case, all three reflect the same cultural influence. The suggestion that their form was dictated simply by the softness of the rock and that the vaulted walls were built to prevent the collapse of the sides of the chamber is not plausible;[24] if this were so, one would expect to find the same precautions taken throughout the site, since the rock is the same everywhere. At other sites in Cyprus where the natural rock is very soft there are shaft graves instead of chambers – such as those at Angastina and Akhera – but not built 'tholoi'. No doubt the builders of these tombs were following a foreign model which may be of Near Eastern origin. A suggestion has been made that its prototype may have been the funerary architecture of Megiddo in the Levant, dated to the end of the Middle Bronze Age.

Rock-cut chamber tombs of various types continue to be the standard form during the Late Cypriot II period,[25] but again Enkomi

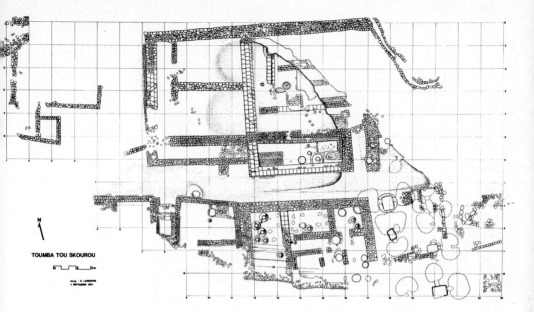

TOUMBA TOU SKOUROU

has several exceptions. Seven built tombs are constructed of fine ashlar limestone blocks. One of them, found by the British Mission at the end of the century, consists of a rectangular chamber. The roof is partly corbelled, with a flat top, and is covered with large slabs. The stomion is on the central axis of the chamber and its threshold is above floor level. Four other tombs were found by the same mission and two by the French Mission. They have stepped dromoi – one is 1.7 m in length with three steps – and resemble the funerary monuments of the same period at Ugarit.

49 Plan of Toumba tou Skourou (excavated by an American Mission, 1973). Remains of workshops for pottery-making, built on an artificial oblong mound; on the southeastern part of the site are chamber tombs.

Toumba tou Skourou

Toumba tou Skourou in the Morphou bay would have been a promising site for the study of Late Cypriot I architecture, had it not suffered considerable destruction. Excavated remains include a potters' quarter, established *c.* 1600 BC on an artificial oblong mound.[26] A terrace wall, over 30 m long, was first constructed along the north slope of a platform of soft rock, in what may originally have been a swampy area. Workshops along this wall were divided by low walls, resembling benches. After a destruction in *c.* 1550 BC, new workshops were built on an elevated mound of debris. Kilns, basins and benches were constructed on the new floors which, together with lumps of various clays found there, suggest a lively ceramic industry. Products of this potters' area may be seen among the grave-goods excavated in the tombs of the area. A second installation for pottery-making was constructed along the south side of the same mound; it is a large room measuring 14.5 × 6 m, with access to it by a pebbled ramp. Basins with plastered ridges, and pithoi buried up to their rims in the floor, may suggest a workshop for refining clay; three sacks of clay were found on the floor. Houses were located in the lower area on the other side of the ramp, and southeast of them were chamber tombs.

49

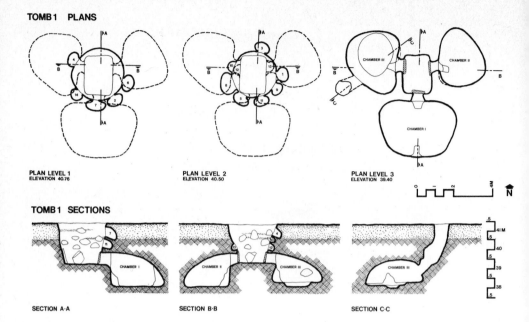

PLAN LEVEL 1
ELEVATION 40.76

PLAN LEVEL 2
ELEVATION 40.50

PLAN LEVEL 3
ELEVATION 39.40

TOMB 1 SECTIONS

SECTION A·A

SECTION B·B

SECTION C·C

50 Toumba tou Skourou: plans and sections of a large chamber tomb of the second half of the 16th century BC. It consisted of a circular shaft which contained thirteen niches for infant burials all round it. The tomb-gifts included fine Cypriot vases as well as pottery imported from Crete and the Near East.

51

Of the tombs, chamber I is of particular importance. It consists of a circular shaft which contained thirteen niches for infant burials around its sides in superimposed rows. At a lower level there are three chambers cut into the bedrock, in which about three dozen adults were buried. This tomb was used for about one century. The earliest burials took place c. 1550–1525 BC. Of the eight hundred objects found in this tomb one should mention vases of various wares, shapes and sizes, gold, silver and ivory objects, and so on. Noteworthy are a Tell el-Yahudiya juglet with engraved nilotic birds and lotus flowers, and several Bichrome Wheelmade vases. But of particular importance are the vases and the sherds of Late Minoan ware which belong to at least thirteen vessels, dated c. 1525–1475 BC.[27] This is the period when the Cypro-Minoan script was introduced to Cyprus. Further connections with the Aegean are attested in the tombs of Ayia Irini, on the coast northeast of

51 Cup of Late Minoan or Late Helladic II ware, found in a tomb at Ayia Irini on the northwestern coast (excavated by an Italian Mission, 1970–4). The cup is decorated with the 'double axe' motif. Similar vases were found in tombs at the neighbouring site of Toumba tou Skourou. Ht 6.9 cm; diam. 10.6 cm. Cyprus Museum, Nicosia, Ayia Irini, Tomb 3, no. 16.

Morphou, where Late Helladic (?) I and Bichrome Wheelmade vases have been found together with a rich variety of local wares.[28]

Although excavations at Toumba tou Skourou and Ayia Irini have increased considerably the number of objects known to have been imported from the Aegean during Late Cypriot I, they are outnumbered by those from the Near East. In the same way, Late Cypriot I objects in the Aegean are very few indeed compared with those found in Syria, Palestine and Egypt. It is often argued that the commodities exported in the greatest quantities from Cyprus were raw copper and probably foodstuffs, but this cannot in any way be substantiated. More plausible is the suggestion by Merrillees that trade during this period was in the hands of entrepreneurs who did not base their transactions on official trade agreements of balance but on profit.[29]

The ceramic industry

Artistic productivity in Cyprus at the end of the Middle Cypriot period was rather poor because of the troubled conditions the island was experiencing. But as soon as peace and trade relations were established, innovations began to appear in Cypriot art, including two new important ceramic wares: White Slip ware, which has a hard core and a smooth surface of thick white slip with an orange, brown or bichrome

52 Jug of White Slip I ware decorated with geometric patterns in dark brown-orange paint on a white background. This fabric appears during Late Cypriot I and predominates until the very end of the 13th century BC, having passed through various phases of development. From a tomb at Perakhorio (Nisou), south of Nicosia. Ht 29.4 cm. Cyprus Museum, CS.2414/85.

52

53 (*Left*) Jug of Base Ring I ware with a long neck and beak-shaped mouth. The body and neck are decorated with 'rope' ornament. The shape, fabric and decoration recall metal prototypes. Base Ring ware vases, together with those of White Slip ware, were very much favoured on the foreign market, perhaps because these fine vessels were handmade whereas the potter's wheel was in use in the Near East. Ht 44.5 cm. Cyprus Museum, Nicosia, no. A1156.

54 (*Right*) Hollow terracotta figurine of Base Ring ware, representing a nude female figure with the arms bent against the chest below the breasts. The genitals are prominently shown with grooves and paint. Such figurines are usually found in tombs, perhaps as symbolic companions for the male dead. Ht 22.2 cm. Cyprus Museum, Nicosia, no. A53.

55 Composite vase of Base Ring I ware consisting of two juglets (bilbils) joined together and bridged by a common handle. Such vases have also been found outside Cyprus, mainly in Egypt and have been associated with the export of opium. In fact their form resembles a poppy head. Ht 14 cm. Cyprus Museum, Nicosia, no. 1946/XII–14/1.

56 (*Left*) Large spindle-shaped bottle from Enkomi in Red Lustrous Wheelmade ware. This ware probably originated in Anatolia at the beginning of the Late Bronze Age but was current in Cyprus during the Late Bronze Age II period. This is the largest bottle of its kind so far discovered in Cyprus. Ht 79 cm. Musée du Louvre, Paris, Enkomi, Tomb 2, no. 2.

57 (*Above*) Bowl of Base Ring I ware, with conical body and raised wishbone handle. The surface is dark brown and has a lustrous appearance. The walls are thin, giving the impression of an imitation of a metallic prototype. Such bowls were very popular in Cyprus during the Late Bronze Age I period and were also exported, mainly to the Near East. Ht 13.2 cm; diam. 16 cm. Cyprus Museum, Nicosia, Inv. no. 1933/IV–14/2.

58 (*Below*) Bowl of Proto-White Slip ware with hemispherical body, round base and wishbone handle. The white surface is decorated with horizontal straight and wavy bands in brown paint. This fabric became very popular in Cyprus during the Late Bronze Age I and II periods. The present example is one of the earliest (Late Bronze Age I). Ht 9.5 cm.; diam. 12 cm. Cyprus Museum, Nicosia, Inv. no. 1963/VII–18/17.

53, 54 decoration, and Base Ring ware, with dark thin walls and a shiny surface. They are both handmade, though in neighbouring countries the potter's wheel was already in use. Nevertheless, they were popular in many foreign lands, perhaps because of their primitive appearance. Base Ring ware has a metallic quality which is accentuated by the type of relief decoration used, and by the vase forms. No doubt there existed metallic prototypes, mainly of bronze, which have not survived.

55 Particularly well known are the Base Ring ware *bilbils* which were exported chiefly to Egypt. They resemble inverted poppy-heads with the stem uppermost, and it has been suggested that they contained opium and that their shape was a kind of trade mark.[30] Both the White Slip and Base Ring wares are deeply rooted in Middle Bronze Age traditional shapes, and no foreign influence is recognizable in either of them. They continued through the Late Cypriot I and II periods, but degenerated towards the end of Late Cypriot II. During the 14th and

56, 57, 58 13th centuries BC the characteristic bowl with a wishbone handle manufactured in both wares was copied, with variations, even by Mycenaean potters.

Northwestern Cyprus (Morphou-Pendayia-Myrtou) developed a very important regional ceramic style, illustrated particularly by the handmade White Painted technique. Apart from some interesting

59 anthropomorphic vases from this region, there is a distinctive range of

59 Jug of White Painted ware, with additional purple paint. The mouth is in the form of a human face; two opposed projections on the shoulder suggest the arms of a human figure. The surface of the vase is decorated with geometric patterns. The rendition of anthropomorphic features on Middle Bronze Age vases is quite common. End of the Middle Bronze Age. From Morphou. Ht 23.5 cm. Hadjiprodromou Collection, Famagusta.

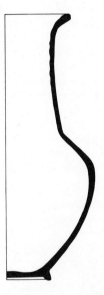

60 Jug of Bichrome Wheelmade ware, decorated with an armed warrior (there are also traces of a second human figure) and geometric patterns. It was found in a tomb of the Late Cypriot I–II period at Dromolaxia, Larnaca District. Pictorial compositions, particularly human figures, are rare on such vases; the commoner motifs are fishes, birds and linear patterns. Such vases may have been made in Cyprus by foreign (perhaps Syrian) artists in the 16th century BC. Dromolaxia-*Trypes* T.1/58. Ht 24 cm. Larnaca District Museum.

jugs bearing a human or animal protome on the shoulder opposite the handle.[31]

Of the new wares introduced to Cyprus after 1600 BC, the most important are Bichrome Wheelmade ware, which is outside the ceramic tradition of Cyprus both with regard to its wheelmade forms and decoration, and Tell el-Yahudiya ware. Though the prototype may have originated in Syria, recent research has shown that Bichrome Wheelmade ware is made of Cypriot clay.[32] Examples of Tell el-Yahudiya ware found in Cyprus were imported from Syria and Palestine.[33]

60

Trade relations between Cyprus and the Aegean, Egypt and the Near East have already been mentioned, as well as the steady increase in the number of imports to Cyprus, and in the number of Cypriot objects, mainly pottery, found outside the island. Relations with the Aegean, however, are still slight, particularly during Late Cypriot IA, though they develop during Late Cypriot IB.

Mycenaean connections

Relations with the Aegean are very close from *c.* 1400 BC, and are marked by an influx of Mycenaean pottery, though some Aegean wares appear already from *c.* 1450 to *c.* 1400 BC. Events in the Aegean, often referred to as the 'fall of Knossos' which is now dated to *c.* 1380 BC, brought the Mycenaeans as successors to the Minoans in the East Mediterranean. The copper of Cyprus, and the wealth of the Near East in general, attracted the new lords of the Aegean, who very soon established emporia along the eastern and southern coasts of Cyprus from which they traded safely with the Syro-Palestinian littoral. The tombs at sites such as Enkomi, Pyla, Hala Sultan Tekké, Maroni and Kourion have produced considerable quantities of Mycenaean pottery, 61 particularly of large vessels – amphorae and open craters – decorated in the pictorial style.[34] This style is dominated by Aegean motifs such as chariot groups, compositions of human figures, octopuses and bulls, though occasionally one may detect certain Near Eastern elements.[35] A Mycenaean IIIA1 open crater from Enkomi is decorated with a scene which may be connected with the Near Eastern myth of the chase and final capture of the monstrous bird Enzu. Another Mycenaean IIIA1 open crater from Pyla-*Verghi* is decorated with chariot compositions. One of the chariots has a six-spoked wheel, whereas the normal number for a Mycenaean chariot is four. Furthermore, the harnessing of one of the horses is rendered with incisions, a feature alien to Mycenaean vase-painting. Another vase decorated with a famous composition is the Mycenaean IIIA1 amphoroid crater from Enkomi known as the

61 Mycenaean IIIB bell-crater decorated on one side with a bull and human figure (perhaps an echo of bullfights) and on the other with a bull and calf. The animal's outlined body is divided into various sections filled with small abstract motifs recalling tapestry or weaving, a technique which prevailed during the 13th century BC, when pictorial composition became more decorative and lost its previous vigour. Ht 28 cm; diam. 30 cm. G. G. Pierides Collection, Nicosia.

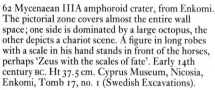
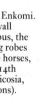

62 Mycenaean IIIA amphoroid crater, from Enkomi. The pictorial zone covers almost the entire wall space; one side is dominated by a large octopus, the other depicts a chariot scene. A figure in long robes with a scale in his hand stands in front of the horses, perhaps 'Zeus with the scales of fate'. Early 14th century BC. Ht 37.5 cm. Cyprus Museum, Nicosia, Enkomi, Tomb 17, no. 1 (Swedish Excavations).

'Zeus crater'. It illustrates a long-robed human figure holding 'scales', in front of warriors in a chariot before they depart for battle. This has been related by Nilsson to the well-known scene in the *Iliad* where Zeus holds the 'scales of destiny'. If this interpretation is correct, then here is one of the earliest representations of a Greek mythological scene.

Though chemical and neutron-activation analysis of Mycenaean vases found in Cyprus suggests that they were made on the Greek mainland and mostly in the Peloponnese from where they were exported to Cyprus,[36] there are scholars who believe that Mycenaean pottery of the pictorial style could have been made in Cyprus by potters who accompanied traders there at the beginning of the 14th century BC or even later. In fact, there are examples of Mycenaean vases of both the 14th and 13th centuries BC which copy distinct Cypriot forms. There are also Mycenaean vase forms which are specific to Cyprus and the Near East and have never been found west of Rhodes, such as the lentoid flask with a rounded base – a form which has a long tradition in the ceramic repertoire of the Near East – the handleless chalice with carinated profile and the jug with trefoil mouth and carinated shoulder, to mention only a few. To say that these were made in the Argolid with the Cypriot market in mind does not sound very convincing. Whatever the case may be, the role of Cyprus in the formation of the pictorial style of Mycenaean vase-painting must have been considerable. The Cypriots have always had a taste for pictorialism and exuberant styles in pottery forms and decoration. And the Mycenaean pottery, with its fine, shiny fabric and glossy paint, and above all its imaginative decoration, must have appealed strongly to Cypriot taste. We have already detected the hand of a number of vase-painters to whom works have been attributed. Some painters may have worked both in the Aegean and in Cyprus, for their work is found in both places. Furthermore, artists must have travelled quite extensively.

Mycenaean vases, especially large craters decorated in the pictorial style, have been found in the cosmopolitan centre of Ugarit and as far east as Amman. It is probable that they were exported from Cyprus, as they are usually found together with large quantities of Cypriot pottery. During the 14th century BC the predominant compositions are of chariot groups and of bulls, often in association with human figures. Gradually the figured compositions are crowded with subordinate

63 (*Above, right*) Mycenaean IIIB pilgrim flask with lentoid body, decorated on both sides with concentric bands and rings. This is a form which had a long tradition in the Near East but is unknown in the Aegean. It belongs to the so-called specifically Levanto-Helladic class of Mycenaean pottery. Ht 17 cm. Cyprus Museum, Nicosia, no. 1933/V–6/5. (*Above, left*) Mycenaean IIIB bowl with wishbone handle. The outside is decorated with horizontal parallel bands and a horizontal zone of parallel chevrons; the inside is undecorated. This form may be an imitation of the Cypriot White Slip ware bowls. Ht 9.5 cm; diam. 16 cm. Cyprus Museum, Nicosia, no. 1955/IV–14/2.

64

64 Silver bowl with a wishbone handle found in a tomb at Enkomi. The exterior is decorated with a horizontal frieze of six bulls' heads with two stylized flowers between them; below is a horizontal frieze of petalled rosettes within a semicircle. The decoration is inlaid in gold and *niello*. A very similar bowl was found at Dendra in the Peloponnese. 14th century BC. Ht 6 cm; diam. 15.7 cm. Cyprus Museum, Nicosia, Enkomi, T.2, no. 4207 (excavated by the French Mission).

65 (*Opposite*) Fragmentary rhyton of faience found in a tomb at Kition. The surface is covered with thick blue enamel and is decorated in three registers with running animals (above), the hunting of animals (middle), and running spirals (below). The decoration is painted in yellow and black and inlaid with red enamel. Aegeo-Oriental style. Preserved ht 26.8 cm. Cyprus Museum, Nicosia, Kition special series, no. 1.

abstract and floral filling ornamentation, and the scenes lose their vigour. In the Mycenaean IIIB period the pictorial style changes character; the main motifs now include bulls, goats, birds and fishes, drawn in outline and filled with small abstract designs which give the impression of embroideries or tapestries. But even in this style there are some very successful creations, such as shallow bowls decorated on the inside with birds and fishes or other motifs, in a whirling pattern. Among the several painters in this style who have been identified, are two of the 13th century BC to whom a large number of works found in Cyprus (Enkomi and Kition) and the Near East (Ugarit) have been assigned. They specialize in bulls and bull protomes and are known as the Protome Painters A and B.

Tombs of the 14th and 13th centuries BC have yielded several outstanding works of art.[37] The hemispherical silver bowl from Enkomi, dated to the 14th century BC, is a case in point. It is decorated in the inlaid technique with gold and niello, with a frieze of six bull-heads alternating with lotus flowers just below the rim, and another of arcaded rosettes around the lower part of the body. It has a wishbone handle, as does another silver bowl from Enkomi with less elaborate decoration. A very similar bowl, with regard to shape and decoration, was found at Dendra in the Peloponnese. They may both have been manufactured by the same artist, but it is not possible to say whether he worked in Cyprus or in the Peloponnese, or whether he was an immigrant artist who settled in Cyprus having first worked in the Peloponnese. A silver cup from a Late Cypriot II tomb at Enkomi bears a striking resemblance to the famous gold Vapheio cups from the Peloponnese.

A remarkable work of art of the middle of the 13th century BC is the conical rhyton from Kition. It is made of thick, hard faience, covered inside and out with a generous layer of blue enamel. The exterior is divided into three horizontal registers decorated from top to bottom, respectively, with galloping animals, human figures chasing bulls, and vertical running spirals. The decoration is either painted in black, yellow and green or inlaid in red enamel. The shape of the rhyton, as well as certain decorative details, are Aegean in origin, but the technique and other iconographical details are Near Eastern. The hunters of the middle register wear kilts and head-dresses of a Syrian type; one of them, raising his arm to strike a bull with a knife, is in a

particularly Egyptian attitude and wears sandals with 'magic knives', a feature which occurs in Egyptian iconography.[38] This vase may have been made in Cyprus or on the Syro-Palestinian coast under strong Egyptian influence. It is a representative specimen of the Aegeo-Oriental stylistic trends which prevailed in Cyprus during the Late Cypriot II period.

Aegeo-Oriental stylistic tendencies in glyptic art during the Late Cypriot II period have already been noted. Some seals in this mixed style may have been made by Cypriots under Aegean influence, as is suggested, for instance, by the cylinder seal from Enkomi representing a kilted young man flanked by lions and *genii*, with flying birds and griffins and other motifs in the background. Another cylinder seal from Idalion, decorated with a procession of long-robed or kilted human figures holding vases, may be the work of an Aegean engraver working in Cyprus.

A mixed style may also be observed in jewelry. Gold diadems decorated in repoussé often appear in Late Cypriot II tombs. While the idea of an oblong rectangular diadem is Cypriot, the repoussé decoration often betrays influences from both the Aegean and the Near East. The characteristic sphinx motif appears both in Aegean and Near Eastern forms. The oval bezel of a gold-plated finger ring from Enkomi is decorated with a lion of Mycenaean inspiration, while the finger ring itself shows Egyptian influence. Noteworthy are the gold pendants from Enkomi in the form of pomegranates decorated with granulated triangles, and the necklaces with beads in the form of figure-of-eight shields, also from Enkomi, or others with beads in the form of pomegranates and dates, from Ayios Iakovos. Of purely Cypriot inspiration are the gold ear-rings in the shape of bull-heads hanging from a loop of thin wire and made from an embossed sheet of gold. A pair of gold ear-rings from Maroni in the form of bull-heads is decorated all over with granulation.

66

67

Catastrophe – The Sea Peoples

The peaceful conditions which encouraged these artistic interconnections and combined styles were to change towards the end of Late Cypriot II. Although we may not accept as entirely accurate the boastful assertion of the Hittites that they exercised control over Cyprus from *c.* 1400 to *c.* 1200 BC, we cannot ignore the fact that during the reign of Shuppiluliuma II conditions in the East Mediterranean could not have been calm. The disruption of the Mycenaean empire, and the collapse of government and well-organized society during the later Mycenaean IIIB period in centres of the Peloponnese such as Mycenae, Tiryns and Pylos, had far-reaching repercussions. About 1200 BC, large numbers of refugees left their homes in these towns to seek their fortunes elsewhere. The route eastwards, which their fathers had taken two hundred years earlier, was no doubt the most familiar and the most promising. In their wanderings, these Mycenaean refugees may have first gone to Anatolia where they were joined by other adventurers before they reached Cyprus. After the catastrophe their aim was survival, and we should not be surprised that they became adventurers and plunderers. It is proposed here, in agreement with

66 Bezel of a gold-plated finger ring, engraved with a lion walking to right, with the head turned to the opposite direction. The animal is naturalistically rendered, recalling Aegean prototypes. From Enkomi, Tomb 18, no. 62 (Swedish Excavations). Max. diam. 3.2 cm. Cyprus Museum, Nicosia.

Desborough and others,[39] to associate the events which preceded the destruction of major coastal towns of Cyprus – such as Enkomi and Kition – with the activities of these wanderers, who are usually known as the Peoples of the Sea or the Sea Peoples. We know from the tablets which constitute the correspondence between the king of Alashiya and Hammourapi, king of Ugarit, that the former was concerned about the frequent appearance of foreign ships, and he advised the king of Ugarit to stand firm and mobilize his army within the city walls. The king of Ugarit reported that seven ships plundered his country when his own troops and ships were in the land of the Hittites. Despite the alliance and the exchange of information about enemy movements between these two kings, a letter from the superintendent of Alashiya states that ships from Ugarit joined forces with the enemy and raided the northern part of Alashiya – such was the confusion and uncertainty then prevailing in the East Mediterranean. Destructions also took place in

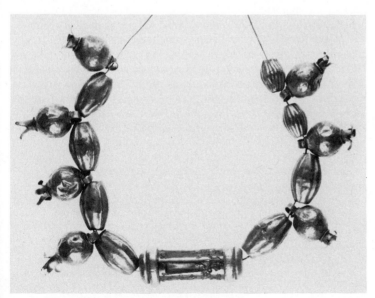

67 Necklace consisting of seven pomegranate-shaped beads and eight in the form of dates. There is a pendant in the form of a Babylonian cylinder seal. The beads are of Aegean type; the pendant is oriental, characteristic of the mixed style in Cypriot art of the Late Cypriot II period. From Ayios Iakovos (Swedish Excavations). L. 19.8 cm. Cyprus Museum, Nicosia.

68 Impression of a conoid seal representing a 'Philistine' wearing a feathered helmet and holding a large shield. From Enkomi, Late Cypriot III period. L. 1.5 cm. Cyprus Museum, Nicosia (excavated by the Cyprus Department of Antiquities), no. 184.

Syria and Palestine. The Sea Peoples were finally defeated by Ramesses III during the eighth year of his reign, c. 1186.

There are still many gaps in our knowledge concerning events in the East Mediterranean c. 1200 and even about the exact identity of the Sea Peoples.[40] The only sure fact is that destructions are evidenced at the end of the 13th century BC when Mycenaean IIIB pottery was in use – that is, at the very end of Late Cypriot IIC. But what happened to the Sea Peoples after the destruction of Kition and Enkomi? Are we to suppose that some stayed behind and settled, as Desborough proposes? The well-known stamp seal from Enkomi,[41] showing an armed warrior wearing the characteristic feathered head-dress of the Sea Peoples as depicted on Egyptian reliefs, and a similar warrior on the ivory gaming-box from Enkomi, may lend some support to this hypothesis. In any case, the destructions at Enkomi and Kition at the end of Late Cypriot IIC are extensive and a sharp decline and even partial abandonment follow.[42] The spacious workshops for copper-smelting in Area I at Kition were deserted, and in Area II, above floor IV which was in use at the time of the destruction, lies a thick layer of alluvial deposit. Enkomi and Kition – and no doubt many other towns not yet excavated – were subsequently completely rebuilt. At Kition a thick layer of greenish clay covers the wall foundations and floors of the previous occupation, sealing the dromoi of the tombs in the courtyards of the houses – some of which were first looted for gold by the newcomers – and a new town was constructed above the buried remains of the earlier settlement. It was at this time that the old mudbrick city wall of Kition was destroyed and on its debris a 'cyclopean' wall was constructed, 50 cm above bedrock. Similar fortifications were built at Enkomi, Sinda and Maa, all of which mark the beginning of Late Cypriot IIIA.

Useful information may be gained from the study of archaeological remains which immediately precede Late Cypriot IIIA, as for example, the material from Kition Tomb 9, upper burial. Above this tomb runs floor III of Late Cypriot IIIA. The roof of the tomb had collapsed after the last upper burial had been placed in it, so those who built above were unaware of its existence. The pottery which this tomb contained is of local manufacture, mainly comprising dishes known as 'Late Mycenaean IIIB' dishes.[43] They are decorated with horizontal bands inside and out and with a spiral at the bottom. The clay is of inferior quality compared with that of Mycenaean ware, and the paint is matt brown. Two skyphoi in the same fabric, found among the pottery of this upper burial, may imitate Late Helladic IIIB2 or IIIC1a prototypes.[44] There is a similar skyphos from a Late Cypriot IIC tomb at Hala Sultan Tekké, which also contained 'Late Mycenaean IIIB' dishes.[45] Pottery of the same type as in Kition Tomb 9, upper burial, has been found in deposits at Palaepaphos-*Mantissa*[46] and at Enkomi Tomb 18.[47] The latter has also produced a bronze sword of the Naue II type and a pair of bronze greaves, both belonging to a Mycenaean warrior; they are of types alien to Cyprus and have western connections.[48] These objects were placed in the tomb shortly before or immediately after the catastrophe mentioned above. It is suggested here that they belonged to a Mycenaean among the Sea Peoples who raided Enkomi.

Another characteristic fabric of the Late Cypriot IIC period is the 'Pastoral Style' (known earlier as the 'Rude Style') which, like 'Late Mycenaean IIIB', was produced in Cyprus when genuine Mycenaean IIIB pottery was scarce on the island, owing to the troubled conditions in the Aegean and the East Mediterranean which made communication very difficult or impossible west of Rhodes. It is probable, however,

69 Bell-crater of the early 'Rude Style' or 'Pastoral Style' from Enkomi. It is decorated on one side with a bull and goat near a bush, and on the other with a bull near a bush. The painter, under the influence of ivory carving, has rendered the anatomical details of the outlined bodies very carefully with thin and thick lines. This style developed in Cyprus at the very end of the 13th century BC, perhaps as a result of the discontinuation of brisk trade with the Aegean; it soon degenerated, however, into a really 'rude' style. Ht 28.7 cm; diam. 27.7 cm. Cyprus Museum, Nicosia, Enkomi, T.19 no. 66 (Swedish Excavations).

that the 'Pastoral Style' began slightly earlier than 'Late Mycenaean IIIB', perhaps originating as a pictorial style imitating engraved representations on ivory plaques or metallic surfaces.[49] This is evident not only in the choice of subjects (usually a bull or a goat in association with a tree, the rendering of the tree having exact parallels in ivory-carving), but also in the technique: anatomical details such as the dewlap of the bull, facial characteristics, muscles and leg veins are all rendered with thick and thin lines. There are some admirable examples of realistic drawing among the earliest products of this style, but it soon degenerated, hence the name 'Rude' which was first assigned to it. Genuine Mycenaean IIIB pottery did not, however, disappear immediately from Cyprus and some pieces are found together with locally produced 'Late Mycenaean IIIB' and 'Pastoral Style' wares, as well as the traditional Cypriot Base Ring II and White Slip II wares. During this period, at Kition, Pyla-*Verghi*, and Enkomi, whole vases or fragments appear of the so-called 'Grey ware' or 'Trojan ware' which must have been imported from the region of Troy.[50] This may be an important argument in favour of the theory that the Sea Peoples came to Cyprus via Anatolia.

69

The transition to Late Cypriot IIIA

Some of these wares are also found at Maa-*Palaeokastro*.[51] The results obtained so far from the excavations at this westernmost coastal site will be described in some detail, since they are related to the transition from Late Cypriot IIC to Late Cypriot IIIA. Maa was built as a fortified outpost on a headland of the western coast.[52] Its steep sides provided a natural fortification, so that only the neck of the headland and the tip of the point needed to be fortified artificially. The promontory is only about 300 m in length and 150 m in maximum width. The choice of this site for a fortified military outpost was deliberate: it was small, washed on three sides by the sea, and naturally defended on two sides, so that any necessary artificial defences could be constructed quickly and at low cost.

The first trial excavation at Maa in 1954 uncovered a limited area with walls and floors of houses associated with Mycenaean IIIC1b pottery, this being the pottery brought to the island by Achaean colonists from the Aegean region. The fortification walls have always stood above ground and their cyclopean character has been compared to the walls of Enkomi, Sinda and Kition.

The 1980 excavation campaign, however, revealed ceramic material in pits which is earlier than Mycenaean IIIC1b, namely Mycenaean IIIB, 'Late Mycenaean IIIB', Base Ring II, White Slip II, White Shaved and Red Lustrous Wheelmade, all wares which were in existence during Late Cypriot IIC. This material is contemporary with that of the upper layer of Kition Tomb 9 and Enkomi Tomb 18. At Maa, sherds were found in pits together with ashes, and must have been thrown there with the arrival of those bringing the Mycenaean IIIC1b pottery found on the house floors. Clearly, this Mycenaean IIIC1b pottery is also contemporary with the site's abandonment, soon after newcomers from the Aegean arrived who may be called Achaeans.

The 1981 campaign revealed that Maa-*Palaeokastro* was in fact inhabited for the first time at the very end of Late Cypriot IIC, at a time when Mycenaean IIIB, Base Ring II and White Slip II pottery were in use. These early settlers built a rectangular building of ashlar blocks very near the dog-leg gate of the north cyclopean wall. This building, measuring *c.* 12.5 × 12.5 m, has a thick floor on which pottery of Late Cypriot IIC was found. Its architectural character, and its proximity to the city gate, may suggest a sanctuary (as at Enkomi and Kition), but it is still too early to judge, since the excavation is not yet complete. Soon after its construction, however, the building was destroyed, and after a few years of abandonment – an alluvial deposit was found on it – private houses with rubble walls were built there, with a pebbled street running across it, separating two houses. Mycenaean IIIC1b pottery was found on the floors of these houses, indicating the date of their abandonment. The houses correspond in character and date to those found during the 1980 campaign; one is of purely Aegean plan, with a central 'megaron' and two lateral narrow rooms.

The history of Maa may be reconstructed as follows, taking into consideration the fact that there was no previous continuity at the site: towards the end of Late Cypriot IIC, when Mycenaean IIIB, 'Late Mycenaean IIIB' and other traditional Cypriot wares were in use, Maa was fortified by foreigners with particular reasons to be cautious and to defend themselves quickly against possible attack, both from land and sea. These, we suggest, were the Sea Peoples, who also raided Enkomi and Kition. Whether they raided nearby regions from this outpost is not known. No major Late Cypriot II settlements are known in the vicinity, and this may have made the site even more attractive for the establishment of a military outpost by foreign warriors, away from any local hostile population. Furthermore, the safe anchorage of the well-protected bay on either side of the headland, and the nearby water supply from a perennial spring, made it an ideal choice. These early settlers, of an heterogeneous culture and including perhaps Anatolians as well as the Aegeans who formed the majority, were responsible for the cyclopean wall and for the ashlar building. One of their first preoccupations was the accumulation of supplies (including water, wine, oil), hence the discovery of an extraordinary quantity of large pithos sherds at the site; some of these sherds, as mentioned earlier, were used during the second period of occupation as building material. A similar abundance of pithos sherds may be observed at the site of Pyla-*Kokkinokremos*, which also served as a military outpost. They abandoned the site, however, about two decades after their arrival, and settled at Palaepaphos. They were succeeded by a new wave of settlers, who introduced Mycenaean IIIC1b pottery and built houses with rubble walls. These may also be responsible for the blocking of the dog-leg gate and for the triangular inner fort. A safe criterion for dating the construction of this second period is the use of large pithos sherds as building material. We believe the second settlers to have been 'permanent' Achaean settlers. There are no signs so far that there was a violent succession from the first to the second period of settlement, for there is evidence for a short abandonment, as mentioned above. The second wave of settlers were of a more homogeneous culture, not accustomed to monumental buildings of ashlar blocks – hence the disuse of the earlier ones. These settlers, in their turn, did not stay long, but abandoned the site in the early years of the 12th century BC, at a time when Mycenaean IIIC1b pottery was in use.

If this reconstruction is valid, it would explain why there are no large quantities of Mycenaean IIIC1a pottery in Cyprus; the real influx is represented by Mycenaean IIIC1b, left by the second wave of settlers. It is probable that after the abandonment of their site, when Mycenaean IIIC1b pottery was in use, the inhabitants of Maa went to Palaepaphos, the nearest urban centre, since pottery of exactly the same style has been found there (mainly skyphoi with solid painted interiors, the outsides of which are decorated characteristically with antithetic stemmed spirals).[53]

The settlement of Maa, occupied for no more than fifty years at two periods, will no doubt prove, as the excavations continue, of the utmost importance for dating the Achaean colonization of Cyprus and the ashlar block buildings of Enkomi, Kition and Hala Sultan Tekké.

The history of the fortified settlement at Sinda,[54] west of Enkomi in the Mesaoria plain, is strikingly similar to that of Maa. The settlement of Period I at Sinda was 'destroyed' at the end of Late Cypriot IIC. According to the excavator's preliminary report, 'the oldest city had undergone a violent destruction'. In the northwestern excavation area an ash layer above the rock was all that remained of the houses, and no walls had been preserved except the city wall itself. That this enceinte was built when the town was founded is clear from the evidence in the city gate area. The same catastrophe had caused the destruction of the massive building adjoining the gate which served in its defence. After this catastrophe, new floors were laid everywhere, over the burnt remains of the earlier ones.[55] Though the elucidation in detail of the real events at Sinda awaits the final publication of the excavation results, one may tentatively suggest that Sinda, like Maa, was first constructed as a military outpost, whence the Achaeans moved on to Palaepaphos and Enkomi, both of which were already flourishing Late Cypriot II urban areas. Those Sea Peoples and Achaeans who settled at Sinda may have come from the Aegean along the southern coast of Asia Minor, landed somewhere near the 'shore of the Achaeans' (*Achaion Akte*) on the northern coast of Cyprus, and crossed the Kyrenia mountains on their way to Enkomi, as Dimitrios Poliorketes was to do at the end of the 4th century BC when he marched against Salamis. It is possible that there was a Late Cypriot II settlement at Sinda, or nearby, which the Sea Peoples destroyed before settling there, though the apparent absence of walls may preclude this.

One may suggest a similar explanation for the settlement at Pyla-*Kokkinokremos* – on the south coast east of Kition – situated on a plateau and defended on all sides by a massive casemate wall. Dikaios carried out a very limited excavation at this site; the settlement was established at more or less the same time as Maa, and was abandoned before Mycenaean IIIC1b pottery was introduced. It has been suggested that the low ground between the plateau and the coast, which is now marshy land, may have been a harbour.[56] If the settlement at *Kokkinokremos* was a military outpost like Maa and Sinda, then we may suggest that its occupants moved to the already flourishing town of Kition after they had departed.

Late Cypriot IIIA

It is not certain when Late Cypriot IIIA begins, though this period follows a few years after the catastrophe of Late Cypriot IIC. Desborough has suggested that either some of the Mycenaeans (Sea Peoples) who took part in the events leading to the first destruction remained behind and settled, or that others from the same ethnic stock, who may be called Achaeans, took advantage of a weakened population to penetrate the island and establish themselves at key points. There is no indication that this process entailed domination of the local population, at least at first, though the newcomers may not always have been welcome and there may have been occasional friction. It has been suggested that the settlers lived on equal terms with the local population and they may have intermarried. That domination was not involved is clear from the fact that the Achaeans adopted several cultural elements from the local population, including architectural styles, aspects of religious activity and script.

Excavations at Enkomi have revealed a second catastrophe that took place at the end of Late Cypriot IIIA1, which is associated by some scholars with the raids of the Sea Peoples. In the extensive excavations at Kition, however, no such catastrophe has been observed. It is true that there are two phases of floor III, but the layer between the two is very thin and the earlier floor IIIA is not found throughout the site. In any case, on floors III and IIIA the same Mycenaean IIIC1b pottery was discovered. It is only at the end of Late Cypriot IIIA that changes occur in the buildings, such as the construction of floor II on which 'Granary Style' pottery with the characteristic wavy band was found. Desborough suggests that this destruction resulted from a continued struggle between the local Cypriot population and the Achaeans, and that further groups of Achaeans came to help their kinsmen.[57] Several years later, c. 1100 BC,[58] groups of Minoans arrived. There are indications of an even later, final wave of Achaean settlers who landed c. 1075 BC, judging from the style of pottery found in a tomb at Idalion-Ayios Georghios.[59]

The Sea Peoples, or what was left of them, finally settled in Palestine after causing widespread destruction in the Levant. As a result, refugees from this region fled to Cyprus where they joined the Achaean settlers. This explains the mixed character of the culture of Cyprus during Late Cypriot IIIA, particularly in ivory-carving and glyptics, and later in a number of forms of Proto-White Painted ware.[60]

The disaster which put an end to the Late Bronze Age occurred between 1075 and 1050 BC. At Kition the mudbrick superstructure of the cyclopean walls and the rectangular bastions tumbled down onto an adjacent street, burying Proto-White Painted pottery. A violent destruction is also evidenced at Enkomi.

Shortly before this catastrophe, Wenamon, an Egyptian priest, is described as visiting Alashiya by an Egyptian narrative.[61] He was sent to Byblos c. 1075 BC, and on his return was shipwrecked, whereupon he and his crew sought refuge in Alashiya. The inhabitants, according to the Egyptian record, neither understood the Egyptian language of Wenamon nor the Syrian language of the crew and intended to kill them. Wenamon succeeded in finding his way to the princess of the town Heteb, to whom he explained, through someone who could understand Egyptian, that if he and the members of his crew were killed, the king of Byblos would take revenge by killing ten sailors from Alashiya. Though the rest of the story is not known it raises some interesting points: it provides additional evidence in support of the argument that Alashiya is in Cyprus and not in Syria; and the fact that at least one person understood Egyptian indicates that either there were Egyptians on the island or that contacts with Egypt continued into the 11th century BC, as is corroborated by archaeological evidence.

After this short historical survey of the Late Cypriot IIIA period, it is to archaeological evidence that we must now turn. The arrival of the Achaeans opened a new era in the political, economic and cultural life of Cyprus, and well-organized cities succeeded the ruined towns of Enkomi and Kition.

Cities and fortifications

ENKOMI

Enkomi was fortified with a 'cyclopean' wall,[62] the lower part of which consists of two parallel rows of large, unhewn blocks, c. 1.5 m high. Those of the outer row are larger than those of the inner row and the core was filled with rubble. The superstructure of the wall was of mudbrick. There were several towers built at irregular intervals against the south, west and north sides, constructed of large stone blocks with a rubble core. Their dimensions vary from 4–5 m in length and 2–3 m in depth. The structure identified by the excavator as a large rectangular tower outside and adjacent to the north city gate may in fact be a sanctuary.[63] It is interesting to note that the date given by Dikaios for the construction of this wall is the very end of Late Cypriot IIC, which makes it contemporary with the cyclopean walls of Kition, Maa and Sinda. The city wall of Enkomi has largely been exposed, so the extent of the whole city is known. It measures c. 400 m from north to south, and 350 m from east to west. Straight streets cross the city from one side to the other, connecting opposite gates and intersecting at right angles, forming a regular grid which recalls Hellenistic town planning. At about the centre of the town there is a paved open space.[64]

KITION

At Kition the city wall was constructed on the mudbrick debris of the wall destroyed at the end of Late Cypriot IIC. Mycenaean IIIB and Late Cypriot II pottery were found in the debris. Its course is irregular, to judge by the portions that have been uncovered and by a surface survey of the area. The city enclosed by this wall is c. 1500 m long and c. 700 m wide. Only two of the bastions, at the northernmost part of the city, have been fully uncovered. They already existed in Late Cypriot II and their mudbrick superstructure may have been destroyed and reconstructed or repaired. The new cyclopean wall, of which about

100 m have been uncovered in Area II, is *c.* 2.4 m wide. The height of
the stone structure is *c.* 1.25 m and above this lie the mudbrick courses
of which several partially survive. A large stone anchor, measuring
c. 1.3 × 1.07 × 0.32 m, was built into the city wall, parallel to which a
street runs on the outside and along the façade of one of the bastions.
This street is 3 m wide, and its outer edge was marked with a row of
large stone blocks perhaps to provide a boundary along the edge of the
marshes. It was constructed on the mudbrick debris of the Late
Cypriot II wall. Its surface is hard, made of gravel and crushed animal
bones, a style also found within the city and at Enkomi. On the street
the tracks of vehicle wheels were clearly visible at the time of
excavation. In the northeastern part of Area II the city wall turns
southwards at right angles. A rectangular tower is located at the corner
against the wall, but this is still to be excavated. A short distance south
of this tower is a gate through which a street runs. To the left, on
entering the gate, are the rubble foundations of an approximately
rectangular tower. This part of the city wall, however, including the
gate and the two towers, is seriously damaged, perhaps as a result of
stone-robbing at later periods.

SINDA

Sinda also has an irregular, polygonal plan, measuring *c.* 250 m from
east to west and *c.* 200 m from north to south. At the northern part of
the town is a gate which was protected by a guardhouse with strong
walls. Those who entered the gate had to expose their uncovered right
flank. The rest of the wall resembles the cyclopean walls of Enkomi and
Kition in its structure. Air photography, however, has shown that there
may be another wall in front of the main one, which served perhaps as
an advance fortification. The excavator believes that the origins of this
type of fortification should be sought in Anatolia.

MAA-PALAEOKASTRO

Maa is a formidable fortress, combining both manmade and natural
features. The stretch of wall constructed across the neck of the
promontory to protect the settlement from the land side is of the usual
cyclopean type. It measures *c.* 3.5 m in width and has two gates situated
not far from each other. One of the gates is a simple aperture between
two opposing stretches of wall, the other formed by two overlapping
stretches of the wall. The seaward side, which is low land, was also
defended by a wall *c.* 3.5–4 m wide. It is curved slightly to follow the
contour of the promontory, and at one point, where the wall turns at an
angle, a rectangular tower is located. The north and south ends of the
wall correspond to the points where the slopes of the promontory begin
to be precipitous. Apart from these two stretches of the city wall there
are other fortified structures within the walled promontory. Near the
seaward side there is a large triangular enclosure built of thick rubble
walls of which only the foundations survive; this may have been used as
a guardroom or as a place where chariots or horses were assembled.

Buildings in ashlar

Late Cypriot III is marked not only by the building of monumental
fortresses but also of 'palaces'. At Enkomi there is one of the most

outstanding structures of Late Bronze Age domestic architecture, known as 'Bâtiment 18' and identified by its excavator as a 'palace'. No doubt it was not an ordinary residence. Its four sides open onto streets, i.e., it occupies a whole block. Its principal façade, on the south, is more than 40 m long and has four doors that are each more than 2 m wide, and four windows. The manner of wall construction is new to the island. On a rubble foundation there is an embossed block serving as a socket, on which rests a large ashlar block forming the first course. The blocks occasionally measure more than 3 m in length, 1.4 m in height and 0.7 m in width. The top is cut to receive two smaller blocks set parallel to one another, like orthostats, and at a small distance from one another; the space between them was probably filled with soil and/or rubble. At the top of the second course there was a horizontal slab. The ashlar blocks of local hard limestone have perfect points and are set dry without mortar. The inside compartments of the building, arranged around an inner court, are constructed of thinner walls, but again with ashlar blocks. This building was constructed at the very beginning of Late Cypriot IIIA, but at the end of the period it was divided by rubble walls into smaller compartments and was used as a workshop for copper-smelting. Its large windows were also blocked with rubble.

The introduction of ashlar-block construction at Enkomi, as well as in other main urban centres such as Kition, Palaepaphos, Hala Sultan Tekké and Maa-*Palaeokastro*, coincides with the arrival of the first Achaean settlers, but it is a building fashion alien to the Aegean that could not have been introduced by them. Since the technique was known in Anatolia and at Ugarit (in the Temple of Baal and the Palace), it is not impossible that it was introduced to Cyprus by builders from these regions, in particular from Ugarit.[65] We know that refugees from there must have left their country after the destruction of their city and have settled in Cyprus *c.* 1200 BC.

At Kition (Area I) are traces of ashlar-block construction in a private house, in which the walls are built of small ashlar blocks resting on a low rubble wall *c.* 50 cm above floor level.

Sacred architecture

ENKOMI

At both Enkomi and Kition, ashlar-block constructions are used for
70   sanctuaries. The sanctuary of the first 'horned god' at Enkomi consists of a hall, the roof of which was supported on two rectangular pillars.
71   From this hall there was access to two inner cult rooms to the east, in one of which the bronze cult statue of a 'horned god' was found. In the hall, around the sacrificial altar and offerings table, were a large number of skulls of oxen and of other horned animals such as deer and goats. There were also quantities of bowls which must have been used for pouring libations.

To the east, adjacent to the large sanctuary of the 'horned god', there was a smaller sanctuary of the same period consisting of an outer hall, with a hearth altar close to an offerings table in the centre, and an inner room in which a small bronze statuette of a double-headed female divinity was found; she may have been the consort of the male god. A

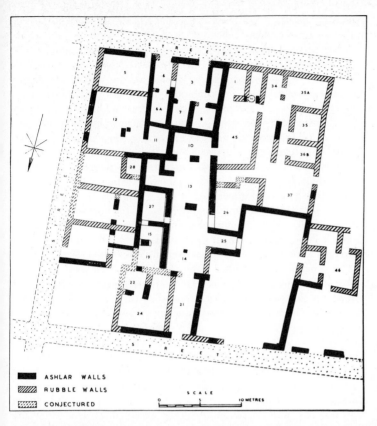

ASHLAR WALLS
RUBBLE WALLS
CONJECTURED

SCALE
0   5   10 METRES

70 Plan of the sanctuary of the 'Horned God' at Enkomi (in solid black). It was built of ashlar blocks and its ground plan may show affinities to the megaron type of Aegean architecture. End of the 13th century BC. (After P. Dikaios, *Enkomi* vol. IIIB (1969), pl. 275.)

71 General view of Enkomi. In the central part of the photograph is the sanctuary of the 'Horned God'. Sanctuaries and other public buildings were erected at Enkomi towards the very end of the 13th century BC, usually constructed with ashlar blocks. In this particular sanctuary the bronze statue of the cult – a horned god – was found.

similar phenomenon may have existed, as has already been suggested, in the sanctuary of Ayios Iakovos.

Another sanctuary at Enkomi, also built of ashlar blocks, consists of a propylaeum (main porch) and a cella (shrine). In the central part of the cella near a well is the rectangular stone base of a pillar, which may recall the pillar cult in Aegean religious architecture. A capital with a stepped profile was found nearby. Such capitals are known from other Late Cypriot III sanctuaries at Kition, Palaepaphos and Myrtou-Pigadhes.[66] The third sanctuary at Enkomi,[67] constructed c. 1150 BC, consists of a rectangular courtyard in which a hearth altar and two free-standing stone blocks were found. One of them is pierced in the upper part, perhaps for tethering sacrificial animals which were slaughtered on the other block, the upper part of which is hollow. Benches against the walls served for the deposit of offerings. At the northeastern corner is a small cella where the bronze statue of the second 'horned god' of Enkomi, known as the 'Ingot God', was found. On the floor of the courtyard were numerous skulls of oxen, used for ritual purposes.

The sanctuaries and other public buildings at Enkomi lie in the centre of the town. Along the northernmost part, near the city wall, are workshops for copper-smelting, situated so that the prevailing south winds would blow the poisonous fumes away from the residential area.

KITION

The same phenomenon also appears at Kition, but there the sacred area is located at the northernmost part of the town, for a reason to be explained later. As already stated, during Late Cypriot II there were 72 two sanctuaries (Temples 2 and 3) in the northernmost part of the town near the city wall; between them lay a sacred garden. After the destruction of these temples at the end of Late Cypriot IIC, the sacred area was not only maintained but was extended. The small Temple 3 was abolished and its foundations covered by the floor of an open sacred courtyard (Temenos A); next to it was built a large temple of ashlar blocks, enclosing part of the sacred garden. This is Temple 1, which measures 33.6 m east to west and 22 m north to south. It consists of a large rectangular courtyard with two lateral entrances. One of these, in the east, has a kind of propylaeum in front of it with sockets on the floor on either side, probably to hold poles for banners as in Egyptian temples; the other, to the south, is reached by a ramp and a staircase. Along the south side runs a long narrow corridor. The holy-of-holies is along the western part. It consists of a long narrow corridor along the whole width of the building and is 5.3 m deep; it is divided into three compartments which do not communicate with one another, but which each open onto the main courtyard to the east. Near the central doorway, and within the courtyard, there is a well from which several channels run, connecting the pits of the sacred garden. These must have been intended for small bushes rather than trees; they are c. 30 cm deep and c. 30 cm in diameter. A rectangular pool, almost in the centre of the courtyard, measures 4.6 × 1.8 m and is 0.9 m deep. It is cut into the bedrock and has a pebbled floor. The pool, together with the well, must have helped irrigate the garden, but the pool may also have contained 'sacred fishes' in the fashion of the 'sacred lakes' in Egyptian

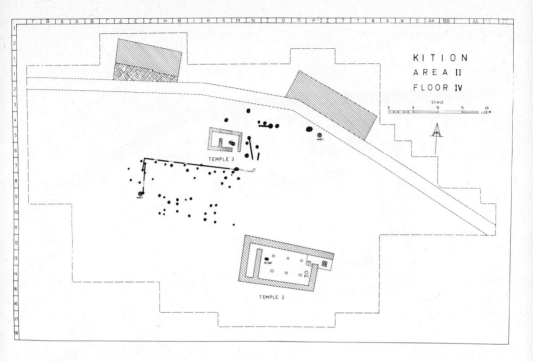

KITION
AREA II
FLOOR IV

temples of the 18th and 19th dynasties. The walls of Temple 1 consist of two parallel rows of ashlar blocks with drafted edges. These are particularly large along the outer façade of the south wall; the largest block measures 3.5 m in length and 1.5 m in height. The inner façade contains smaller blocks, the floor of the courtyard inside the temple being higher than that of the courtyard outside. The space between the two parallel rows of blocks was filled with rubble. The foundations of the south wall are built of unhewn stone blocks with a flat top, to bear the embossed ashlar blocks of the base, or socle. There is no socle on the other sides.

Temple 2 was not exactly rectangular so was remodelled, although its original dimensions were more or less retained: 14.5 m east to west and 9 m north to south. The walls are built of ashlar blocks of which only the embossed socle is preserved, resting on a rubble foundation. The screen wall which separates the holy-of-holies from the outer courtyard of the temple is also of ashlar blocks. Two lateral openings give access to the holy-of-holies. Along the south wall of the courtyard a bench was constructed for the deposit of offerings. There were also several other alterations and additions to the original plan, among which the construction of a low offerings table next to the hearth altar is worthy of note.

Temples 1 and 2 form one architectural unit that also includes an open rectangular courtyard, Temenos B, which lies north of Temple 2 and east of Temple 1. The east enclosure wall of this courtyard, also of ashlar blocks, passes parallel to the east façade of Temple 2, forming a narrow corridor in front of it. This wall – the façade of the sacred complex (Temples 1 and 2 and Temenos B) – is 23.5 m long and

72 Plan of Kition, Area II, showing the course of the city wall, the two rectangular bastions against it and, *intra muros*, Temples 2 and 3. Between them the black spots indicate the pits of the 'sacred garden'. Beginning of the 13th century BC. (Kition floor IV, *c.* 1300–1200 BC.)

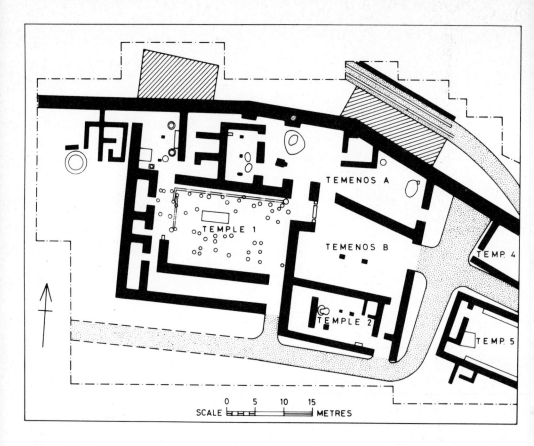

73 Plan of Kition, Area II, showing the cyclopean city wall with its rectangular bastions, Temples 1, 2, 4 and 5 and the workshops for smelting copper between the north wall of Temple 1 and the city wall. (Kition floor III, *c.* 1200–1150 BC.)

73

consists of one course of orthostats resting on a socle of embossed ashlar blocks. The main entrance to Temenos B from the east is 4.2 m wide. From Temenos B one could proceed to Temples 1 and 2. Along the south wall of Temenos B there must have been a portico, the roof of which was supported by two perhaps wooden pillars. The stone bases of the pillars and their stone capitals with stepped profiles have been found on the floor of Temenos B.

From Temenos B one could also proceed to another open courtyard through an opening in its north wall. This is Temenos A, whose cemented altar, slightly higher than the level of the floor, was meant for animal sacrifices (quantities of carbonized bones were found on and all round it, as well as fragments of bowls mixed with ashes). Next to this altar was a rectangular offerings table of ashlar blocks, near which a pair of stone 'horns of consecration' was found, that had obviously stood originally at the top. A second pair of stone 'horns of consecration' was found reused in a later wall in Temenos B. The same religious symbol is also present at the top of the altar of the sanctuary at Myrtou-*Pigadhes*,[68] and a fragmentary one was found at the site of the Temple of Aphrodite at Palaepaphos.[69]

In front of the east façade of Temenos B is an open triangular space which separates Temples 1 and 2 from a second complex, that of Temples 4 and 5. Temple 4 is situated along the inner side of the city wall, and is separated from Temple 5 by a street; the same street then turns twice at right angles, to run parallel to the south façade of Temple 2 and then reach the south lateral entrance to Temple 1. Temple 4 is built of small ashlar blocks along its north wall, which is in fact the inner façade of the city wall, but there is no evidence for the use of ashlar blocks in the rest of this temple. One should mention, however, that the foundations of the south and west walls are constructed of stone anchors, perhaps so that their flat top would provide a base for ashlar blocks. The temple consists of a rectangular courtyard, with one opening on the west and another on the east. The holy-of-holies is on the east, unlike all the other temples in this area which have their holy-of-holies on the west. It consists of two small adjacent rectangular rooms, one of which contained a group of ivory objects; in the other, bowls on the floor were probably used for libation. In the northwestern courtyard of the temple, below the floor, two unfinished bronze tools and a large bronze peg were discovered, obviously part of a foundation deposit. The bronze peg has parallels in inscribed clay from the ancient Near East. In approximately the centre of the courtyard is an offerings table and a sacrificial altar. The door in the east wall of the temple leads to a paved area which was largely destroyed by a Hellenistic water cistern. The few stone flooring slabs that survive are heavily burnt. To the same paved area belongs a rectangular stone-lined well for lustral purposes which may have formed part of the sacred area. This area is in the immediate proximity of the city gate at the northwestern corner of the city wall. One may suggest that there were yearly festivals during which the gods were invited to enter the city which they protected.[70]

The walls of Temple 5 are of rubble foundations with mudbrick superstructures. Its holy-of-holies, along the western part, is a long

74 Aerial view of Kition Area II (northernmost part of the town). *Intra muros* lie the sanctuaries and workshops. Excavated by the Cyprus Department of Antiquities.

narrow compartment reached from the courtyard through a small lateral opening. There is a side entrance to the courtyard in the northeastern corner. A rectangular offerings table, measuring 2 × 1.8 m, lay in the western part of the courtyard against the screen wall of the holy-of-holies. A votive stone anchor was found leaning against its south side. Along the north and south walls of the courtyard were porticos, the roof of which rested on wooden pillars of which the stone bases have been found. The parts of the floor of the courtyard open to the sky had burnt patches and a thick ash layer, probably the remains of sacrificial altars. On one of them the antlers of a *Dama mesopotamica* have been found. A bench constructed along the north wall was for offerings.

On the floor of the temple several skulls of oxen and other horned animals were found; some of them may have been used as masks during ritual performances. There was also a stone anchor standing upright on the floor.

The architectural plan of all the temples at Kition remained unchanged in Late Cypriot II and III: incorporating a rectangular courtyard and a holy-of-holies, with one or two porticos in the courtyard and a hearth altar and offerings table. This type of sanctuary is common in Levantine sites such as Lachish, Tell Farah and Tel Qasile.

An important feature in the sacred area of Kition is the proximity of the temples to an industrial quarter along the north wall of Temple 1 74 and west of Temenos A. This area is defined to the north by the city wall. In fact one could walk from Temenos A, through the workshops to Temple 1 by an opening near the northwestern corner of its courtyard. Furnaces with ashes, fragments of crucibles and tuyères, as well as quantities of copper slag found on the floors of these workshops, indicate that they were used for copper-smelting. They must have been open to the sky, so that poisonous fumes could be blown away from the residential quarter by the prevailing southerly winds, as was noted at Enkomi.

West of these workshops and behind the holy-of-holies of Temple 1 were storerooms where bone ash was kept. This was used as a fluxing material during smelting, and a furnace was found there for roasting bones. Other storerooms contained tools such as querns and pounders, as well as loomweights and spindle whorls. No doubt all these served the needs of the temples.

PALAEPAPHOS

Another major sanctuary of the Late Cypriot III period is that of Aphrodite at Palaepaphos, which until very recently was considered of Roman date. It is now known to be comparable both chronologically and architecturally with Temple 1 of Kition, though little of its plan has 75 survived.[71] Its walls were constructed of large ashlar blocks resting on socles. Partition walls within the sanctuary were again of ashlar blocks with drafted edges; there were also rectangular stone pillars, of which one survives *in situ*, which had stone capitals with a stepped profile of the kind encountered at Kition and elsewhere. The 'horns of consecration' found in the area of the temple have already been noted.

All these features, as well as a large Late Cypriot III pithos half-buried in a rock-cut pit below the floor of the sanctuary and a clay bath-tub, testify to its Late Bronze Age date. The tripartite plan of this temple is often discussed in terms of temples appearing on the reverse of some Roman coins or on gems and sealings. In the central cella of the holy-of-holies a conical object is shown, usually identified with the betyl (a dark conical stone) which was discovered on the surface in the area of the sanctuary. On either side of the central cella are two free-standing pillars topped by 'horns of consecration'. It is unlikely, however, that the Late Bronze Age plan of the sanctuary remained unaltered down to the Roman period. However, Kition Temple 1 does present a tripartite arrangement.

75 Remains of the Late Bronze Age Temple of Aphrodite at Palaepaphos. The large orthostats recall the walls of the Kition and Enkomi temples. Excavations by a Swiss-German Mission. These remains, formerly thought to be of the Roman period, are now correctly dated to *c.* 1200 BC.

MYRTOU-PIGADHES

We have already mentioned the sanctuary at Myrtou-*Pigadhes* with its monumental altar, over 2 m high. According to the excavators it was built *c.* 1300 BC but was in use until *c.* 1175 BC. A rectangular stepped altar with horns of consecration on top was constructed of ashlar blocks in the western courtyard of the sanctuary *c.* 1200 BC. In the eastern part of the same courtyard was a bench with pierced stone blocks above it inserted in the wall for fastening sacrificial animals.

76

GOLGOI

Finally, the sanctuary on the outskirts of Golgoi should be noted.[72] Hundreds of miniature vases were found in it, as well as nodules of copper slag and bronze objects in various stages of manufacture. It is quite possible that here, as at Kition, was a cult connected with metallurgy. Indeed, Golgoi may have been on the route by which

76 Reconstructed altar in the sanctuary of Myrtou-*Pigadhes* in northwestern Cyprus. At the top of the altar which is built of ashlar blocks are 'horns of consecration', a symbol of Aegean religion. The altar was constructed *c*. 1200 BC.

copper ore was transported from the Troodos mines to Kition. The sanctuary, built in the 14th century BC, continued in use until the Late Cypriot III period.

Religious beliefs

The importance has already been stressed of the divinities associated with fertility in the development of the prehistoric religion of Cyprus, from the Chalcolithic and Early Bronze Age periods onwards. The Cypriots have always been conservative in their religious beliefs, and they preserved the essential elements of their religion over a long period. Thus, the divinities of fertility reappear, though in different forms, during the Late Cypriot period. In the early part of Late Cypriot, and even in Late Cypriot II, there are representations of divinities that can be associated with a cult. Terracotta figurines of a nude female divinity holding an infant or pressing her breasts, are usually found in tombs or in private houses but not in sanctuaries. They may represent the 'Great Goddess', or a female companion for the dead. There are two types of terracottas: the earliest, with a bird-face, has Near Eastern precedents, and the later one of the 13th century

BC with naturalistic facial characteristics which may indicate Aegean influences. Bull figures, either in the form of a rhyton or in terracotta, appear quite often in tombs as well as in sanctuaries such as Enkomi, Idalion and Ayia Irini. There are also terracotta and bronze representations of a bull accompanied by human figures (occasionally riding on a cult vehicle) and who lead the animal for sacrifice. The bucrania (or bulls' heads or skulls) found in sanctuaries such as Enkomi and Kition, may have been worn as masks[73] as already mentioned – the wearer acquiring some of the qualities of a bull. This custom survived into the Cypro-Archaic period as is attested by terracotta figurines found in sanctuaries, which represent human figures in the act of putting bull-masks on their heads.

The main period for the construction of temples and sanctuaries is no doubt Late Cypriot III, when public buildings appear in the major towns and large sanctuaries at Enkomi, Kition and Palaepaphos. Though these sanctuaries coincide with the arrival of the first Achaean colonists, it is surprising how little of their religion these settlers brought with them from the Aegean. They apparently borrowed considerably from the local population, both in religious architecture and practice. The introduction to Cyprus of the 'horns of consecration' as a religious symbol is, however, an exception. This symbol is well known in Crete and the Mycenaean mainland at sites such as Gla and Pylos. It appears at Myrtou-*Pigadhes*, Kition and Palaepaphos and also on a limestone trough from Pyla-*Kokkinokremos*, though in Cyprus it differs slightly from those in the Aegean.[74]

Religious life was conservative in Cyprus, where conservatism is strong in all aspects of culture. Several elements in Cypriot religion were not alien to the new settlers, including the religious significance of the bull and votive anchors, and thus a radical change did not take place; on the contrary, there was every reason for a gradual fusion. At the time of the arrival of the Achaean settlers, religious architecture in the Aegean was not so developed nor was it significantly different. The recent excavation of a sanctuary at Phylakopi may even suggest some resemblances.[75] Later in the 12th century BC, when more Achaeans and other Aegeans had settled in Cyprus, Aegean elements in Cypriot religion became more conspicuous, as we shall see.

Evidence for the cult performed in the sanctuaries at Enkomi is as follows. Horned animals were sacrificed in large numbers in the sanctuaries of the two horned gods, and some of their skulls may have been worn as masks by worshippers or hung on the walls. Libations are suggested by the numerous bowls found in the sanctuary of the first horned god. It is noteworthy that cult statues were found in both sanctuaries, unlike other sanctuaries in Cyprus of the same period. The first horned god is represented as a beardless, youthful, muscular figure, wearing a horned cap of animal skin and a short kilt.[76] He has been identified with the Greek god Apollo Keraeatas of Arcadia, a god of cattle and shepherds. A Hellenistic inscription from Pyla, near Larnaca, mentions the worship of Apollo Keraeatas, obviously a survival of the Late Bronze Age god whose worship may have been introduced by the first Achaean colonists, and quickly established and identified with the old fertility god of prehistoric Cyprus. The facial

77

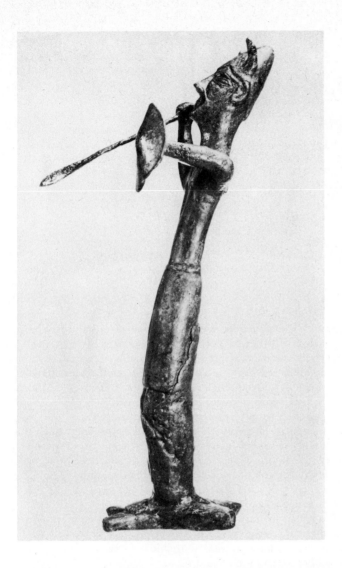

78 Bronze statue of a bearded god, cast solid, found in the cella of the sanctuary of the 'Ingot God' at Enkomi. The god wears a kilt and a close fitted vest. He also wears a conical helmet with horns. He is fully armed, with a shield in his left hand and a spear in his right. His legs are protected by greaves. The god stands on a base in the form of an oxhide ingot – hence his name – and has been identified with the god who protects the copper mines of Cyprus. Beginning of the 12th century BC. Ht 35 cm. Cyprus Museum, Nicosia (excavated by the French Mission, 1963), no. 16.15.

77 (*Opposite*) Bronze statue of a youthful god, cast solid, found in the sanctuary of the 'Horned God' at Enkomi. He wears a short kilt and a helmet with two horns springing from the sides. The facial characteristics recall Aegean prototypes, while the attitude is Near Eastern. This god has been identified as Apollo Keraeatas or Alasiotas (the god of Alashiya). This is a fine example of Cypriot bronzework of the very end of the 13th century BC, and is the largest bronze statue of this period so far found on the island. Ht 54.2 cm. Cyprus Museum, Nicosia (excavated by the Cyprus Department of Antiquities, 1948), no. 19.

characteristics of the god are very 'Greek', though there are Near Eastern parallels for the attitude of the arms. Others have identified this god with Apollo or Reshef of Alasia, based on a 4th-century BC inscription from Tamassos which mentions Apollo Alasiotas. The bronze statue of the second horned god is perhaps even more important for the religious cults of Enkomi. It is 35 cm high and the figure wears a short kilt, chiton and belt, and a horned helmet.[77] He has greaves on his legs and holds a shield in his left hand, while in his right he brandishes a spear. The figure stands on a base in the form of an oxhide ingot and is thus known as the 'Ingot God'. He has been identified with the god who protects the copper mines of Cyprus. A small bronze statuette of a female divinity of the 12th century BC, now in the Ashmolean Museum at Oxford and of Cypriot origin, stands on a similar base. She has been identified with the goddess who symbolizes the fertility of the copper

79 A copper ingot in the form
of an oxhide, with a sign
impressed on its surface. This
is how copper was exported
from Cyprus. Such ingots
were found in a 12th-century-
BC shipwreck off the coast of
southwest Anatolia and are
represented on bronze stands,
being carried by Cypriots on
their shoulders. They were
considered a standard
'monetary' unit before the
invention of coinage. From
Enkomi, c. 1200 BC. Weight
86 lb. 6 oz. L. 72 cm. Cyprus
Museum, Nicosia, no.
1939/VI–20/4.

81 (*Opposite*) Ivory plaque
carved on both sides in the
ajouré technique, representing
the Egyptian god Bes. Tenons
at the top and bottom show
that it was meant to decorate a
piece of furniture. The lower
tenon bears an inscription in
Cypro-Minoan script. Bes
was the god of the household
and protected women in
pregnancy. From Kition,
Temple 4 (holy-of-holies),
c. 1200 BC. Ht 22 cm. Cyprus
Museum, Nicosia, Kition
Area II, no. 4252.

mines.[78] The armed, horned god is doubly significant. Not only is he associated with the copper mines, but he is ready to protect them effectively at a time when the copper trade was endangered by troubled conditions in the East Mediterranean. The connection of metallurgy with religion is also attested in Cyprus by the discovery at Enkomi of small votive ingots engraved in Cypro-Minoan.

The existence in Cyprus in the 12th century BC of two divinities connected with metallurgy is of manifold significance. Such was the importance of the production and export of copper for the economy of the island that the copper industry was put under the protection, and hence the control, of religion and the religious authorities. A similar phenomenon is known at Late Bronze Age sites such as Timna in Palestine and Kea in the Aegean. The association of a male 'smith-god' with a female divinity is also significant. The worship of twin divinities in twin temples in Cyprus has been mentioned. The association of the smith-god Hephaestos with Aphrodite in Greek mythology may thus be neither irrelevant nor accidental.

The connection of metallurgy with religion is also evident in the sanctuary at Myrtou-*Pigadhes*, in the Temple of Aphrodite at Palaepaphos where copper slag has been found, and in the sanctuary at Golgoi. It is most clearly illustrated at Kition, where the temples actually communicate with workshops for copper-smelting. The twin Temples 1 and 2 at Kition, with the open temenoi, form one architectural unit, as already described. Though no cult statue was found in either, it may be that the large Temple 1 was used for the worship of a goddess of fertility; in the Phoenician period it was rebuilt for the cult of the goddess Astarte.

Little is known of other religious rituals in the temples at Kition other than the performances with animal-masks. It is possible that divination was practised, as an inscribed bronze votive kidney from Temple 2 would suggest. This recalls inscribed votive livers of clay

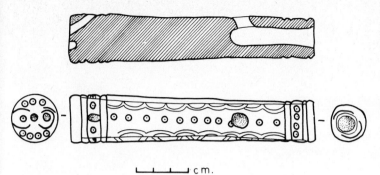

```
                    cm.
```

80 Ivory pipe found in the holy-of-holies of Kition Temple 4. It is partly tubular with an outlet to the side. Its surface is engraved with several circles, semi-circles, and also with an inscription in Cypro-Minoan script. This instrument, the earliest of its kind, may have been used for smoking opium for medicinal purposes in the temple; *c.* 1200 BC. Kition Area II, no. 4262. L. 14 cm. Cyprus Museum, Nicosia.

from the Near East,[79] and the shoulder blades of oxen, engraved with groups of parallel notches.[80]

The second complex at Kition, Temples 4 and 5, are constructed close to each other, and are separated only by a street. In the holy-of-holies of Temple 4 an ivory pipe was discovered which may have been used for smoking opium.[81] Here was also an ivory plaque of the Egyptian god Bes (a healing god, protecting the household and pregnant women).[82] The practice of opium-smoking for medical purposes is known from antiquity and it has even been suggested that opium was exported from Cyprus from the early Late Bronze Age. It is not known which divinity was worshipped in Temple 4, but the discovery on an Early Iron Age floor of a terracotta female figurine with uplifted arms and prominent breasts would indicate a goddess.

Temple 5 may have been dedicated to a male god, a Baal for sailors, to judge by the votive anchor at his offerings table. The worship of such a god would have been quite appropriate for the harbour town of Kition whose economy depended heavily on the export of copper. For the same reason graffiti of ships were incised in the ashlar blocks of the south façade of Temple 1. The bull-skulls on the floor of Temple 5 are also suggestive of a male god. The discovery in the courtyard of Temple 5 of an inscribed cylindrical vase with opposed perforations in the lower part is also connected with the practice of opium-smoking. It has been interpreted as a receptacle in which opium was burnt and inhaled. A similar vase was found in a sanctuary at Gazi in Crete, where the goddess is represented with opium poppies in her hair.

Terracotta anthropomorphic masks, some life-size, were found in a deposit, known as a bothros, of Temple 5. They date to the Early Iron Age and show that apart from bull-masks the priests and worshippers also wore anthropomorphic masks, perhaps mythological in character, during ritual performances. Similar masks have been found in Near Eastern sanctuaries such as Hazor and Tel Qasile in Palestine.[83] Temple 5 has produced terracotta figurines of horseriders of later periods, which may be an additional indication of the worship of a male god, the consort of the goddess who was worshipped in Temple 4.

It is obvious, therefore, that religious practices in Cyprus during Late Bronze Age III were rich and intense. The basic feature was still the old cult of the divinities of fertility, though some new concepts were introduced by the Achaean settlers. But it is a case of fusion with local

80

81

82 Part of the south façade of Kition Temple 1, constructed with large ashlar blocks. Graffiti of ships are clearly seen on their surface. This wall was built on the foundations of a Late Cypriot II wall, probably a boundary wall for the 'sacred garden' between Temples 2 and 3.

religious traditions rather than innovation. The real innovation, which was based on local Cypriot conditions and necessities, was the association of religion with metallurgy.

Metallurgy

The Achaean settlers brought new vigour to the already flourishing culture of Cyprus. This is particularly conspicuous in metallurgy where new techniques were introduced. The two statues of horned gods, cast in solid bronze, are outstanding achievements both in their size and artistic merit. There are other smaller bronze statuettes worth mentioning, such as that of a nude female divinity seated on a chair from Enkomi; two Egyptian figurines, one in silver with inlaid decoration in gold from Enkomi,[84] and the other of bronze;[85] bronze bull figurines from Enkomi and Myrtou-*Pigadhes*; a number of bronze weights in the shape of bulls or goats, filled with lead; and the realistically rendered seated lion from Ayios Iakovos.[86]

Other remarkable finds include cast parts for three large amphorae, of which two have rims and handles with relief ornamentation.[87] The handles are decorated with groups of antithetic *genii* holding jugs, and with bull-heads and octopuses respectively. The flat parts of the rim are filled with a frieze of lions pursuing bulls and with seventy beak-spouted jugs respectively. Their Aegean character is undisputed. Catling suggests that they were made by Aegean craftsmen during the first half of the 12th century BC. They echo earlier, particularly Cretan pieces.

Few complete bronze vases have survived. There is a jug with a beak-shaped mouth from Enkomi[88] and another type of jug with a vertically ribbed body (the prototype for the Bucchero jugs) from Kition[89] and Hala Sultan Tekké.[90]

83   Another class of bronze objects worth mentioning comprises rod and cast tripods and four-sided stands supporting a ring at the top.[91] The latter are decorated either in relief or in the ajouré technique, and demonstrate the remarkable degree of technical and artistic excellence attained by Cypriot craftsmen. The four sides of the stands bear pictorial compositions such as the well-known scene of a Cypriot standing with a copper ingot in his hands in front of a sacred tree; a

83 Bronze stand, probably from Episkopi (Kourion). It consists of a ring at the top resting on four legs supported on wheels. The four sides of the stand are identically decorated in the *ajouré* technique with animals in three registers: a bull and lion, a bull and griffin; there are also pendant birds on all four sides. Cyprus has produced a number of such stands, dating mainly to the 12th century BC. The *ajouré* decoration may have been influenced by ivory carving. Ht 19 cm. Cyprus Museum, Nicosia, no. 1978/XI–21/1.

recently illustrated fragmentary stand of the same group also represents an ingot bearer,[92] together with human figures and sphinxes. Other scenes include a lyre-player, chariot scenes, running animals, antithetic sphinxes and bulls fighting with lions and griffins. Their style often reflects a combination of Aegean and Levantine elements. Some of these stands are on four wheels.

Finally, two wall brackets should be mentioned, one of them found at Sinda. They are decorated with spirals made of bronze wire and applied to the arm.[93] A large trident from a tomb at Hala Sultan Tekké recalls similar objects from the Near East.[94]

84 Bronze trident found in a Late Cypriot III tomb at Hala Sultan Tekké. It has a tubular socket and barbed points. Such tridents have been found in the Near East and may have been used for sacrifices. L. 86 cm. Cyprus Museum, Nicosia (Swedish Excavations).

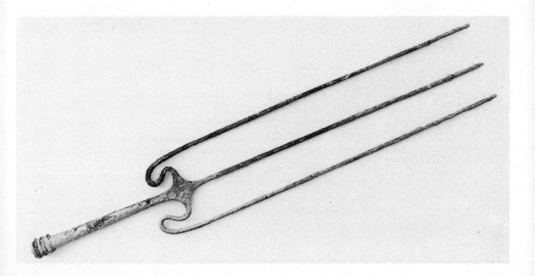

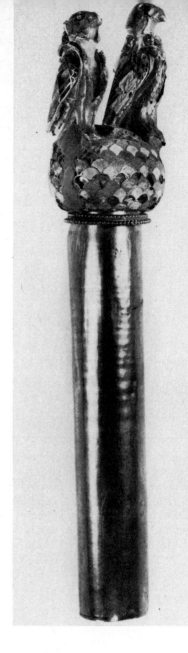

Arts and crafts

Ivory-carving also attained a high degree of artistry.[95] Those Aegean and Levantine elements evidenced in metalwork are also to be observed, as on the draught box from Enkomi. Bulls in relief, shown couchant under an olive tree on one of the short sides of the box, constitute an exquisite scene of Mycenaean carving, while the style of the scenes on the long sides, showing animal-hunting with a chariot, is obviously Near Eastern in inspiration. One of the human figures in this composition wears a feathered head-dress of the 'Sea Peoples' type. Fine-quality carving in relief appears also on the upper broad part of two mirror handles, one from Enkomi and the other from Palaepaphos,

85

with scenes including a hero fighting a lion, and a griffin and a lion attacking a bull. It is interesting to observe the influence which the technique and style of ivory-carving in relief exercised on the ajouré decoration of the bronze stands mentioned above.[96] There are also a number of finely engraved compositions, both figured and abstract, on ivory discs. Compositions with lions on discs from Kition and Palaepaphos, and a plaque in the form of a lion in flying gallop from Kition,[97] betray Aegean influences, as does a box in the shape of a miniature bath-tub from the upper level of Kition Tomb 9.[98] To a period slightly earlier than 1200 BC belongs a small ivory plaque from Kition-*Bamboula*;[99] it represents a seated female figure holding a mirror. Reference has been made to the ivory plaque of Bes from the holy-of-holies of Kition Temple 4, which stylistically recalls examples from Megiddo and imitates Egyptian prototypes, as well as the ivory pipe from the same temple. Ivory-carving must have been a flourishing industry in Cyprus, and there is evidence for workshops at Palaepaphos and Kition.

Jewelry continues the fine Late Cypriot II tradition. The cloisonné technique now appears, of which the bezels of gold finger rings from Palaepaphos are examples.[100] The cloisons, forming curvilinear ornaments, are filled with white enamel. This technique was also used for the globe and the falcons which top the tubular gold shaft of the sceptre from Kourion, dated to the beginning of the 11th century BC. The cloisons are filled with white and greenish (originally blue) enamel.

Glyptics during the Late Cypriot III period are dominated by the conoid stamp seal, of which many fine examples have survived. Aegean influence is frequent, both in the execution of figures such as bulls, lions and stags, and in their grouping, though the form of the conoid seal itself is not Aegean. We have already mentioned the conoid seal

85 (*Opposite, left*) Ivory handle of a mirror from a tomb at Palaepaphos. The flat part of the handle is decorated in relief on both sides with a hero wearing a short kilt and holding a dagger with which he is slaying a rampant lion. End of the 13th century BC. Ht 21.5 cm. Cyprus Museum, Nicosia, Palaepaphos, *Evreti* Tomb 8, nos 7, 26, 34 (British Excavations).

86 (*Opposite, right*) Sceptre from a tomb at Kourion-*Kaloriziki*: a gold tubular shaft topped by a globe on which stand two falcons. The globe and falcons are decorated in the *cloisonné* technique and are inlaid with white and blue enamel. This technique is very rare and is also encountered in the decoration of finger rings of the 12th century BC from Palaepaphos. No doubt this was the sceptre of a king, and was a symbol of authority. Early 11th century BC. Ht 16.5 cm. Cyprus Museum, Nicosia, no. J.99.

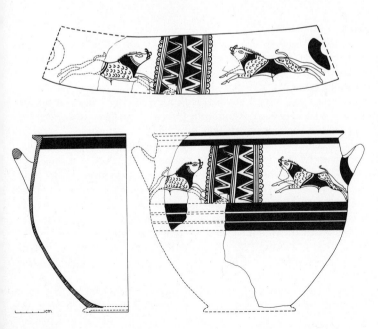

87 Fragmentary bell-crater decorated in the Mycenaean IIICıb style, from Kition. Such vases, locally made under strong Aegean influence, are usually decorated with abstract motifs. Pictorial compositions are rare. This crater is decorated on both sides between the handles with leaping antithetic wild boars within rectangular panels. From Kition, Area II, Temple 5, no. 1107. Ht 28 cm; diam. 31 cm. Cyprus Museum, Nicosia.

depicting a warrior wearing the feathered head-dress of the Sea Peoples, and another with the head of a helmeted warrior, both from Enkomi.[101]

Styles of pottery and of vase-painting introduced by the Achaean settlers gradually ousted the traditional Cypriot wares. Locally made Mycenaean IIIC1b pottery predominates, particularly skyphoi decorated with antithetic spirals and other abstract motifs.[102] There is also a flourishing local Mycenaean IIIC1b pictorial style, mainly of 87 birds and fishes, but also occasionally including horses and human figures. The style of figure-drawing and the motifs themselves are of pure Aegean inspiration. Side by side with this, however, there is another local style which is possibly influenced by the 'pleonastic' style of Crete, as well as by that of the Near East.[103] Large vessels are usually decorated in this way; its characteristic motifs are abstract, but there are occasionally pictorial motifs such as fishes and birds.

The 'Pastoral Style' disappeared during the early years of Late Cypriot III. One of the last productions was a crater fragment from Morphou, decorated with a human figure in a chariot box.[104] The light, open chariot is of an Aegean type of the 12th century BC, very different from the three-sided chariot boxes of the Mycenaean IIIA and B periods.

Before the end of the 12th century BC the so-called 'Granary Style' was introduced to Cyprus by a further influx of Achaean settlers.[105] The characteristic motif of this style is the double or triple horizontal wavy band around the body of vases, mainly skyphoi and cups. After this new wave of colonists the Mycenaean element in Cyprus was perhaps considerably strengthened, and from now on, the island is largely Hellenized. The Greek language, religion, customs and culture spread in Cyprus at a time when the Mycenaean culture was about to die in the Aegean.

Cretan elements

After the 'Dorian invasion' of the Aegean *c.* 1100 BC there was an influx of Cretans to Cyprus who established themselves in places such as Enkomi and Kition and introduced certain artistic styles and even religious elements from Sub-Minoan Crete.[106] A case in point is the 88 terracotta figurine of a goddess with a cylindrical body and uplifted arms – a style of long duration in Cyprus from the 11th century BC onwards and associated with the local goddess of fertility.[107] She has the characteristic flat tiara of the Aegean prototypes, as well as swollen eyes, pointed nose and painted necklaces and bracelets. The breasts are usually prominent and there are painted discs or spots on the face. Such figurines have been found at Enkomi in the last phase of the Temple of the Ingot God, and also on floor I of the Kition temples. The clay models of sanctuaries (naïskoi) are similarly of Cretan inspiration.[108] There are also two double-headed monsters from the Temple of the Ingot God at Enkomi; they have the body of a quadruped (perhaps a bull) and a human face. They have been compared to the centaurs from Ayia Triadha in Crete.[109]

Cretan elements are plentiful in the ceramic industry of Cyprus between *c.* 1100 and 1075 BC. The Proto-White Painted style was

88 Terracotta figurine from Limassol of the goddess with uplifted arms. Representations of this goddess appear in Cyprus from the 11th century BC onwards; she must have been introduced to the island by Cretan immigrants after *c.* 1100 BC, together with other religious and artistic elements. She was gradually identified with the local fertility goddess and survived down to the Classical period. 11th century BC. Ht 17.5 cm. Limassol District Museum, no. 580/6.

developed locally, combining Aegean, Cypriot and Near Eastern elements in shape and decoration.[110] Decorative motifs are applied in orange or dark brown matt paint. They are geometric, but occasionally figurative: birds, quadrupeds and especially the wild goat with long back-curved horns which is popular in Cretan iconography. A kalathos (or wide, two-handled bowl) from Palaepaphos is decorated inside and out with pictorial and geometric motifs in a bichrome technique. This type of pottery is known as Proto-Bichrome ware. The shape itself is Aegean, but most of the decorative motifs are Near Eastern.[111] An amphora from Lapethos is painted with two human figures in a boat,[112] and a hunting scene appears on an amphora from Enkomi.[113] Though the figure-drawing and compositions are often crude, they compare with the Mycenaean pictorial style of the 14th and 13th centuries BC.

92

These are the first signs of a revival of pictorial vase-painting in Cyprus which was to flourish especially during the Late Geometric and Archaic periods.

THE ALAAS CEMETERY

Alaas, a cemetery in eastern Cyprus northwest of Salamis, has several tombs with representative material from Late Cypriot III.[114] The tombs are of Mycenaean type, with a small, approximately rectangular chamber and a long narrow dromos filled with soil and rubble. The stomion is also blocked with rubble. There is a single burial in the chamber, following the Mycenaean tradition. Apart from Proto-White Painted and Proto-Bichrome pottery the tombs contained imported pottery, mainly pilgrim flasks of Syrian origin. This indicates that relations with the Syro-Palestinian coast had not been interrupted. Syro-Palestinian influence extends also to Proto-White Painted and Proto-Bichrome shapes such as the bottle with a cylindrical body, ring-vases, imitations of the Canaanite jar, and even to decoration, as in the case of a lotus flower on a Proto-Bichrome pyxis from Alaas. Basic shapes as well as the decoration, however, are Aegean. A very common decorative motif is the composite triangle, often containing concentric semi-circles, which is popular on Sub-Minoan pottery. The cylindrical pyxis with opposed, raised horizontal loop handles, which frequently occurs in the ceramic repertory of this period, is also of Cretan origin.

The tombs of Alaas contained a few gold objects, mainly ear-rings. Though the first half of the 11th century BC may not be a period of great prosperity, it cannot be denied that severe poverty is unknown and that peaceful conditions favoured communication with both the Aegean and the Near East and encouraged a lively artistic development.

Abandonment and new developments

Following the catastrophe, probably a natural phenomenon such as an earthquake which brought to an end the Bronze Age in Cyprus, Enkomi was abandoned and its inhabitants moved gradually closer to the sea where they built Salamis, a new city around a natural harbour. Kition, according to the evidence in Area II, was also destroyed, but the inhabitants remained and rebuilt the temples. By the end of the second millennium, however, c. 1000 BC, Area II was abandoned and a new city built nearer the sea. The same catastrophe may also have caused the abandonment of Hala Sultan Tekké, whose inner harbour, like those of Enkomi and Kition, may have been silted up. Only Paphos continued to flourish without a break.

The destruction and abandonment of Late Bronze Age cities and the construction of new towns is alluded to in the foundation legends of a number of Cypriot cities. According to these traditions Greek heroes came to Cyprus and founded cities 'after the end of the Trojan war'. Among these were Teukros the founder of Salamis, and Agapenor the founder of Palaepaphos.

Events during the short period between c. 1075 and 1050 BC are also worthy of consideration. This is the period when a transition from Sub-Mycenaean to the Proto-Geometric period takes place in the Aegean. The pottery of Attica is occasionally influenced in shape and decoration by Cypriot wares, though no Cypriot vases of this period have so far been found there. New shapes appear in the Sub-Mycenaean repertoire, such as the bottle, the ring-vase and the pilgrim flask. Decorative patterns on vases become richer. These changes have been attributed by Desborough to Cypriots who emigrated to Athens and took with them new fashions in ceramics as well as in metalwork.[115] Iron pins with ivory heads of distinctly Cypriot type appear in two tombs of the Kerameikos, dating to the late Sub-Mycenaean and the early Proto-Geometric period respectively; another pin was found in a Sub-Mycenaean tomb at Tiryns. Iron swords and daggers of Cypriot type appear at Tiryns and elsewhere. Iron objects, admittedly few, appear occasionally in Cyprus during the 12th century BC, but their numbers increase towards the end of Late Cypriot IIIA and particularly during the 11th century BC, as we shall see below.[116]

Iron oxide ores may already have been extracted in Cyprus at the end of Late Cypriot IIIA, as an iron dagger from floor II at Kition would suggest. It is difficult to determine which factors gave an impulse to iron production. Were there difficulties in the supply of tin for tin-bronze, or had the Cypriots already discovered that iron objects were harder than bronze? The first iron artefacts produced in quantity were knives, secured initially with bronze rivets. Daggers and swords followed. It is interesting that the first iron cut-and-thrust swords in Cyprus were flange-hilted, of the so-called Naue II type, the bronze version of which was introduced from the Aegean at the very beginning of Late Cypriot IIIA. The appearance in Greece of iron swords and daggers in Proto-Geometric and Early Geometric contexts may justify Desborough's suggestion that the knowledge of iron was brought to Athens by Cypriots.[117] One might suggest, however, that it was not Cypriots who fled to Athens c. 1075–1050 BC, but Achaeans already settled in Cyprus who decided to return to the mainland, perhaps after the catastrophe which destroyed the Bronze Age cities. It is not improbable that the beginning of ironworking in Cyprus should be credited to the metallurgical skills of Achaean immigrants. Examination of certain iron knives of the end of Late Cypriot IIIB have shown the high technological level attained during this period. The knives were carburized, quench-hardened and tempered, which gave their blades the hardness of modern steel. A survey by Snodgrass of the earliest iron knives in Cyprus and Greece established that in Cyprus they outnumber those of bronze, whereas during the same period in Greece exactly the opposite occurs. Snodgrass too is in full agreement with Desborough about the transmission of ironworking from Cyprus to Greece.[118]

6

The Early Iron Age

Cypro–Geometric I

89 The transition to the Iron Age is marked not only by an era of cultural innovation but also by the appearance of new cities.[1] Salamis is an example, symbolizing a break with the old world. At Kourion, Lapethos and elsewhere new sites were chosen for the Iron Age settlements, although these were not far from the old ones, since arable land, water supply and other economic resources were still important.

Political life during early Cypro-Geometric I must have been centred round the king and the Mycenaean aristocrats who ruled the large cities. By now the Hellenization of Cyprus had progressed considerably. Those Eteocypriots who objected to the rule of the Achaean Greeks gathered at Amathus where they kept their own Eteocypriot (non-Greek) language and the indigenous Cypriot culture until the late Classical period.

Relations with the Near East continued, as the material from the Alaas tombs and Salamis Tomb I has shown. In the tombs at Kaloriziki the so-called 'Red-and-Black' flasks are Syro-Palestinian imports, as are vessels from the tombs at Palaepaphos-*Skales*. Apart from imported Canaanite jars and their local imitations the tombs at Palaepaphos-*Skales* have produced a number of other jugs and flasks of Syro-Palestinian wares, such as Black-on-Red (as at Kaloriziki) and White Painted wares as well as a faience bowl. There are also Egyptian imports: a paste stamp-seal with hieroglyphs and a large stone scarab of Amenophis III bearing a hieroglyphic inscription commemorating his exploits in lion-hunting. This scarab must have been treasured as an heirloom for a long period by a family which once had strong connections with Egypt.

Relations with the Aegean are attested by Cypriot and Near Eastern objects found at Lefkandi in Euboia and by Cypriot influences on the development of the Early Proto-Geometric pottery of Athens and Euboia. Desborough has suggested that these Near Eastern imports and influences are due to traders from the East Mediterranean.[2] Others, however, have argued that Euboean merchants were responsible for the establishment of these trade relations, as were their descendants 150 years or so later, when they established a trading colony at Al Mina on the Syrian coast.[3]

Cypro-Geometric I was doubtless a period of wealth and prosperity, in which peaceful conditions permitted trade with the Near East.
90 Relations with the Aegean included the copper trade. The large

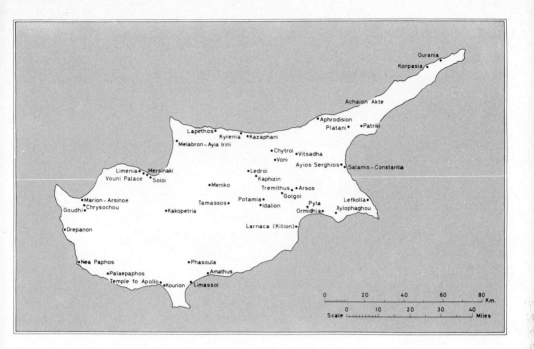

89 Iron Age sites in Cyprus.

number of bronze bowls of various types and sizes, including a tripod cauldron, as well as bronze spearheads and other bronze objects found at Palaepaphos-*Skales*, suggest that metallurgy flourished more than ever. The same may be said for the manufacture of iron objects, including daggers and swords of a Greek type. This confirms Desborough's and Snodgrass' suggestion that the knowledge of ironworking must have been exported from Cyprus to Greece. Several examples of the characteristic flange-hilted dagger and sword (one of them 'killed' so as not to be used again) have been found. One dagger has its half-moon-shaped ivory pommel intact. There are also a large number of iron knives, some with bronze rivets, as well as iron spearheads.

SALAMIS

It seems that the inhabitants of Enkomi began abandoning their homes *c.* 1075 BC, after a disaster caused by an earthquake. This movement of population to the new city must have lasted for about twenty-five years. The Temple of the Ingot God at Enkomi was in use as late as the beginning of Cypro-Geometric I. According to the 'nostoi' – Greek texts including myths – however, Teukros, son of the king of the island of Salamis in Greece, founded the town of Salamis in Cyprus after the end of the Trojan war.[4] Together with his comrades he landed on the north coast, probably at the site which is known as *Achaion Akte* or the 'shore of the Achaeans', and from there he proceeded to the Bay of Salamis, where he founded a city which he named after his own fatherland. He also built the Sanctuary of Zeus of which he became the first high priest. This became the official cult of Salamis and as such it survived down to the Roman period.[5] Teukros is a hero with Greek as

90 Large bronze bowl from Palaepaphos-*Skales*. It has two horizontal loop handles rivetted onto the body and bridged with it through spirally twisted wire. The top of the handles is decorated with large goat protomes. The inspiration for such vessels may be Near Eastern. The Palaepaphos-*Skales* necropolis has produced a number of large bronze bowls, demonstrating the high quality of Cypriot bronzework during the 11th century BC, obviously due to the metallurgical skills of the Achaean colonists. Ht 20 cm; diam. 37.1 cm. Cyprus Museum, Nicosia, Palaepaphos-*Skales*, Tomb 49, no. 1.

well as Anatolian connections and he may symbolize the Graeco-Anatolian groups who invaded Cyprus *c.* 1200 BC. The foundation myth, of course, was a much later invention by the Athenians.[6]

Yet the discovery at Salamis of a mid-11th century BC tomb (known as T.I) within the boundaries of the later city has demonstrated what was hitherto believed but not proven, namely that Salamis succeeded Enkomi.[7] As in the case of the Early Bronze Age, our knowledge of the Early Iron Age is based largely on such evidence from tombs. It is unfortunate that recent events in Cyprus have made impossible the continuation of archaeological research at Salamis to discover more of its early life.

The Bay of Salamis offers an ideal natural harbour. The city must have developed around the harbour[8] and there are indications that it was defended by a wall. The cemetery, to which the 11th-century BC tomb (T.I) referred to above belongs, was *extra muros*. As the city expanded the cemetery moved westwards, and in the 9th century BC it already lay about half a mile farther west. Material found in tomb T.I is most informative.[9] The richness of its contents suggests that by the middle of the 11th century BC the city was firmly established and supported a prosperous community. Apart from the Proto-White Painted and Proto-Bichrome wares, this tomb contained Cypro-Geometric I wares as well as pottery imported from the Syro-Palestinian coast. The discovery of a White Painted I amphora, decorated with compass-drawn concentric circles, betrays influences from Athenian Proto-Geometric pottery,[10] while Bichrome jugs with rounded body and funnel mouths, as well as amphorae imitating the 'Canaanite' type, indicate strong Near Eastern influence. A number of gold and faience objects found in this tomb should be attributed to the same region. It is thus relevant that, according to one tradition, Teukros took possession of Salamis with the aid of Belos, King of

Sidon. The tomb itself is of Mycenaean type, following the tradition noted at Alaas twenty-five years earlier.

KITION

The continuous use of the temples at Kition for about fifty years after the catastrophe represents a prolongation of Late Cypriot III architectural styles, without any real innovations. The city wall was not reconstructed after its collapse *c*. 1075 BC. The cult of the fertility goddess continued, to judge by the discovery of a number of terracotta figurines of the goddess with uplifted arms in the sacred area. But the cemetery of the Cypro-Geometric I period moved outside the city boundaries. Tombs of this period, with rich ceramic material dating to *c*. 1050–1000 BC, have been found on the western outskirts of Kition outside the limits of the Late Cypriot town. Occupation of Area I at Kition also continued. The walls of the new houses (floor I) often have a different orientation to that of the Late Cypriot III houses, but sometimes the foundations of the older houses were reused. The excavated surface of Area I, however, is small and no complete houses have been uncovered. The material in use in the temples of Area II must have been abandoned on the floors and was later covered by the debris of the fallen roofs, or by silt deposited as a result of an abandonment lasting about 150 years. When the Phoenicians rebuilt some of the temples in the 9th century BC they found this material, some still in good condition, including small dishes, terracotta figurines of the goddess with uplifted arms and anthropomorphic masks – and they stored it in bothroi, outside the reused temples. Similar objects were found on the uppermost floor of the Temple of the Ingot God at Enkomi, a fact which suggests a homogeneity of cult.

It is interesting that no Greek foundation legend exists for Kition, unlike for all other kingdoms of the 1st millennium BC. This may be explained by the fact that when these legends were formed Kition was a purely Phoenician city and could not possibly have been given a Greek foundation legend.

LAPETHOS

Lapethos, with her well-irrigated valleys, regained the importance which she had enjoyed during the earlier part of the Bronze Age. The Cypro-Geometric I tombs excavated by the Swedish Cyprus Expedition make it clear that there were two communities living there side by side: the Greeks and the autochthonous Cypriot population.[11] According to the foundation legend for this city, some Laconians, headed by King Praxandros, were her first Greek settlers. Tombs in the Greek cemetery at the site of *Kastros* are of Mycenaean type, as is the case at Salamis. Tombs of the indigenous population at the site of *Plakes* follow the Cypriot tradition. A similar distinction may have existed in the settlement site. A characteristic tomb type is that of a chamber with an adjacent shaft-dromos from which it is separated by a screening wall of rubble. Such a tomb was discovered in the Late Cypriot IIIB cemetery of Alaas.

A noteworthy burial custom appears during this period in Lapethos: the sacrifice of slaves to serve their dead master in the second life. Three tombs of the Cypro-Geometric I period (T.412, 417, 420) provide evidence for this custom.

KOURION

Kourion did not receive any Achaean-Anatolian settlers in Late Cypriot IIIA. Herodotus recalls a legend that the inhabitants of this city believed themselves to be descendants of the Argives, but he may be referring to the second wave of Greek colonization in Late Cypriot IIIB. These new settlers brought the custom of cremation to Kourion, as can be seen in the Kaloriziki cemetery.[12] The tombs are of Mycenaean type and date from Late Cypriot IIIB onwards. The tombs in the cemetery are consistently orientated. This, together with the practice of cremation and the deposit of the remains in an incinerary vessel, is considered by Benson as evidence that these settlers came to Cyprus via Rhodes, or from Rhodes itself where cremation and the consistent orientation of tombs existed slightly earlier than on the Mycenaean mainland, that is before the Sub-Mycenaean period.[13] The presence of an amphora of Rhodian fabric in one of the Kaloriziki tombs supports this suggestion. Both inhumation and cremation were practised in Late Cypriot IIIB and Cypro-Geometric I tombs. If tombs were reused, the cremated or inhumed skeletal remains of the earlier burials were put in large urns, as already mentioned, which were deposited along the sides of the chamber. Skeletal remains of the same individual would frequently be placed in more than one recipient.

PALAEPAPHOS-SKALES

Recent excavations by the Department of Antiquities of a number of tombs at Palaepaphos-*Skales* have brought to light much evidence for funerary architecture, burial customs and culture in general of early Cypro-Geometric I.[14] The tombs have a consistent orientation (to the south) as at Kaloriziki. The chambers are approximately rectangular and fairly large in size; the dromoi are long and narrow and are filled with soil and rubble; the stomia are also blocked with rubble. They were used for multiple burials – inhumation being the common practice – but there are also a few cases of cremation. The skeletal remains of the previous burials were deposited in one or more large

91   vessels whenever a subsequent burial took place. Shallow graves were used for infant burials, and in one case such a grave was dug at the entrance of the dromos of a tomb. The tombs at Palaepaphos-*Skales* constitute a further development from the Late Cypriot IIIB small

92   rectangular chamber at Palaepaphos-*Xerolimni*, where there was only a single burial.

Though the material from Lapethos and Salamis reflects the wealth of the Cypro-Geometric I period, the tombs at Palaepaphos-*Skales* emphasize this prosperity not only in the quantity but also in the quality of the tomb-gifts. Gold objects are found in almost all of them, including, apart from ear-rings and finger rings, a number of gold discs decorated with embossed rosettes, thin rectangular sheets with chariot scenes and figures in repoussé. These sheets, known also from the early Cypro-Geometric I Tomb 417 at Lapethos, may have formed part of tiaras worn by women. There is also a gold needle, not unlike the one

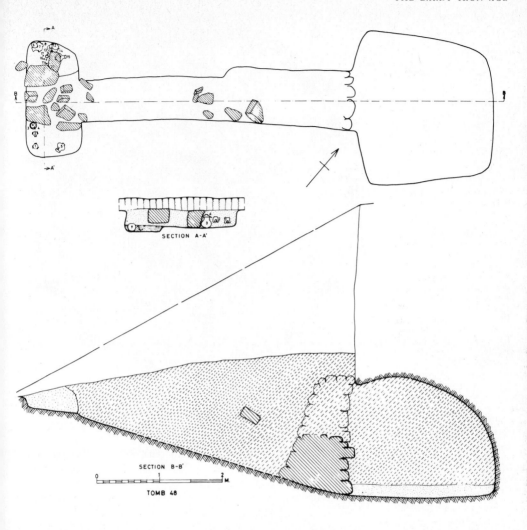

SECTION A-A'

SECTION B-B'

0   1   2
└─┴─┴─┴─┴─┴─┴─┴─┴─┤M.

TOMB 48

from Salamis Tomb I, bronze pins with a gold head and so on. Most tombs produced bronze fibulae of the D-type. Such ornaments, unknown in Cyprus before the Late Cypriot III period, are fashionable in the tombs of Alaas and in all the Cypro-Geometric I tombs. At Palaepaphos-*Skales* there are also a few iron fibulae and one in silver decorated with gold beads. The fibula must have been introduced to Cyprus by Achaean women in the 12th century BC. A certain type of fibula, with a swollen bow decorated with two mouldings, may have been taken to Greece in the 11th century BC, as recent discoveries at Lefkandi in Euboia suggest.[15]

Another interesting object from an 11th-century BC tomb at Palaepaphos-*Skales* is a life-size limestone bath-tub. It contained bowls and other vases, and as the skeletons in the tomb were on the floor, it had clearly not been used as a sarcophagus. Whether its occurrence in the tomb has a practical explanation or a lustral, ritual significance, is difficult to determine. The fact remains that in the 11th

91 Plan and sections of Tomb 48 of the 11th century BC at Palaepaphos-*Skales*. The chamber is roughly rectangular, the dromos is long and narrow. At the dromos entrance there is a shallow grave of an infant. The stomion of the chamber was blocked with rubble. This style of funerary architecture is Mycenaean in character, the first to appear in Cyprus.

92 The inside decoration of a Proto-Bichrome ware kalathos from Palaepaphos-*Xerolimni*. It is decorated with human, animal and floral motifs within panels, including a goat attended by a human figure, a lyre-player, a palm-tree etc. The iconography and decoration betray a mixed Aegean and oriental style; the form of the vase is Aegean. Beginning of the 11th century BC. Ht 15 cm; diam. 22 cm. Cyprus Museum, Nicosia, Palaepaphos-*Xerolimni*, Tomb 9, no. 7.

93

93 Detail of a bronze obelos from a tomb at Palaepaphos-*Skales* (Tomb 49, no. 16). Near the socket are five signs of the Palaeopaphian Cypriot syllabary of the 11th century BC, representing the genitive of the Greek proper name Opheltes in a form of the Arcadian dialect. This is the earliest evidence for the use of the Greek language in Cyprus. L. of obelos 87.2 cm. Cyprus Museum, Nicosia.

century BC bath-tubs were used in Palaepaphos, whereas in the Aegean this custom, which was known in earlier periods, had been forgotten during the Dark Ages.

One of the major contributions of the Palaepaphos-*Skales* material to the history of this city and of Cyprus in general is an inscribed document from a tomb, the contents of which belong entirely to the Cypro-Geometric I period. This is one of three bronze obeloi (skewers or spits), found together. Such objects usually occur in tombs of warriors from the Cypro-Geometric I period onwards and have been discovered at Paphos, Lapethos, Salamis and elsewhere. They are symbols of prestige and indicate the high social rank of the deceased. The inscribed obelos bears five signs of the Cypriot syllabary, engraved near the socket, which read from left to right: *o.pe.le.ta.u*. These syllables have been read as the genitive form of the Greek proper name *Opheltes*. In Mycenaean Greek one would expect the genitive form to end in -o, but the -u ending is characteristic of the Arcadian dialect. The implications of this discovery are far-reaching. This is the earliest evidence for the use of Greek so far in Cyprus, thus confirming that by the middle of the 11th century BC it was the language of at least part of the population, and that at Paphos the form of Greek generally used

was the Arcadian dialect. Thus, the myths acknowledging Agapenor, leader of the Arcadians in the Trojan War, as the founder of Paphos take on a new dimension. The same is true for the later associations between Tegea and Cyprus; we know from Pausanias that at Tegea there was a Temple of Aphrodite Paphia.

The material from the Palaepaphos-*Skales* tombs throws much light on the period usually known as the Dark Ages. But considering the wealth of the gifts in other tombs of the same period in Cyprus, and the fact that the script had not been forgotten, it appears that, unlike in the Aegean, this period in Cyprus was one of prosperity, and was not at all 'dark'.

The ceramic industry

Cypro-Geometric I pottery is a development from Proto-White Painted ware, with some shapes, such as the stirrup jar, gradually disappearing and others becoming more fashionable, for example the cup, shallow dish and footed bowl. Decoration is applied in black matt paint. Bichrome decoration develops from the Proto-Bichrome technique, but is rather rare at first. The decorative motifs are geometric and arranged in strict symmetry, with occasional pictorial motifs such as fishes, birds and quadrupeds. A most unusual

94

94 White Painted I ware shallow dish from Palaepaphos-*Skales*. The base is decorated with a two-headed monster which two human figures, armed with a bow and knives respectively, are attempting to kill. No doubt the vase-painter intended to represent a specific theme, probably a myth, recalling that of Heracles and Iolaos slaying the snake of Lerna. 11th century BC. Ht 5 cm; diam. 28.3 cm. Cyprus Museum, Nicosia, Palaepaphos-*Skales*, Tomb 58, no. 104.

composition appears on the base of a dish from Palaepaphos: two human figures attempt to kill a large two-headed snake with arrows and knives. No doubt the vase-painter had a mythical scene in mind, and if so, this may be one of the earliest representations of a motif which appears in Greek mythology as the killing of the snake of Lerna by Heracles and Iolaos. The clay tripod, either of medium size or in miniature, is common at Palaepaphos. The discovery of two bronze rod tripods may suggest that such metallic objects were extensively used and were the prototypes of those in clay.

The discovery at Palaepaphos of Syro-Palestinian jugs and flasks has been noted. The surface of the Black-on-Red vases is covered with a red slip, and the decoration (horizontal bands on the shoulder or concentric bands around the sides) is applied in black and occasionally also white paint. This ware is imitated by Cypriot potters during Cypro-Geometric II, using a much harder clay with a semi-lustrous red-slip surface, often plain but occasionally decorated. During the Cypro-Geometric III period this fabric developed into what is known as Black-on-Red and Bichrome Red wares. The origin of these wares has been discussed at length.[16] Palaepaphos has now thrown light on both their origin and development.

Another ware which was very popular throughout the Cypro-Geometric period is the Black Slip or Bucchero ware, used mainly for jugs and occasionally for small amphorae. It is a developed version of the ribbed 'Base Ring' ware of the later part of Late Cypriot II and III.

Cypro–Geometric II

Cypro-Geometric II (c. 950–850 BC) follows the previous period with very few cultural changes.[17] The sharp distinction between the Eteocypriot and the Mycenaean cultures, so clearly illustrated by the different tomb types used in the two separate cemeteries in Lapethos, gives way to a gradual fusion with the Eteocypriot element gaining ground. It is significant that in the Greek cemetery of Lapethos-*Kastros* there are shaft tombs of the type used in the Eteocypriot cemetery at Lapethos-*Plakes* during Cypro-Geometric I and II. At Palaepaphos-*Skales* the dromoi of the tombs become wider and shorter. The dynamic Greek element which characterizes the beginning of the Cypro-Geometric period in general now gives way to the less sophisticated traditional Cypriot culture. This can be seen in the rather unimaginative character of the decoration and the heavy outlines of vases.

Trade relations

Relations with the Aegean continue, though on a smaller scale than before. Two Greek Late Proto-Geometric (10th century BC) vases from Amathus, probably imported from Euboia,[18] are evidence for trade connections, as is the discovery of a Cypriot Bichrome flask of the same period at Lefkandi in Euboia. A bronze macehead of the early 9th century BC found recently at Lefkandi is clearly of Cypriot origin.[19] Whether the initiative for these trading links came from the Cypriots or from the Euboians is, again, difficult to determine. At the end of the

10th century BC the plain hemispherical bronze bowl was introduced from Cyprus to Athens where it became common in the Kerameikos cemetery.[20] A few Cypriot imports appear in 9th-century BC tombs at Ialysos on Rhodes.[21] Cypriot wares may have also influenced certain 10th-century-BC pottery found in the Dodecanese, such as the duck-vase, pilgrim flask and open-work kalathos. But the region with which Cyprus maintained frequent relations was Crete,[22] and interconnections were already strong during the 11th century BC. Apart from iron spits (obeloi) of a Cypriot type from a tomb of the 10th century BC at Knossos (similar obeloi are known from the Lapethos and Palaepaphos tombs), Cyprus exported bronze rod tripods and open-work stands to Crete; the latter were imitated even in clay during the 11th century BC. Bronze rod tripods are known in Crete from the 10th and 9th centuries BC. The recent discovery in the region of Knossos of a 10th- to 9th-century-BC bronze bowl bearing a Phoenician inscription may indicate that it was the Phoenicians who carried Cypriot objects to Crete and throughout the Aegean during this period.

Relations between Cyprus and Crete continued into the 8th century BC when Cypriot pottery was still exported to Crete and where it influenced various Cretan wares. This is also the time when orientalizing scenes appear on Cretan shields, which may have been made under strong Cypriot or Phoenician influence.[23]

The Phoenicians and Cypro–Geometric III

About three centuries following the final influx of Mycenaean colonists to Cyprus, the fusion of the Eteocypriot and Greek cultures was complete, with the Cypriot becoming increasingly stronger. It was at this point in the mid-9th century BC that the Phoenicians arrived from Tyre to stir the stagnant waters of Cypriot culture and to draw Cyprus closer to the Levant. This date also marks the initial stage of the third phase of the Cypro-Geometric period. They established their first colony at Kition at the beginning of their westward expansion.[24] Gjerstad has convincingly shown that the name Qarthadast (new city) was given to Kition by the Phoenician colonists.[25]

KITION

By the middle of the 9th century BC the Phoenicians were well established at Kition. At Kition-*Bamboula* a sanctuary was built, which is the predecessor of the Sanctuary of Heracles-Melqart of the Cypro-Archaic period. It is possible that it was originally dedicated to the same god.[26] On the foundations of Temple 1 at Kition (Area II), which was abandoned *c.* 1000 BC, a new temple was now built. It retained the dimensions of the earlier structure (33.5 × 22 m) but had a different interior arrangement. The large courtyard was now furnished with two porticos along the north and south walls respectively; the roof of each portico was supported on two parallel rows of wooden pillars, of which the stone bases with rectangular sockets on the top have survived *in situ*. There were seven pillars in each row, making a total of twenty-eight. The ground plan of the holy-of-holies remained as it was, but lacking the dividing walls. On either side of the central opening there were two

95

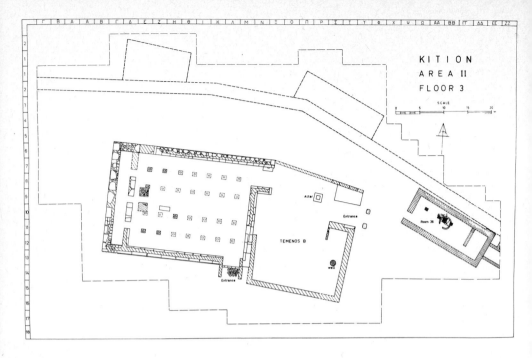

95 Plan of the Phoenician
Temple of Astarte at Kition.
In front is a large rectangular
open courtyard, and to the
east the smaller Temple 4.
Floor 3 is illustrated here,
which corresponds to the
period *c.* 850–800 BC. The
Temple of Astarte was built
on the ruins of the Late
Bronze Age temple and is one
of the largest in the
Phoenician world. In front of
its long, narrow holy-of-holies
were two porticoes, each
supported on two rows of
wooden pillars of which the
stone bases survive.

96 Fragmentary bowl of Red
Slip ware (Phoenician), with
an engraved Phoenician
inscription. It mentions the
sacrifice at the Temple of
Astarte by a certain *ML* from
Tamassos. End of the 9th
century BC. Ht 5.8 cm;
restored diam. 25 cm. Cyprus
Museum, Nicosia, Kition
Temple 1, no. 1435.

rectangular free-standing stone pillars, recalling the biblical pillars of
the Temple of Solomon in Jerusalem, called Jachin and Boaz. It should
be mentioned that the Jerusalem temple was also built by Tyrian
masons. An inscription on a Red Slip bowl found on the earliest floor of
the Kition temple, and dating from before the period of its first
destruction by fire *c.* 800 BC, mentions, according to Professor A.
Dupont-Sommer,[27] a Phoenician called *ML* who went from Tamassos
to Kition and made sacrifices in honour of Astarte. This interpretation
has not been accepted in its entirety by all Phoenician scholars, but
most accept the reference to Astarte. So the temple was most probably
dedicated to this goddess, whose cult was instituted as the official cult of
the Phoenicians by King Ethbaal, who reigned between 887 and
856 BC, and was high priest of Astarte before he ascended the throne of

97 Wall-bracket or incense-burner decorated with abstract motifs in the Bichrome III technique and with a nude female figure in relief with arms bent forward. Above her, near the suspension hole, are two bull-heads. The female figure, wearing a tiara, is an adaptation of the Cretan goddess with uplifted arms who was, by the 9th–8th centuries BC, identified with Astarte. Such objects were used in sanctuaries during the Late Bronze Age. In later periods they are also found as votives in tombs. This is the largest clay wall-bracket known so far from Cyprus. Ht 70 cm. Hadjiprodromou Collection, Famagusta.

Tyre and Sidon. It is thus quite natural that the largest temple in this first Phoenician colony should be in honour of Astarte.

Representations of this goddess now appear very frequently in
97 Cypriot art. A typical example is Astarte depicted in relief on a wall bracket from the Famagusta District. The nude goddess is shown with uplifted arms, wearing a tiara and with spots on her face.[28] These are all characteristics of her predecessor, the 'goddess with uplifted arms', who was represented from the 11th century BC onwards, but not as a nude. The great Temple of Aphrodite at Paphos must have had a similar history to that of Kition. Inscriptions of the late Classical period also refer to Aphrodite Paphia as Astarte Paphia. A late Classical inscription painted on a small marble slab at Kition enumerates the personnel employed in the Temple of Astarte there, namely guards, servants, bakers, barbers and sacred prostitutes. It is interesting to note the existence of sacred barbers in connection with the cutting of hair and the dedication of it in a bowl to Astarte. This custom is also described in the account of the visit to the temple by *ML* from Tamassos mentioned above. The same custom survived until the days of Lucian, who, in his book on the Syrian Goddess (*De Dea Syra*), states that when he visited the Temple of Astarte at Hierapolis in Syria, he cut his hair and dedicated it to her in a silver bowl on which his name was inscribed. Another feature of the cult at Kition already mentioned
98 is the use of masks or bucrania in Temple 5 and in the two main temples at Enkomi during the end of the Late Bronze Age. It is not surprising to find a survival of this custom in a community which, in spite of the presence of the Phoenicians, must have retained many elements of its own Eteocypriot religion. A pile of bucrania was found on the earliest floor of the Temple of Astarte.

This temple was destroyed by fire *c.* 800 BC. The twenty-eight wooden pillars of the courtyard, together with the beams of the roof of the porticos, were burnt, depositing a thick layer of ashes and charcoal over floor 3, mixed with sherds of 'Samaria' ware bowls, including a double bowl of ritual character.

Soon after the first Temple of Astarte was destroyed by fire the Phoenicians rebuilt it with changes to the courtyard. The wooden pillars were either too expensive to replace or were considered too dangerous; the four rows were replaced with two rows of thick rectangular pillars of masonry, resting on large bases. In the southwest corner of the courtyard an animal, probably a lamb, was sacrificed, and a large number of small unguent juglets and bowls of Black-on-Red and Black-and-Grey Lustrous ware were offered as a foundation deposit, to ensure that the second temple would not suffer the same fate as the first.

Of the other Late Bronze Age temples of Area II in Kition, Temple 2 was covered and the ashlar blocks of its walls reused elsewhere. In its place a large open courtyard was constructed with an altar near its entrance. This courtyard occupied the space in front of the great Temple of Astarte. Temple 4 was rebuilt with approximately the same ground-plan, but Temple 5 was remodelled. It was reduced to a small rectangular cella with an altar in front of it, within an open courtyard. Fragments of a Greek Middle Geometric trefoil-lipped oenochoe as well as sherds from a Cycladic Sub-Geometric skyphos were found on

the floor of this courtyard.²⁹ These Greek sherds both indicate relations with the Aegean at a time when the Phoenicians were masters at Kition, and confirm the 9th-century-BC date suggested for the Phoenician restoration of the Late Bronze Age temples.

By the end of the 9th century BC the Phoenicians must have asserted their domination not only over Kition, but perhaps over other parts of the island also. Some of the material from tombs at Amathus dating to the end of the 9th century BC is either Phoenician or of Phoenician inspiration. The fact that *ML* in the inscription on the 9th-century-BC Red Slip bowl is mentioned as coming from Tamassos, may indicate that Phoenician merchants had already penetrated inland and were in control of the copper mines. A few years later they were carrying Cypriot copper to the Aegean (perhaps to Lefkandi in Euboia) and other Cypriot goods to the Dodecanese. In Kos, side by side with the local Middle Geometric pottery, there are slow-pouring flasks of Black-on-Red ware which most probably contained perfume and of which there are local imitations. It has been suggested³⁰ that Phoenician perfume-makers may have established themselves in the Dodecanese and that local potters were producing the characteristic flasks for the Phoenician perfume. This is also the time at which Cypriot wares influenced Greek pottery, in the form of concentric circles used as a decorative motif by certain potters in Rhodes, Crete, Eretria and Athens.

98 Fragmentary anthropomorphic mask from Kition, painted in red and black from a deposit in Temple 5. Such masks were used as votive objects in temples, e.g. at Enkomi and several Near Eastern sites, and date approximately to the 11th century BC. Both anthropomorphic and bull-masks were used in temples during ritual ceremonies. Ht 16.7 cm. Cyprus Museum, Nicosia, Kition, Area II, no. 3809.

7

The Cypro-Archaic period

Exactly when the Cypro-Geometric period ended is not certain. There are indications that the Cypro-Archaic period begins before *c*. 700 BC, the date originally suggested by the Swedish Cyprus Expedition; the general opinion now is that it begins *c*. 750/725 BC.[1] The Phoenicians continued to dominate the political life of Kition, and their economic and cultural influence extended over a wider area. Further epigraphical evidence attests their presence at Kition in the 8th century BC. On two bronze bowls, said to have been found at Mouti Sinoas near Limassol, there are inscriptions mentioning 'the Governor of Qarthadast [Kition], servant of Hiram, King of the Sidonians, to Baal of Lebanon, his Lord'. This is King Hiram II of Tyre who paid tribute to King Tiglatpileser III of Assyria (745–727 BC) in 738 BC.

In art there are bronze and silver bowls decorated with figured compositions in a combined repoussé and engraved technique. A bronze bowl found in a tomb in the Kerameikos cemetery in Athens and dated to the mid-9th century BC is said to have come from Cyprus.[2] This Kerameikos bowl, like others from Cyprus of a slightly later date, is decorated with cult scenes probably inspired by ritual performances and festivals in the great temples of Astarte at Kition and Palaepaphos. Similar bowls, of silver or gilded, continue to be produced in Cyprus during the two following centuries, as will be seen below.

In vase-painting, pictorial decoration develops further, side by side with geometric motifs. Some ambitious vase-painters at Chrysochou in northwest Cyprus portray complicated compositions which may be ritual scenes, as well as horse-riders and musicians.[3] Some of these representations may have been taken from scenes engraved on ivory and in bronze. The Hubbard amphora from Platani and the Ormidhia amphora (from the site near Larnaca) are decorated with similar ritual scenes, the central figure being seated while other figures bring gifts.[4] This ritual appears on metal bowls at the end of Cypro-Geometric III. The scene with dancers on one side of the Hubbard amphora may have been influenced by Greek Late Geometric vase-painting. Similarly, certain scenes on decorated metal bowls may have inspired the iconography on some Greek Late Geometric vases. Such vases must have been traded by the Phoenicians in the Aegean, and allusions to them are often found in Homer (e.g. *Iliad*, XXIII, 740–5).

The role of the Phoenicians in Cyprus during the 8th–7th centuries BC must have been far greater than can be seen in the arts. The forests of Cyprus provided vast quantities of timber for shipbuilding, enabling them to trade throughout the Mediterranean. Cyprus is mentioned by

Eusebius as one of the 'thalassocracies' of the 8th century BC.[5] The Phoenicians are found as far west as Huelva on the Atlantic coast of Spain, trading in copper from there and perhaps in silver from Cartagena, further east.[6] This period saw the peak production of 'Cypro-Phoenician' silver bowls, some perhaps made by Phoenician artists in Cyprus. The discovery of Cypriot objects in Spain – and the horse and chariot burials recently found at Huelva recall those of Salamis[7] – suggests that Cypriots may have accompanied the Phoenicians in their westward adventures.

Assyrian rule

At the end of the 8th century BC in Cyprus there occurred an event for which there is epigraphical evidence. In the year 707 BC the kings of Cyprus submitted to King Sargon II of Assyria (722–705 BC) and paid tribute to him in gold, silver, utensils and valuable furniture.[8] This event is recorded in inscriptions from the palace at Khorsabad as well as on the famous stele from Kition which is now in Berlin. Seven kings submitted to Sargon according to this inscription, but their names are not stated. It is later, on the prism of Esarhaddon dated to 613/2 BC which commemorates the rebuilding of the palace at Niniveh, that there is any information on those who were forced to contribute. Among them are ten kings of 'the land of Iatnana, of the middle of the sea'. In this inscription Kition is mentioned as Qarthadast, though after the conquest by Sargon II the bonds between Kition and the metropolis of Tyre would have been broken. The names of the other cities have been tentatively identified as Idalion, Chytroi, Paphos, Kourion, Tamassos and Ledroi. Sillua and Sillu may be identified with Salamis and Soloi, but Nure is still unknown, though Amathus is a possibility.[9] Certain names of kings sound almost Greek and have been identified with Eteandros, Damasos, Onasagoras and Pylagoras.

Assyrian rule does not seem to have been particularly hard, and as long as the Cypriot kings paid their tribute they were left to exercise their own local authority. In fact, the built tombs of Salamis, which mostly date to the end of the 8th and to the 7th centuries BC, demonstrate that the Salaminian kings had so much wealth and were accompanied to their final abode with so much splendour and pomp that it is difficult to imagine they were servants to the Assyrian king. On the contrary, they tended to imitate his taste for luxury.

The king must have been the central figure around whom political and cultural life centred, especially if he was also a high priest, as were Teukros and Kinyras in earlier periods. The palace would have been the centre of all cultural activity. Epic poetry was flourishing, as is known from the epic *Kypria* whose author, Stasinos, is said to have married Homer's daughter. It has even been suggested that some 'Homeric' aspects in the burial customs of the 'royal' tombs of Salamis may have their roots in the revival of the Homeric epic in Cyprus. One must also account for the festivals with musicians and epic poets in the great temples of Aphrodite-Astarte at Kition and Paphos. The temple at Paphos, erected in the 12th century BC, was known to Homer as a sanctuary of Aphrodite. Festivals in honour of Aphrodite and Adonis would have been important cultural events. Her high priest Kinyras is mentioned by Pindar as 'favoured by Apollo'. The Homeric 'Hymn to Aphrodite' is said to have been written for the Adonia and Aphrodisia festivals of Paphos. The Cypriot Euklos is known among the prophet-bards of the 7th century BC. Some of his prophecies were collected by Pausanias, but only one has survived: that of the birth of Homer at Salamis in Cyprus to a peasant woman, Themistô. This is significant since it underlines the intensively 'Homeric' or 'epic' atmosphere of Salamis, which could even claim to be the birthplace of Homer.

THE 'ROYAL' TOMBS OF SALAMIS

The splendour of the 'royal' tombs of Salamis is an almost unique phenomenon in Cyprus. Apart from a few other extraordinary cases, such as the tomb of a warrior at Palaepaphos,[10] tomb architecture outside the main urban areas is modest: no more than traditional chamber tombs unconnected with Greek funerary architecture. At Salamis there is evidence for a built tomb in the 9th century BC, but this was mostly destroyed in later periods to provide building material for other constructions.[11] The first complete tomb which was excavated in the 'royal' necropolis (Tomb 1) has a built chamber with a façade of ashlar blocks and a cornice along its upper part, of an Egyptianizing type. This tomb may date to the 8th century BC. It contained, apart from local Cypriot pottery, a large Greek Middle Geometric crater and a whole 'set' of bowls and dishes, and Sub-Proto-Geometric skyphoi and plates. It has been suggested that they belonged to the dowry of a Greek princess who was married to a member of the royal family of Salamis.[12] Her body was cremated in the Greek fashion and her necklace of gold and rock-crystal beads was found in a bronze cauldron, together with her incinerated skeleton.

Similar Greek imported pottery has been found in tombs of the same date excavated at Amathus: up to now they include two Middle Geometric craters and several skyphoi.[13] During the 8th–7th centuries BC there is a preference in Cyprus for Greek drinking cups, no doubt by those who could afford to buy luxury imported goods. The same was true in Levantine towns such as Al Mina. They include East Greek, Cycladic and Euboian cups which are often imitated locally. It is not easy to determine whether these goods were exported to Cyprus and the Levantine region directly from the Aegean, or whether they were traded by the Phoenician merchants for other luxury goods during their dealings in the Aegean area. Apart from skyphoi and medium-size craters, Euboia sent to Cyprus a masterpiece of one of her painters, a Late Geometric I crater found at Kourion of c. 750 BC date.[14]

The 8th century BC is the period of direct contacts between Cyprus and the Aegean. At the end of the 9th century BC the Euboians had already begun their eastward trade expansion and had established a trading-post at Al Mina on the north Syrian coast. It has been suggested that part of the population of Al Mina may have come from Cyprus, and that it was they who led the Greeks there.[15] There must have been strong links between Cyprus and Euboia. Thus Cyprus once again plays her central role as she did in the 14th and 13th centuries BC as an outpost of the Mycenaeans in the East Mediterranean.

The 'royal' tombs of Salamis have added a new chapter to the history and archaeology of Cyprus in the 8th and 7th centuries BC. Architecturally there are no immediate predecessors for them, though built tombs appear at Enkomi during the Late Bronze Age. There is evidence, however, of Anatolian influence on the tomb architecture of Salamis (Tomb 3) and Tamassos during the 7th and 6th centuries BC.[16] Burial customs dictated the special features of these tombs, and particularly the sacrifice of horses with their chariots in honour of the dead.[17] This took place in the dromos in front of the chamber, explaining the exceptionally broad dromoi with a sloping cemented floor. The chambers were relatively small with a flat or corbelled roof, built of ashlar blocks with particular emphasis on the façade. There was usually a straight-topped propylaeum in front of the chamber, with a staircase leading from the dromos. The walls of the dromos were often built of stone or mudbrick. Numerous gifts were found in the dromoi, but the chambers had been looted earlier. The chambers, where the body was deposited, also contained the personal belongings of the dead. A silver bowl with engraved decoration was found in a corner of the chamber of one of the smallest 'royal' tombs (Tomb 2), which escaped the attention of the looters.

The richest tomb is Tomb 79. Among the objects discovered on the floor of the dromos were several pieces of furniture, three thrones and one bed. They were made of wood and decorated with ivory plaques. One, covered in thin sheets of silver and decorative silver nails with gilded heads, was accompanied by a similarly decorated stool. The resemblance of this to the 'silver-studded' throne of Homer is remarkable. One of the thrones is of special importance. Its backrest bears vertical bands of ivory guilloche pattern and horizontal friezes of

99 General view of the dromos of Salamis Tomb 79, dating to *c.* 700 BC. The tomb was used twice for burials. It is the most important of all the built tombs of the 'royal' necropolis of Salamis, because of the wealth of the objects found in the dromos; these include ivory pieces of furniture, bronze cauldrons and masses of pottery. Horses and chariots were sacrificed on the floor of the dromos, with all their metal harness.

99

100

100 Throne from Salamis Tomb 79 (restored), made of wood covered with ivory plaques; the upper part of the backrest was decorated with thin sheets of gold. Under the arms are two carved ivory plaques in the *ajouré* technique, representing a sphinx and a composite lotus flower respectively. The backrest was decorated with guilloche pattern and inlaid palmettes. This throne corresponds very closely to that of Penelope as described by Homer. *C.* 700 BC. Ht 90 cm. Cyprus Museum, Nicosia, Salamis, Tomb 79, throne 3, no 518.

inlaid anthemia of ivory. The upper part was covered with a thin sheet of gold. The sides of the throne, decorated with two plaques in the cut-out technique, one representing a sphinx, the other a composite lotus flower, are carved on both sides. They are decorated with blue and brown paste placed in cloisons, the walls of which are covered in thin sheets of gold. This throne closely resembles that of Penelope described by Homer. Such thrones are also described in the Linear B tablets. The reconstructed bedstead of the bed in Tomb 79 is decorated with ivory plaques representing various figures taken from Egyptian iconography, namely Bes and Heh. The upper part of the bedstead is decorated with a purely decorative frieze of Egyptian hieroglyphs inlaid in blue paste, but without any meaning. No doubt they were the work of Phoenicians who could not understand them. The style of the ivories is Egyptianizing Phoenician, recalling the technique of the ivories found in the palace of Nimrud in Syria. The pieces of furniture from Salamis Tomb 79 may have been made in a workshop in north Syria, if not in the same one which produced those of Nimrud. Near Eastern literature refers to the beds and thrones of ivory which were prize possessions of kings and rich families in the East Mediterranean, and Homer described such pieces in detail.

Tomb 79 was used twice, the first burial taking place at the end of the 8th century BC and the second shortly afterwards. In both cases chariots and horses were sacrificed in honour of the dead. The corpse was carried on a hearse, the war chariots being a symbol of the high social rank of the deceased. Of particular importance are the bronze and iron horse trappings as well as the actual chariots and hearses, which have been reconstructed. The horses were decorated for the ceremony with bronze front bands and blinkers. They also wore breastplates and side pendant ornaments decorated in repoussé with scenes and monsters from Egyptian and Near Eastern iconography. A frequent theme is a winged sphinx or a winged lion striding over a fallen human figure, symbolizing the victorious Pharaoh dominating his enemies. The style of these bronzes, which were probably made by local artists familiar with the various styles prevalent in the East Mediterranean during the 8th and 7th centuries BC, culminated in a *koene* of Phoenician, Egyptian and even Urartian elements. The same may be said for the style of a monumental bronze cauldron standing on an iron tripod. The cauldron is decorated around its rim with eight cast griffin protomes and four double-faced hammered sirens. The cauldron itself, which is hammered out of a double sheet of bronze, is 51 cm high; the height of the iron tripod is 65 cm. The total height, including the attachments, is 125 cm. This is the first time that a cauldron of this type has been found anywhere in the Near East, though the origin of 'griffin cauldrons' has always been considered Near Eastern. Those found in the Aegean and Etruria, even though locally made, must have been inspired by Near Eastern prototypes.

Another 'heroic' element from Tomb 79 is the pair of iron firedogs and the bundle of twelve obeloi (skewers or spits). Such objects are

101

102

101 Skeletons of two horses lying on the floor of the dromos of built Tomb 50 of the Salamis necropolis. The horses were sacrificed while yoked together (the wooden yoke and pole left impressions in the soil; the chariot box or hearse must have been detachable). The horses are of a short race known as *Equus aegyptiacus*.

102 Bronze cauldron hammered out of two metal sheets. There are 8 cast protomes of griffins and 4 double-headed 'sirens' rivetted around the rim of the vase. The cauldron is supported on an iron tripod decorated with lilies. Such vases have been hitherto known from Etruria and Greece; this is the first to appear in the East Mediterranean. The ultimate origin of the style may be Urartian with Phoenician influences, *c.* 700 BC. Total ht 125 cm. Cyprus Museum, Nicosia, Salamis, Tomb 79, no. 202.

known from tombs of warriors at Palaepaphos and Patriki in Cyprus, at Argos and Nauplion on the Greek mainland and at Kavousi in Crete. Skewers without firedogs have a wider distribution. The particular form of the firedogs as mentioned above – a stylized version of a warship – may not be accidental. Coldstream suggests that Cyprus is where firedogs and spits were invented, since they have been found there in tombs of warriors from the 11th century BC, such as those at Palaepaphos-*Skales* and Lapethos. Whether their presence in the tomb had any religious significance or was simply utilitarian is difficult to determine. It is suggested that they mark the distinct rank of the deceased. Homer was fond of describing in detail the roasting of meat – the meal of a hero *par excellence*.

Tomb 3 is another important built tomb of the 7th century BC. It has connections with Anatolian funerary architecture, as mentioned above, and may have been built by itinerant masons from Anatolia who would also have been responsible for the tumulus of earth which covered it, since large tumuli are quite alien to the funerary architecture of Cyprus. In the dromos of the tomb, which is 24.6 m long and 5.2 m wide, a chariot and two horses were sacrificed in honour of the dead as in Tomb 79, recalling again the funerary customs described by Homer at the funeral of Patroklos (*Iliad* XXIII, 170–6). Apart from the usual harness and decorative metal ornaments for the chariots, the tomb contained a warrior's shield, a spear and quiver and evidence for a bow. Of particular interest is the iron sword, 92 cm long, bearing traces of its wooden sheath. It had a pommel of perishable material which left its impression in the soil. This was fixed to the tang with silver-plated bronze nails which correspond to the Homeric description of the 'silver-studded' sword. Among the numerous vases offered to the dead and piled up against the wall of the dromos (some of them may have contained food), there was a large amphora with a painted inscription below one of the handles. It is in the Cypriot syllabary and mentions 'olive oil' in Greek. This is yet another element from the Homeric description of the funerary pyre of Patroklos in the *Iliad*. According to Homer, Achilles also placed on the same pyre the bodies of twelve Trojans whom he had sacrificed. Evidence for such a sacrifice was revealed in the fill of Tomb 2: a human skeleton with the hands bound in front of the body was found near the surface in the dromos. Other details recalling Homeric descriptions have been found in Tomb 47, including blinkers and front bands of a perishable material (perhaps leather) covered with thin sheets of gold, resembling the harness used by the gods.

The common practice at Salamis was inhumation, but there are two instances of incineration: in Tomb 1, already mentioned, and in Tomb 31 where the incinerated remains were found in an amphora.

The built tombs of the necropolis of Salamis are confined to one area reserved for members of the royal family and the nobility. In another part of the necropolis, to the south, ordinary citizens were buried in plain rock-cut tombs with a rectangular chamber and a stepped dromos.[18] The chamber and the dromos were confined within a block-built enclosure within which there was often a pyre. This usually contained small broken vases, imitation clay jewelry, as well as carbonized seeds and fruit, recalling the Greek funerary custom of *panspermia* or *pankarpia*, according to which the first-fruits are offered to the gods. There were also clay snakes, offerings to the divinities of the underworld.

In the same part of the cemetery several infant burials were discovered in jars of which some are imported. Similar burial customs are not unknown in the Greek world and it may well be that a large portion of the population of Salamis preserved their Greek ancestral customs.

103 Iron sword with traces of a wooden sheath, from inside the chariot box found in the dromos of Salamis Tomb 3. The pommel, probably of wood and now restored, was fixed on the tang with bronze rivets, the heads of which were silver-plated. This recalls the 'Homeric' silver-studded swords which were thought to be much earlier. 7th century BC. L. 92 cm. Cyprus Museum, Nicosia, Salamis, Tomb 3, no. 94.

104 Jug of Bichrome IV ware, decorated in the 'free-field' technique (against an empty background). The whole body surface opposite the handle is occupied by the figure of a warrior, armed with a spear, axe and sword; he wears an Egyptian head-dress. This style flourished particularly in the 7th century BC; decorative motifs usually comprise birds, fishes and quadrupeds, but there are also ambitious compositions with human figures. Ht 15 cm. Pierides Foundation Museum, Larnaca.

Of the pottery found in these tombs several Greek storage jars of the 'SOS' type are worthy of note. One, dating to *c.*700 BC, bears an engraved inscription in the Greek alphabet. The individual buried with this amphora must have been of some importance, since a horse was sacrificed in the dromos, as in the 'royal' tombs. In another instance there is evidence for the sacrifice of a slave to serve the deceased master. East Greek pottery and local imitations have also been found in these tombs.

Foreign influence and local creativity

In the 7th century BC Salamis must have been one of the largest and most prosperous cities in the East Mediterranean, with a cosmopolitan culture combining the exuberance and wealth of the Near East with Greek undertones. That the Salaminians, more than other Cypriots, maintained close connections with the Aegean, is reflected by the archaeological discoveries. Greek traditions would have been current among citizens of Greek descent in other cities as well. It is noteworthy that at the end of the 7th century BC a Cypriot dedicated a bronze tripod to the Temple of Apollo at Delphi. His name, Hermaios, is engraved in the Cypriot syllabary on a leg of the tripod.[19] Connections with the Aegean are particularly apparent during the second half of the 7th

105 Amphoriskos of White Painted V ware, from Amathus. It is decorated on one side with a horse and rider and a second human figure walking in front of the horse; the other side depicts two winged sphinxes confronted on either side of a 'sacred tree'. The decoration is in silhouette, with grooves indicating details, in the fashion of Attic Black Figure vases which inspired the technique and often the iconography of the so-called 'Amathus style' of the 6th century BC. Ht 13.5 cm. Limassol District Museum, Amathus, Tomb 251, no. 8.

century BC, when large quantities of East Greek and Rhodian pottery appear in Cyprus. This period coincides with the end of Assyrian domination after 650 BC, following the collapse of the Assyrian empire c.669 BC. The Greeks themselves renewed their interest in Cyprus, and some developed a taste for Cypriot works of art. Cypriot terracotta figurines and limestone statuettes are found among the votive offerings in the Temple of Hera at Samos,[20] together with orientalizing bronzes, including Cypriot candelabra.[21] At a slightly later date, similar objects, particularly limestone statuettes, appear in Rhodes and Naukratis. They may be local imitations or the work of immigrant Cypriots.[22]

Though the ivories and bronzes of Salamis and the silver 'Cypro-Phoenician' bowls do not reflect purely Cypriot art, this is not the case for vase-painting, an everyday art which is deeply rooted in popular tradition. The tendency towards pictorialism in the Cypro-Geometric period is now developed even further with the introduction of the 'free-field' style: stylized birds, fishes, quadrupeds and human figures are successfully adapted to the curved surface of vases against a free background, hence the name of the style.[23] Bichrome paint is fully applied for a more striking effect. The figures are usually rendered in outline and filled with purple paint. Reserved spaces are left within the body to show anatomical details such as the ribs and the dewlap of

104

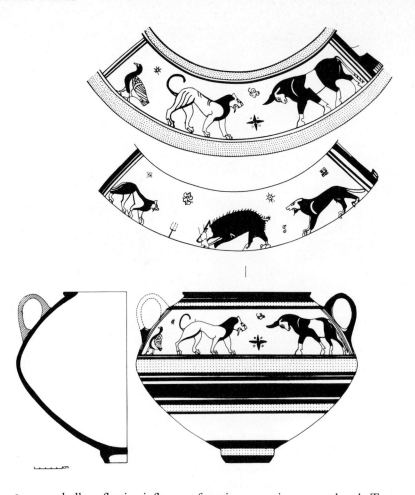

106 Fragmentary jar of Bichrome V ware, from Goudhi (Paphos District). It is decorated with animal figures (a lion, bull, duck, boar etc.) in a style which imitates Rhodian vase-painting of the end of the 7th century BC. Rhodian vases of the 'wild goat style' have been found in Cyprus. Beginning of the 6th century BC. Preserved ht 29.5 cm (foot missing). Paphos District Museum, no. 2235.

bulls, reflecting influences from ivory-carving or metalwork. Tapestry and weaving may also have influenced the technique of some of the pictorial compositions. Themes such as groups of human figures, usually women in a procession holding flowers, may have been borrowed from the decoration on metal bowls inspired by festival scenes or ritual performances in temples. There are some instances where the Cypriot artist tries to imitate the 'animal style' of Rhodian vase-painting,[24] but the most noteworthy achievements are those where the true Cypriot spirit prevails. Compositions like that on a jug showing a bull smelling a flower, or a large bird in front of a stylized lotus flower, or with a fish in its beak, are purely decorative. Unlike his Greek contemporaries, the ambition of the Cypriot vase-painter was to adorn the vessel rather than to produce fine artistic compositions on the curved surfaces.

Egyptian rule

After the collapse of the Assyrian Empire *c.* 669 BC, the Egyptians became increasingly powerful in the East Mediterranean. By 570 BC the

Egyptian King Amasis had become the effective ruler of Cyprus,[25] and the easy period of Assyrian rule, during which Cyprus developed into an almost independent country, was over. Though Egyptian rule, which lasted for about twenty-five years, was more severe than that of the Assyrians, the Cypriots continued their cultural development unhindered as long as they paid tribute regularly to the Egyptian king. Their relations with the Aegean progressed undisturbed and a national consciousness now began to arise, which heralded the political developments of a few decades later. It is during this period of Egyptian domination that the Athenian philosopher Solon is said to have visited Cyprus and to have advised his friend Philokypros, King of Aepeia, to move his city, Soloi, to a healthier site, which he did. This visit may never have taken place,[26] of course, and recent discoveries have shown that Soloi existed as a town in the same area from the 11th century BC onwards.[27] Nevertheless, this tradition demonstrates the lively interest the Greeks had in Cyprus. It is also said that Solon dedicated an elegiac poem to Philokypros.

If Egyptian influence on the development of Cypriot sculpture was considerable, equally strong was that from Ionia. In fact, influence from both these regions was so strong that Cypriot art began to lose the power to absorb and remould foreign traits. The Egyptian presence in Cyprus is attested in various monuments and works of art. At Salamis the vaulted Tomb 80, built of ashlar blocks in the middle of the 6th century BC not far from the 'royal' necropolis, is decorated inside with painted lotus flowers in black, red and blue paint applied directly to the smooth surface of the stones of the walls and ceiling.[28] At Kourion, a small bronze situla, dedicated to the Temple of Apollo, bears an inscription 'to the god' in the Cypriot syllabary and in Egyptian hieroglyphs.[29] In sculpture, a Cypro-Egyptian style is introduced in which the Egyptian dress and head-dress as well as the facial expression are often imitated.[30] At the same time, however, Greek influences cause the development of a Cypro-Ionian style.[31] These Cypro-Egyptian and Cypro-Greek tendencies in sculpture are characteristic of Archaic Cypriot culture in general, which fluctuates between the Orient and the Occident.

Greek imports continue to reach Cyprus, particularly vases from Athens, Corinth, Rhodes and Chios as well as 'naukratite' vases (from the site of Naukratis in Egypt). These, however, are found in the main harbour towns, particularly Amathus, Salamis and Marion.[32] Amathus lies on the route to Naukratis, the Greek colony in Egypt, and would have been a port of call for Greek ships sailing to the Delta. Relations with Greece are also proven by the dedication at Delphi of two bronze shields of a purely Cypriot type, known from Idalion and Paphos. Were they deposited by enemies of Cyprus who had been victorious over one of her kingdoms, or by a Cypriot king who had defeated another?[33]

Sanctuaries and religious beliefs

The 7th and 6th centuries BC are the heyday of rural sanctuaries. Whereas the main urban centres are continuously open to new cultural influences from abroad, the Cypriot countryside remains very conservative. Its religion is deeply attached to the prehistoric divinity

of fertility, often symbolized by the bull. The sanctuaries often consist of a small cella, an altar and a large courtyard. The god or gods combine many qualities: they are healing gods, weather gods, war gods, fertility gods. Offerings are made to them of statues and statuettes of stone or, more frequently, of baked clay, as well as smaller gifts such as scarabs, amulets and bronze artefacts. The statues represent human figures, often holding an animal or playing a musical instrument for the pleasure of the divinity. These are substitutes for the worshippers, and their presence in the sanctuaries is a permanent reminder to the god of their gift and prayer. There are also animal figures, usually bulls, as well as horses and riders, chariot models and so on. Images of a divinity are rather rare. The terracotta figures usually have a wheelmade or handmade cylindrical body, with a moulded or handmade head. They are plain, but occasionally they are decorated with black and purple paint, like the vases of the same period. The vast majority are small, but figures of large size, even overlife-size, are also made in one or two or even more pieces. Terracotta votive offerings in sanctuaries are usually found in large numbers. The sanctuary at Ayia Irini, which flourished mainly during the 7th and 6th centuries BC, produced about two thousand.

The terracotta figures are placed on benches around the altar or on an offerings table in the courtyard of the sanctuary. Every time these were full the priest would dig a pit in the vicinity of the sanctuary and bury the surplus so as to make room for new gifts. Such a deposit was found near the Sanctuary of Apollo at Kourion, which was first constructed in the 8th century BC. Large numbers of clay figurines – horses and riders, chariot models, and groups of human figures wearing anthropomorphic or bull-masks – were found in a deposit (bothros) in the precinct of the sanctuary.[34] Recent excavations near the altar of the

107

Archaic precinct have produced terracotta figurines of bulls as well as two small bulls of gold and silver respectively.[35]

THE SANCTUARY OF AYIA IRINI

The sanctuary of Ayia Irini was constructed at the end of the Late Bronze Age and was in use until *c*. 500 BC.[36] The Cypro-Archaic I phase, which concerns us here, consists of an irregular temenos which is fenced with a peribolos wall of rubble. At the centre stands an altar on which the cult symbol was placed. This was a smooth oval stone, probably a survival from the Late Bronze Age sanctuary. A similar cult symbol was found in the Cypro-Archaic II sanctuary at Meniko, as described below. It should be considered as the abode of the power of fertility, though this deity was also symbolized by the bull. Near the altar was a small structure of two rectangular 'rooms' which have been identified as enclosures for sacred trees. There are also remains of substructures for wooden posts which probably supported the roofs of two shelters. There are thus two separate units within the sanctuary, an open courtyard on the one hand, and an inner courtyard on the other, with the altar, shelters and enclosures for the sacred trees. It follows the model of the older open-air rustic sanctuary from Vounous.

The divinity worshipped in this sanctuary was connected with fertility, explaining the presence of clay bull-figurines and also of bisexual centaurs, or minotaurs who were the demons accompanying the divinity. But the offerings also include clay models of war chariots and armed human figures – which suggest that the same god was also worshipped as a god of war. The ex-votos were arranged in concentric semicircles around the altar. Though little is known of the cult practices within the sanctuary, it may be inferred from terracotta figurines wearing bull-masks that the priests and perhaps the

107 One gold and (*on facing page*) one silver bull figurine, from the Archaic altar of the Sanctuary of Apollo at Kourion. Other votive figures found on and around the altar include clay bull figurines, horses and riders, chariot groups etc. A large bothros (deposit) of figurines was found in the vicinity of the altar. The technique of the gold and silver figurines betrays Anatolian influences. 7th century BC. L. of gold figurine 4.9 cm; L. of silver figurine (tail missing) 6.4 cm. Cyprus Museum, Nicosia.

108

109

108 Group of terracotta figures of various sizes from the sanctuary of Ayia Irini. They represent about half of the votive figures found in this sanctuary (the other half is in the Cyprus Museum, Nicosia). They are mostly human figures, but there are also chariot models, bull figures, centaurs and horse figures. In the foreground a round 'sacred stone'. 7th–6th century BC. Medelhavs-museet, Stockholm.

worshippers wore such masks during ritual performances, thus presenting the theriomorphic aspect of fertility as is known from the Bronze Age.

The human figures are of different sizes. There are many small ones in the 'snowman' technique, which were perhaps the poor man's gifts. Richer worshippers, however, would offer larger or life-size figures of themselves bearing gifts. One bald, bearded figure may even be an attempted portrayal of a particular worshipper. This is certainly the case with a small terracotta of a standing male with a cylindrical body, holding a large Egyptian *ankh* symbol.[37] His facial characteristics are African. No doubt this is a representation of an Egyptian adherent to the cult. He may even have been an Ethiopian since, as we know from Herodotus, a group of Ethiopians settled in Cyprus in connection with the Egyptian domination (Herod. VII.90).[38]

Remains of several other sanctuaries have been excavated. Their architecture varies from the primitive type, like that of Ayia Irini, to the more advanced, with an enclosed temenos and a roofed chapel, as in the sanctuaries at Idalion and Voni.[39] The quantity of material collected from these sanctuaries is enormous.

The cults of Cypro–Archaic II

Apart from archaeological evidence concerning religious architecture and practices in Cyprus during the late Archaic and Classical periods,

109 Terracotta figurine of a human figure wearing a bull-mask. Such figurines have also been found in sanctuaries of the 6th century BC, e.g. at the Sanctuary of Apollo at Kourion, and represent priests or worshippers. The custom of wearing bull-masks during ritual performances in Cyprus dates back to the Bronze Age. The idea was to acquire the qualities of the bull (fertility, virility). 6th century BC. Ht 13.2 cm. Limassol District Museum, Amathus, Tomb 200, no. 1.

there is epigraphical and other evidence which is of importance. Numerous divinities were worshipped in the island during this period, and their character corresponds to the ethnic distribution of the population. By now the majority of the Cypriots were Greeks, but we know that the Phoenician element was strong and the Eteocypriot substratum still considerable. Furthermore, in the rural areas prehistoric religion continued to form the basis of religious belief and practice.

The Greek gods of Olympus were gradually introduced to Cyprus,[40] some of them as early as the initial stage of the Achaean colonization. Zeus was worshipped at Salamis, and the origins of his cult must reach back to the foundation of the city, since Teukros is said to have introduced the cult and to have become the first high priest of the sanctuary. The remains of a monumental Temple of Zeus of the Hellenistic and Roman periods were uncovered in the central part of

110 Salamis some years ago. The father of the gods was also worshipped at later periods in cities such as Marion, Chytroi and Golgoi. An Archaic limestone statue from Kition portrays the god holding an eagle and brandishing a thunderbolt (Zeus Keraunios).

Hera had a sanctuary at Palaepaphos (which was built by King Nicocles) and was also worshipped at Amathus and Idalion. In addition, King Nicocles built a temple to Artemis at Paphos. She was worshipped at Kition as Artemis Paralia.

Apollo had a sanctuary at Kourion of considerable importance, as already mentioned. The god was worshipped there as Apollo of the woods (Hylates). Under the names Mageiros and Lakeutes (connected with sacrifices and divination) he was worshipped at Pyla near Larnaca.

Athena was worshipped at the Palace of Vouni, at Soloi, Kakopetria, Mersinaki and Idalion, according to archaeological remains and inscriptions.[41]

Aphrodite was the principal goddess of Paphos where she is never mentioned by her name but as Anassa (the Lady). Her sanctuary, built in the 12th century BC and known to Homer, remained down to the Roman period one of the most famous on the island. At Amathus she is known as Kypria, the goddess of Cyprus.

Heracles was worshipped more as a god than a hero. Numerous representations of him have survived, and at Kakopetria he was worshipped together with Athena.

Reference is elsewhere made to other gods such as Kybele and Hermes.

The Phoenician population worshipped Astarte, whose cult was introduced to the island in the 9th century BC. Though several purely Phoenician gods, such as Eshmoun, Melqart, Reshef and Mikal Baal, are mentioned in Phoenician inscriptions from Kition, several Greek gods are assimilated with their Phoenician equivalents, such as Aphrodite-Astarte, Athena-Anat, Heracles-Melqart. We have already referred to the worship of Baal Hamman.

The Eteocypriot element of the population, however, retained its own divinities, which had appeared at the dawn of Cypriot prehistory. The 'Great Goddess' associated with fertility continued to be worshipped side by side with a male fertility god. Both are anonymous, but sometimes they fuse with Greek or Phoenician divinities such as Apollo Keraeatas, a god of cattle, whose name occurs in an inscription at Pyla and who may be identified with the Late Bronze Age horned god. The same Late Bronze Age god may have survived as Apollo Alasiotas (the god of Alasia = Cyprus) known from a 4th-century-BC inscription from Tamassos.[42]

During the Egyptian occupation certain Egyptian elements may have infiltrated Cypriot religion, for example, the god Bes, who is represented in Cyprus as early as the 12th century BC. The Egyptian pantheon flourished in Cyprus particularly from the 3rd century BC when the island was under the domination of the Ptolemies.[43]

THE SANCTUARY OF MENIKO

Worthy of mention in some detail is the sanctuary dating from the end of the Cypro-Archaic period excavated at Meniko, west of Nicosia,

110 (*Opposite*) Limestone statue of Zeus Keraunios (the Thunderer), from Kition. The god wears a long tunic and mantle (*aegis*) over his shoulders. In his raised right hand he holds the thunderbolt, while in his left hand he held an eagle, of which only the claws survive. He is bearded and has the expression of Archaic Cypro-Greek sculpture of *c*. 500 BC. Ht 56 cm. Cyprus Museum, Nicosia, Kition, Temple of Heracles (Swedish Excavations) no. 139.

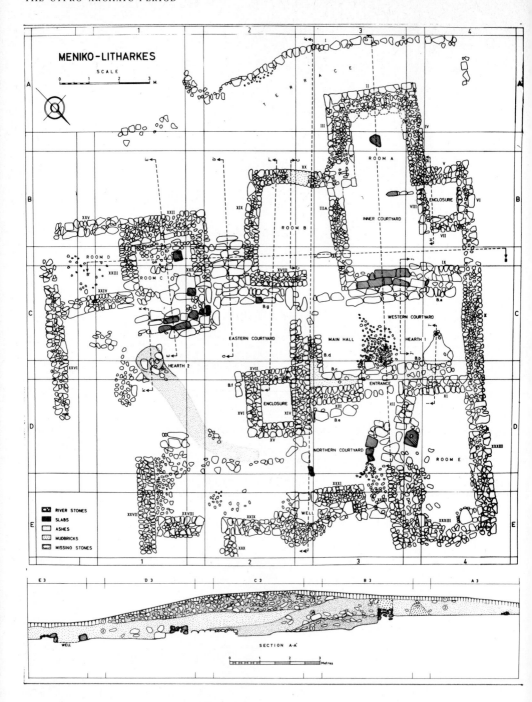

111 Plan of a rural sanctuary at Meniko-*Litharkes*. It is a double sanctuary, one part for the god Baal Hamman (right) and the other for his companion Tanit (left). They have a common courtyard with built enclosures for sacred trees. A large number of votive terracotta figurines were found in it. Though one may identify with certainty the main divinity who was worshipped in the sanctuary as Baal Hamman, the character of this Phoenician-Punic god was adapted by the Cypriots who attributed to him certain qualities of the old fertility divinity who had a long tradition in prehistoric Cypriot religion.

112 Terracotta figurine of a bearded Baal Hamman, wearing a long robe and seated on a throne with his feet resting on a stool; he has ram's horns. From the cella of his sanctuary at Meniko-*Litharkes*. 6th century BC. Ht 18.5 cm. Cyprus Museum, Nicosia, Meniko sanctuary, no. 1.

firstly because the architectural remains are very well preserved, and secondly because of the unusual character of the objects it contained.[44]

Meniko is still an agricultural area, just as it must have been when the sanctuary was in use. Its walls are of igneous river boulders at foundation level, with mudbrick superstructures. In its second period of construction it consisted of two architectural units, parallel to each other and separated by a staircase. The first and largest of these units comprises an open-air outer courtyard, on the floor of which there were patches of burnt soil with ashes, suggesting sacrifices. A staircase led   111
from the courtyard to an inner court with a cella at the far end, the latter probably being roofed. A small rectangular enclosure, on the right on entering the cella, may have been for a sacred tree. Adjacent to the inner courtyard there was another rectangular room, which also opened onto the outer courtyard. In the cella of this first architectural unit a terracotta statuette was found of the god Baal Hamman. He is bearded,   112
with twisted ram's horns, wears a long chiton and is seated on a throne with a stool at his feet. In the same cella two clay and one limestone   113

147

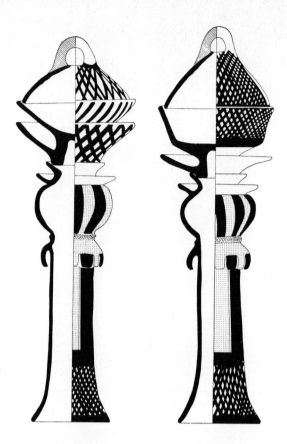

113 A pair of clay stands of incense-burners from the cella of the sanctuary of Baal Hamman at Meniko. The name Baal Hamman means the 'god of the perfumed altar or incense-burner'. This is the first time that such objects (*hammanim*) have been found in a sanctuary dedicated to this god. 6th century BC. Ht 38 cm and 36.6 cm respectively. Cyprus Museum, Nicosia, Meniko sanctuary, nos 21 + 26 + 33 and 22 + 23 + 34.

thymiateria (incense burners) were excavated. Terracottas of human figures were found scattered in various parts of the sanctuary. In addition there were figurines of bulls, horses and riders. Noteworthy is a terracotta group with a large bull being led to sacrifice by two small human figures, one on either side. There is also a terracotta figurine of a ram and a model chariot.

The Meniko god thus combined many qualities. Significantly, there was a cult of Ammon in Libya, since King Evelthon of Salamis maintained particular links with Libya during the middle of the 6th century BC. In Carthage, too, the god Baal Hamman (the god of *hammanim*, or thymiateria) was worshipped in association with the goddess Tanit Pene Baal, who had the same attributes as Astarte in the Near East. There was also a cult of Baal in Syria and Phoenicia, from where his worship could have been introduced to Cyprus. Though several representations of the god, seated on a throne usually supported by rams, are known from the island, this is the first to be discovered with his attributes par excellence, the *hammanim*. Several small thymiateria were found in the sanctuary apart from the three large ones referred to above; they consist of a double bowl with a conical lid perforated at the top. The cult of Baal Hamman must have been widespread in Cyprus, judging from the distribution of his clay and limestone figurines, but this is the first time that a sanctuary dedicated

114 Terracotta group
consisting of a large bull
standing on a flat rectangular
plinth and flanked by two
small kilted human figures.
They are all in a frontal
position. The animal is being
accompanied to be sacrificed,
in the fashion of certain Late
Bronze Age representations in
bronze or terracotta. 6th
century BC. Ht 28.5 cm.
Cyprus Museum, Nicosia,
Sanctuary of Baal Hamman at
Meniko, no. 16.

to this god has been discovered. It is interesting that in the middle of
the 6th century BC there was a Phoenician cult in the centre of Cyprus.
Meniko lies not far from the copper mines and, as already noted, the
Phoenicians had found their way to Tamassos in this mining area by the
9th century BC. The discovery, in the Meniko sanctuary, of clay bull
figurines, warriors and a chariot model demonstrates that the essential
elements of the old Cypriot religion and the concept of a god with
several attributes had not disappeared.

The second architectural unit of the sanctuary is situated
immediately to the east of the first. It consists of two rectangular rooms,
and access to one of them is through a staircase, as for the first unit. The

adjacent room was built during the second period of the sanctuary, probably to provide more space for offerings. There is an open courtyard in front of these two rectangular rooms, and in one corner there is a small rectangular enclosure for a sacred tree, as in the first architectural unit. A thick layer of ashes on the floor of the courtyard in front of the staircase is evidence for an altar. An architectural analysis of the whole complex indicates that these are twin sanctuaries, each with a cella, an additional room, a staircase, an open courtyard, an altar for sacrifices and a sacred tree. It has already been mentioned that the companion goddess of Baal Hamman in Libya is Tanit Pene Baal. The large limestone symbol resembling 'horns of consecration' in the second cella may well be associated with Tanit, rather than representing a survival of the Aegean 'horns of consecration' as was originally believed. If this new identification is correct, then the cult of two purely Phoenician divinities was well established in the main mining area by the middle of the 6th century BC. On the other hand, instead of the worship of Tanit, a Punic deity, one might argue for that of Astarte, whose cult had a long tradition in Cyprus, and indeed the qualities of the old fertility gods of Cyprus are still present.

THE SANCTUARY OF LIMASSOL

A slightly later sanctuary, dating to *c*. 500 BC, was excavated at Limassol-*Komissariato*.[45] It consists of a small semicircular cella where most of the votive objects were found. It could not be ascertained whether this cella was associated with a peribolos wall or a temenos. The character of the votive offerings helps to identify the deity worshipped in this sanctuary. As at Meniko, there is a divinity of fertility, this time associated with phallic terracottas. A clay phallus was found in the central part of the cella, and a large number of stylized bull-shaped zoomorphic vases with prominent genitalia support the identification of this god as one of fertility. There are also a few female figurines which may represent a female companion to the male god, as at Meniko. The discovery of a notched scapula at the Limassol sanctuary is also important. It cannot be proven that these objects were used for divination, but the fact that they first appear in Cyprus in the Late Bronze Age sanctuaries of Enkomi, Kition and Myrtou-*Pigadhes*, and continue to the end of the Cypro-Archaic period, is an additional element of conservatism.

OTHER SANCTUARIES

The study of material from two other sanctuaries in Cyprus, at Kazaphani in the north and Potamia near Idalion, should elucidate the cults during Cypro-Archaic II.[46] The material from Kazaphani comes from a 'favissa' (a deposit of objects from a temple) and ranges from between the 6th or mid-7th century BC, according to the higher chronology for Cypro-Archaic sculpture, and the Classical period. It may have come from a sanctuary of Heracles-Melqart, as far as one can judge from the presence of a limestone statuette of this god and a stamped sherd from a large terracotta representing a hero slaying a lion. The same 'favissa' also produced terracotta figurines of the Astarte type, as well as a terracotta figurine of the Classical period representing the god Hermes.

No doubt the cult in sanctuaries in the main urban areas developed differently from that in the rural areas. At Potamia[47] the cult is first identified in the Cypro-Archaic period and continued down to the 3rd century BC. The offerings are mostly stone sculpture, as good quality limestone was readily available in the vicinity. The divinity was the Greek god Apollo, represented holding a lyre.

In the area of Salamis, outside the city wall near the Monastery of St Barnabas, large numbers of stone sculptures were found, mainly of female figurines holding a flower, fruit or a dove.[48] It has been suggested that the cult with which they were associated was that of Aphrodite, and this is supported by the literary evidence. In the Homeric 'Hymn to Aphrodite' there is already a reference to the cult of the goddess at Salamis, though it is impossible to prove that this material comes from the temple mentioned in the hymn. The sculptures date from the 6th and 5th centuries BC and show the influence of Greek sculpture, especially of the kore type.

At the urban centre of Tamassos, an Archaic sanctuary was found dedicated to Astarte which continued in use to the end of the Classical period.[49] Its courtyard is surrounded by a peribolos wall, a vestibule and a cella. Two altars were revealed, one of them monolithic, measuring 1.4×1.25 m, with a large cavity at its centre surrounded by smaller cavities. This may have been the altar of the 'mother of the gods', Kybele, according to epigraphic evidence. The second altar is of masonry; several terracotta figurines and vases lay on the floor around it. Near this temple there was evidence for metallurgical activity, as at Kition where the connection between metallurgy and religion began in the Late Bronze Age and was revived in the Archaic and Classical periods.

Finally, at the top of the Acropolis of Amathus,[50] two monumental stone vases were discovered, one complete and the other fragmentary. They may be associated with the cult of Aphrodite which is known from later periods. The style of the carved decoration of one of these vases, now in the Louvre, is of the late Archaic period. Both vases may have been covered by a roof supported by wooden pillars; their function was probably lustral.

At Kition the large Temple of Astarte continued to be used, though its interior was largely remodelled. The courtyard was divided into three areas; along the north and the south walls were benches for the deposit of offerings. The eastern entrance to the courtyard was blocked with masonry and a small workshop for smelting was built behind it. A rectangular altar was erected in front of the principal south entrance to the courtyard. The temenos on the east side of the temple was divided into smaller areas, with an altar for sacrifices in one of them.

In connection with the architecture of the sanctuaries we should also mention clay models of the late Archaic period.[51] At Amathus these consist of an abbreviated version of a sanctuary, resembling a window, over the front of which is a 'winged disc' or a crescent. Within the niche there usually stands a nude female figure between two pillars. Two models of sanctuaries were found at Idalion. One shows 'women at the windows' on both sides, recalling the oriental Astarte in the form of a 'sacred prostitute', as she appears, for example, on ivories from the Assyrian palaces. The second model represents a portico in front of the main entrance to the cella, flanked by two pillars topped by capitals in the form of a lotus flower. Inside the cella a winged 'siren' appears through the door.

The above survey demonstrates that cult practices in Cyprus were as diverse as the general cultural trends which prevailed on the island. There was no conflict in worship, but rather a fusion and assimilation of various elements, and often a coexistence.

Funerary architecture

Funerary architecture during the late Archaic period is represented by several notable tombs built of ashlar blocks, of which the most important are the two 'royal' tombs of Tamassos, recalling wooden architecture. We have suggested that they may have been constructed by itinerant masons from Anatolia.[52] They each have a stepped dromos and their stomion is flanked by two pilasters with an 'aeolic' capital, betraying Phoenician influence. One tomb has an antechamber and a chamber, the second only one chamber. The first tomb, which is the best preserved, is decorated inside with miniature friezes of lotus flowers in relief. In both tombs the deceased was buried in a large limestone sarcophagus.

Several other built tombs of the late Archaic period have been found at Amathus. They all have a stepped dromos, one covered with a vault, and the chamber is mainly saddled.[53] The megalithic tomb at Larnaca-*Phaneromeni* recalls the architecture of the 'royal' tombs of Salamis.[54]

Persian rule

By 545 BC the kings of Cyprus submitted voluntarily to Cyrus, King of Persia.[55] This was soon to develop into hard slavery for the Cypriots, especially after 499 BC, that lasted for two hundred years. The Cypriots found themselves suffering the same fate as other Greeks, especially those in Ionia who became the first victims of the expansionist policy of the Persian kings. At first, however, the Cypriots accepted Persian rule. In 525 BC, when Kambyses attacked Egypt, the Cypriots helped him with ships. Similar help was given by the Phoenicians, the Ionians and the Samians. In 521 BC Cyprus became part of the Fifth Persian Satrapy. Nevertheless, for the first five years of Persian domination the Cypriots were free to exercise their own culture as long as they paid their tribute regularly to the Great King, and were ready to place their army at his disposal when necessary.

At this period Ionian sculpture had a decisive influence on the development of Cypriot sculpture, both in stone and terracotta. The 'Archaic smile' of Ionian statues and the characteristic drapery of the korae find their way into the Archaic Cypro-Greek style. Even Greek gods were represented, such as the statue of Zeus Keraunios from Kition referred to above. A limestone head of a bearded warrior wearing a Greek helmet, dated to the end of the 6th century BC, is characteristic of the spirit now prevailing in art, with its distinct

115 (*Opposite*) Slightly larger than lifesize limestone head of a bearded youth wearing a crown decorated with rosettes. The short beard and moustache are neatly trimmed and are grooved; the hair is curly. The Archaic smile betrays the Archaic Cypro-Greek style of *c.* 500 BC. Ht 32.5 cm. Cyprus Museum, Nicosia, no. 1968/V–30/696.

116 A pair of gold ear-rings from a tomb at Amathus. They consist of a crescent-shaped hoop with three berry-shaped appendices which recall Hera's 'skillfully wrought ear-rings with three drops', described by Homer. Cypro-Archaic III-Cypro-Archaic I period. L. 2.85 cm. Limassol District Museum, Amathus, Tomb 321, no. 138.

predilection for Greek fashions.[56] One should mention here the decoration in low relief on the limestone sarcophagus from Golgoi, now in New York.[57] The compositions decorating the two long sides are of a hunting scene and a banquet respectively. One of the short sides represents the myth of Medusa and Perseus and the other a chariot scene. They could all have been copied from Attic vase-painting of the end of the 6th century BC.

116, 117   Statues of women are heavily decorated with jewelry, such as necklaces, ear-rings and earcups. A necklace of granulated gold beads and an agate pendant from Arsos have many parallels in sculptural representations.[58]

Black-Figure Attic pottery occurs in Cyprus from the mid-6th century BC onwards, side by side with East Greek pottery; not only is it favoured by the rich inhabitants of Marion, Salamis, Kition and Amathus, particularly as grave-gifts, but it is also imitated by a group of Amathusian potters.[59] There is now a uniformity in taste for Greek art, not only among the Greek population, but also among the Eteocypriots and even among the Phoenicians.

As already mentioned, the Cypriot kings apparently enjoyed a high degree of autonomy during the early years of Persian domination and were even able to exercise foreign policy independently of the Persian king. This is clear from the story narrated by Herodotos (Herod.IV.162), according to which Queen Pheretima of Cyrene, paid a visit to King Evelthon of Salamis in 530 BC and asked for military assistance in order to reestablish her son on the throne.[60]

Evelthon was the first Cypriot king to issue his own coinage, and for these coins he used the symbol ky (for Kyprion, 'of the Cypriots').[61] This may not imply a sovereignty over the whole of Cyprus, but a kind of superiority over the other Cypriot kings. His association with the Near East is clearly attested on these coins, for his symbols are the Persian ram and the Egyptian ankh. Evelthon is mentioned by Herodotos as having dedicated an incense-burner at Delphi (Herod.IV.162) which could be seen in the Treasury of the Corinthians. Another Cypriot who presented an offering at Delphi was Helicon, son of Akesas of Salamis, who offered a peplos (an outer cloak) woven by himself.[62]

The expansionist policy of Darius and his efforts to dominate the whole of the Greek world changed the attitude of the Persians towards the Cypriots, and their rule became ruthless. Some kings resented this, but others became pro-Persian in order to save their position, like King

117 Gold necklace of forty biconical depressed beads with granulated decoration all over, and a cylindrical pendant of agate with gold mountings. On top is a gold bee and two *urei* (snakes). Such necklaces are often represented on limestone statues of women. 7th century BC. L. 33 cm; L. of pendant 4.5 cm. Cyprus Museum, Nicosia, excavations at the Temple of Aphrodite at Arsos (1917), no. 100.

Gorgos of Salamis. When the Greeks of Ionia decided to revolt against Persian rule in 499/8 BC, the Cypriots agreed to join them, showing that they considered themselves part of the Greek world of the east.[63] This was the outcome of the nationalistic feelings and pro-Greek loyalties which began to be cultivated intensely in Cyprus during the 6th century BC. Herodotos describes in detail the dramatic events which followed (Herod.V. 104, 108–116). All Cypriots joined in the revolt except the Amathusians. Since Amathus was the centre of the Eteocypriot population there must have been a strong Phoenician community there too. Though Greek goods were favoured by Amathusians and Phoenicians alike, when it came to politics; Phoenician affinities were definitely anti-Greek.

According to Herodotos, a pro-Greek member of the royal family of Salamis, named Onesilos, managed to dethrone his pro-Persian brother Gorgos, who then fled to Persia and left Onesilos as leader of all the other Cypriots in the revolt. His first move was to neutralize the pro-Persian Amathusians by besieging their city. But Darius sent his general, Artybios, to subdue the revolt. Onesilos then asked the Ionians for help and the latter sent land and naval forces to confront the united forces of the Phoenicians and Persians. Onesilos was more successful in battle and killed Artybios, his companion having first cut off the legs of the general's aggressive horse. But as the battle turned in favour of the Greek forces, and the Greek warships were winning the upper hand against the Persians and the Phoenicians in the naval battle off the coast of Salamis, the king of Kourion, Stasanor, surrendered to the enemy and was followed by his soldiers and by the war chariots of the Salaminians. Onesilos was killed on the battlefield, as was Aristokypros, son of Philokypros, King of Soloi. The defeat of the Greek army on land obliged their naval forces to withdraw from Salamis. Gorgos had been brought back to Salamis, and the other cities of Cyprus were besieged one after the other. The siege of the pro-Greek city of Soloi lasted for five months, and that of Palaepaphos was also lengthy.

The Persians built a mound at Palaepaphos in order to dominate the defendants near the northeast city gate, and they opened up subterranean tunnels to enter the city.[64] These defences and the siege mound have been uncovered in recent excavations. To build the siege-mound the Persians used stones and sculptures pillaged from the nearby Archaic sanctuary. The discovery of a Greek bronze helmet of Corinthian type at the site of the city gate eloquently illustrates the Greek participation in the defence of Palaepaphos against the Persians. With the surrender of all the Greek cities of Cyprus, Persian rule was firmly established. The Persian garrison at Paphos was billetted in a building constructed in Persian fashion with bossed ashlar blocks.

In order to punish Philokypros, the pro-Greek king of Soloi, a fortress-palace was built on a hilltop overlooking the city and the valley of Soloi, so that the pro-Persian king of Marion could observe the rebellious city. The policy of the Persians was once again to divide and rule. They managed to revive the old pro-Greek and pro-Persian divisions among the Cypriot kingdoms. In achieving this aim they found an ally in the Phoenician community who would gladly collaborate with them against the local population for reasons of political expediency and for profit.

After their revolt, the Cypriots were roughly treated by the Persians in 480 BC. They were obliged to join the forces of Xerxes with 150 ships against the Greeks. Among them, as we learn from Herodotos (Herod.VII.90) was Gorgos, the pro-Persian king of Salamis, who must have tried to please the Persians. According to Herodotos the performance of the Cypriots was very poor (Herod.VIII.68, 100).

Persophile kings were enthroned in all the cities, several of whom may have been Phoenician. The cities of Marion and Lapethos had coins with Phoenician legends, and Soloi ceased to have an independent coinage.

8

The Cypro-Classical period

In the early years of the 5th century BC Cyprus was again caught up in antagonism between Greece and Persia. The Greeks considered Cyprus part of the Greek world and believed it their duty to liberate her from the Persian yoke. Throughout the 5th century BC Cyprus suffered from this and other problems of Graeco-Persian relations. The distance between Cyprus and the Greek mainland rendered it difficult for the Greek army to liberate the island, and these difficulties were increased by the intrigues of the Persians within Cyprus. Moreover, political ambitions and rivalry among the ten independent Cypriot kingdoms made almost impossible any effective resistance against foreign rule.

These ten kingdoms of the 5th century BC were: Salamis, Marion, Lapethos, Tamassos, Idalion, Paphos, Kourion, Kyrenia, Amathus and Kition. Of these, Idalion was annexed by the king of Kition in 470 BC as noted below. Kingship was already a bygone institution in mainland Greece, but Cyprus retained this ancient political system which brought her closer to that of the Orient. Nevertheless, Persian despotism was not favoured by the Cypriots, and kingship in Cyprus evolved differently under the influence of Greek ideals. This, combined with the awakening of a Greek national conscience among the population, led to the birth of an effective force of resistance, at least on the part of the pro-Greek kingdoms. The old Cypriot culture, rooted in the prehistoric past, was now fading with this Greek influence.

The Greek victories at Marathon, Thermopylae and Plataea disproved the myth that the Persian army was invincible. In 478 BC the Athenians sent fifty ships to Cyprus under the Lacedaemonian General Pausanias, who led the Greeks at Plataea, accompanied by the Athenian Generals Aristides and Kimon. The Greek cities which had surrendered to the Persians were easily liberated, but the Persians recovered control after the departure of the Greek army. The island's kings were already divided in their allegiance and the Persians could easily overrun the whole country, having at the same time the prompt collaboration of the Phoenicians.

That Cyprus was often a victim in the efforts of the Greeks to oust the Persians from the East Mediterranean is clear from the events of 459/8 BC, when the Greeks sent a fleet of 200 ships to liberate Cyprus. However, the development of events in Egypt had a disastrous effect. The Athenians considered the revolt of the Egyptians against the Persians as an ideal opportunity to attack the Persians on Egyptian territory, so they abandoned their efforts in Cyprus and sailed to Egypt. But in the summer of 454 BC the Athenians were defeated and Cyprus suffered the consequences. Yet the Greeks never abandoned their plans to liberate the island, and in 450 BC the Athenian General Kimon planned to destroy the Persian navy which, combined with that of the Phoenicians, constituted a formidable power in the East Mediterranean. The principal cities in Cyprus with pro-Persian kings were Marion, Salamis and Kition. Kimon first embarked on the liberation of Marion, and then installed a pro-Greek ruler in the Palace of Vouni. He next proceeded to Kition in order to attack the Phoenicians in the heart of their domain. But in 449 BC, when the Greeks were about to defeat the Phoenicians, Kimon died – either of wounds or of illness – and the Athenians were forced to withdraw. Before sailing for home, however, the Athenian fleet attempted to conquer Salamis, but were repulsed by the Salaminian King Evanthes, and the Athenians finally withdrew altogether from Cyprus. In 449/8 BC the Athenians signed a treaty with the Persians, known as the Treaty of Kallias, by which they agreed to put an end to their animosities. The Greek desire to deal with their own internal problems, rather than engaging in futile wars in the East Mediterranean which won them merely the hostility of the pro-Persian kings of Cyprus, caused them to postpone their dream of liberating the island. A funerary relief from Lysi, west of Salamis, representing a Greek hoplite who was killed while fighting for the freedom of Cyprus, bears silent witness to the events which preceded the Treaty of Kallias.

Greek influences

Fifty years of continuous wars and direct contact with the Greek army strengthened the Hellenic consciousness of the Cypriots. In the Greek literature of this period Cyprus appears as part of the Greek world, and this is attested both in art and in the evidence discovered of daily life. Cypriot women adopt Greek dress fashions, as they appear on funerary stelae, and import their perfume bottles from Athens. In art there is a slavish imitation of Greek styles. Greek architecture may have been introduced in the main towns. Though no temples have yet been discovered, architectural members such as an Ionic capital from Kition may point to their existence.[1] Greek artists may have emigrated to Cyprus, where they produced works of art such as a bronze statue of Apollo, the head of which is now in the British Museum – the so-called Chatsworth Head.[2] It is dated to c. 460 BC and comes from Tamassos where the Greeks obtained their copper supplies. Others maintain, however, that it was imported directly from Athens. The head of a kouros, in island marble, of c. 480 BC,[3] is also the work of a Greek artist, and is often compared stylistically with sculptures from the Temple of Zeus at Olympia. The Cypriots either commissioned their funerary stelae in Athens, or Athenian sculptors carved them locally using Pentelic marble. The epigrams engraved on them are in the Cypriot syllabary but in the Greek language, and are in the style of Greek epigrams, e.g. 'I am [the stele] of Stasis, son of Stasioikos', or 'I am [the stele] of Aristila from Salamis, daughter of Onasis'.[4] A large portion of Greek works of art of this period, both imported and locally made, have been found at Marion, which was the first port of call for Greek ships coming from the Aegean. The local artists of Marion must have had great difficulty in competing with such artists. They produced terracotta funerary statues representing seated or reclining human figures, and attempted to give their facial expressions something of the sadness and indifference which is so characteristic of Greek funerary stelae.[5] In more provincial centres, however, local imitations are naive and unsuccessful. In several places, particularly in eastern Cyprus, the so-called Sub-Archaic Cypro-Greek style flourished in sculpture, but it often seems monotonous and repetitive.

In vase-painting, an effort was made to produce vessels which would attract local clients away from imports; one was a jug with a terracotta female figure on the shoulder opposite the handle, holding a juglet which served as the spout.[6] Surfaces are often decorated with motifs of Greek inspiration. The result, however, is rather clumsy. Greek styles also prevail in terracottas, especially in larger funerary statues, as noted above. Moulds of smaller terracottas were frequently imported from Athens. Artistic production in general either slavishly imitates Greek models or prolongs the Archaic style in a vigourless manner, showing symptoms of exhaustion.

Cyprus was a centre for gem-engraving during the late Archaic period. Greek engravers may also have been active on the island, where these objects were favoured by Cypriots and Persians alike. Boardman has assembled the works of one such master engraver, all found in Cyprus, known as the Semon Master.[7]

Coins of the Cypriot kingdoms differ little from those of other cities of the Greek world, and no doubt Greek artists were responsible for the dies.[8] Despite the fact that the Cypriot kingdoms maintained the Persian standard for special reasons, the coins represent Greek gods and heroes such as Athena, Heracles, Aphrodite, Apollo and Zeus. The name of the king is mentioned, and in some cases that of the city as well, such as Marion or Idalion. This suggests new political notions which betray Greek ideas, such as that the king *and* the citizens represent the authority of the city state, a concept also apparent on the well-known tablet from Idalion which is now in the Bibliothèque Nationale in Paris.[9] Its long engraved text in the Cypriot syllabary covers both sides of the tablet and refers to an agreement made by the king of Idalion with a physician called Onasilos and his brothers. The physician undertook to treat the wounded from the war against the Medes and the Phoenicians of between 478 and 470 BC. In return, the king and the city promised to pay Onasilos and his brothers a silver talent, or to give them 'state' land for which they would not have to pay taxes. If the king and the state were ever to reclaim this land they would pay Onasilos and his brothers for it. The text was placed in the Temple of Athena, who, as patron goddess of the city of Idalion, had her temple on the acropolis, as in Athens. This temple was destroyed by the Phoenicians in 470 BC. The Idalion tablet, apart from being the longest text in the Cypriot syllabary and dialect which has survived, is a document of considerable importance, since it contains evidence for the earliest social security system known so far. The decision for the agreement is taken jointly by the king and citizens, and the silver talent to be offered to Onasilos is called 'Edalion'.

Greek gods and heroes were now worshipped in Cyprus, particularly

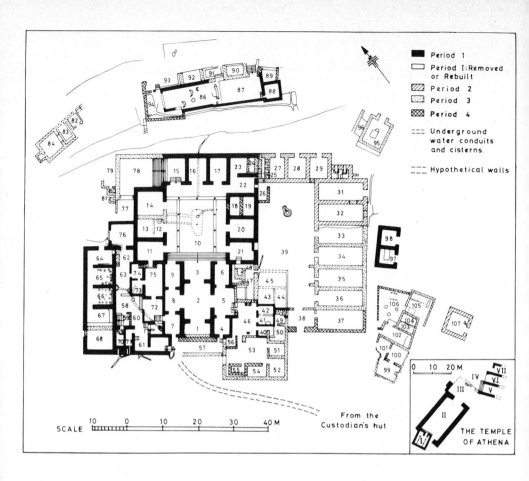

Period 1

Period I: Removed or Rebuilt

Period 2

Period 3

Period 4

Underground water conduits and cisterns.

Hypothetical walls

From the Custodian's hut

SCALE

10   0   10   20   30   40 M

0   10   20 M.

THE TEMPLE OF ATHENA

120 Moulded terracotta head of Heracles wearing a lion's skin. Found in a deposit (*bothros*) at Kakopetria together with a large number of terracotta and limestone votive figures of Athena. It is probable that Heracles shared with Athena a 5th-century-BC sanctuary at Kakopetria. Ht 13 cm. Cyprus Museum, Nicosia (excavated by the Cyprus Department of Antiquities, 1938), no. 53.

in the main towns, as noted above. From the 6th century BC onwards the iconography and cult of Heracles became of particular importance. Cyprus seems to have produced a type of Heracles who betrays both Near Eastern (Phoenician) and Greek elements.[10] The Near Eastern type is often confused with Bes. Representations in sculpture, on metal bowls and on gems offer an interesting variety.

This is the time when the Palace of Vouni was constructed by the King Stasioikos of Marion. After the liberation of the city from the Persians by Kimon, he rearranged the royal apartments to form a 'megaron' – a Mycenaean-style rectangular building with a vestibule – in the central part of the palace, to emphasize his Greek descent.[11] The Temple of Athena, on the higher part of the hill at Vouni, consisted of a large court with a cella – the main part of the temple – at the far end. Near the entrance to the court there was a series of rooms where votive offerings were placed, in the fashion of the Greek 'treasuries' as at Delphi. One of the offerings found in this part of the sanctuary is a bronze cow, said to be a copy of the famous statue by the Greek sculptor Myron.[12] Other offerings include statuettes of Athena wearing a Corinthian helmet.[13] The temple itself, with its Greek-style acroteria, or decorations on the corners of the pediment, must have been visible from a long distance. It may have inspired the cult of Athena at other sites in the Solea valley, and at Kakopetria, an isolated mountainous

118 (*Opposite, above*) Plan of the Palace of Vouni. Built in the 5th century BC by the pro-Persian king of the neighbouring city of Marion, as the headquarters of a garrison to watch over the city of Soloi, which was loyal to the Greeks. The palace consists of state apartments, large storerooms and bathrooms, recalling the spacious palaces of Mycenaean Greece. It is the only palace of the Classical period in Cyprus. Excavated by the Swedish Cyprus Expedition in the 1930s.

119 (*Opposite, below*) View of the courtyard in front of the royal apartments of the Palace of Vouni, with a monumental staircase (right) leading to the *megaron* of the state apartments.

121 Terracotta group representing Athena ready to mount a four-horse chariot. The goddess is dressed in a long chiton and an aegis (or mantle); on her head she wears a helmet. Athena, the Greek goddess *par excellence*, was worshipped in several places along the northwestern coast of Cyprus (e.g. Soloi, Kakopetria, Mersinaki). From Mersinaki (Swedish Excavations). Middle of the 5th century BC. Ht 36 cm. Medelhavsmuseet, Stockholm, no. 8.14.

site on the north slopes of the Troodos mountains, where a deposit of terracottas and limestone figurines of Athena were found;[14] there must have been a sanctuary in honour of the goddess nearby. Athena is crudely represented often in the attitude of Promachos with a shield near her left foot and a spear in her right hand. Among the offerings there was also a bronze votive spearhead and a miniature shield. It is significant that Heracles was also worshipped in the same sanctuary, as was the case in Attica.

Athena was also worshipped in the Temple of Lykios Apollo at Mersinaki between Vouni and Soloi. A terracotta group representing Athena Hippia, ready to mount a chariot, was among the offerings in the temple. It is dated to the early part of the 5th century BC and depicts Athena with a Corinthian helmet and an aegis (or mantle).

The density of Greek penetration around Soloi may not be accidental, for it is close to the copper mines as well as to the forests which provide timber for smelting.

The Phoenicians, Persians and King Evagoras I

While Greek ideas and ideals were flourishing in northwest Cyprus, the Phoenicians were firmly based at Kition and, encouraged by the Persians, extended their rule and influence. King Stasikypros of

Idalion defended his city successfully against the combined Persian and Phoenician forces. The city wall, a large portion of which has been uncovered by recent excavations,[15] may have been reconstructed by this king. The attack, however, was renewed in 470 BC and Idalion finally surrendered. This success strengthened the alliance between the Persians and the Phoenicians. From now on a new factor appears in Cypriot politics – the open hostility of the Phoenicians against the Greek population and their complete alignment with Persian policies. We have already seen the Phoenicians fighting side by side with the Persians against all the very considerable efforts being made by the Greek army to liberate Cyprus.

The Persians tightened their control over Cyprus from 448 BC until the appearance of Evagoras I in 411 BC. A Phoenician from Tyre, called Abdemon, was put on the throne, and the disastrous effects of his rule are narrated vividly by Isokrates, the Greek orator and tutor of Evagoras' son, Nicocles (Isokr. IX). Everything Greek was suppressed and the city became 'barbarous'.

Evagoras, possibly a member of the Teukrid royal family, was born at Salamis in 435 BC. Abdemon, the Phoenician usurper of the throne of Salamis, tried to kill him, but he fled to Cilicia and, having carefully prepared his return, overthrew Abdemon and succeeded to the throne. There was no hostile reaction from the Persian king as Evagoras cleverly hastened to recognize his authority and to pay tribute. His first preoccupation was to protect Salamis anew by fortifying it with walls and building an effective army and navy. He then planned his policy within Cyprus, which was to unite under his leadership all the Cypriot kings against the Persians. His vision extended far outside the island: he aspired to the union of all Greeks under the Athenians, and to make Cyprus the easternmost outpost of Hellenism. His achievements at Salamis and his Greek ideals and aspirations are eloquently – and occasionally exaggeratedly – described by Isokrates. His first act of external policy was to seek an alliance with the Athenians. Already during the first year of his reign he helped the famous orator Andokides, who took refuge in Kition in 415/4 BC after his exile from Athens, by supplying grain and copper. The Athenians, in recognition of Evagoras' help and allegiance, honoured him with a decree which they erected on the Acropolis; they also made him an Athenian citizen and crowned him with a gold wreath.[16] It was natural, after the failure of the Athenians at the battle of Aegospotamoi in 405 BC, that the Athenian Admiral Konon should take refuge in the court of Evagoras. Together they cunningly planned the defeat of the Lacedaemonians, whom they succeeded in overthrowing in 394 BC, with Konon leading the Persian fleet against the Lacedaemonians. This was no doubt part of Evagoras' ingenious diplomacy. He skillfully played the mediator between the Athenians and the Persians while his ultimate goal was the supremacy of Athens in the Greek world. His connections with the Persians and his knowledge and experience of the oriental mentality gave him all the necessary qualifications for such subtle diplomatic manoeuvres. Konon's victory was particularly appreciated by the Athenians, who erected Evagoras' and Konon's statues in the Agora of Athens, next to the statue of Zeus Eleuthereus.

122 Silver stater of King Evagoras I (411–374/3 BC). On the obverse is portrayed the head of the bearded Heracles wearing a lion's skin; on the reverse a seated goat. The name of Evagoras appears both in the Greek alphabet and the Cypriot syllabary. Evagoras I was the first to introduce the Greek alphabet on his coins.

Evagoras combined strength with ambition, the latter sometimes surpassing his capabilities. Influenced by the ideals of the Greek orator Antisthenes, who favoured unified states, he continued to urge the unification of all the kingdoms of Cyprus. His ambition even led to acts of megalomania, such as issuing gold coins to demonstrate that he was equal to the Great King (the King of Persia), the only ruler who had this prerogative. He changed his coinage from the Persian standard to that of Euboia and Rhodes in order to show his independence from the Persians. He was the first to introduce officially the Greek alphabet, which can be seen on his coins: *E* for Evagoras, side by side with the Cypriot syllabary. Greek philosophers and poets were welcome at Salamis during his reign. Artists from Athens must also have worked there and it is certainly one of these who produced the marble statue of 123 Aphrodite or Hygeia, the head of which was found in the ruins of the gymnasium.[17] Though Cyprus did not produce great poets during the Classical period, we should mention Eudemos the philosopher, who was a friend of Aristotle and whose name became known even outside the island. He went to Athens and became a disciple of Plato.

In trying to bring all the kings of Cyprus under his authority Evagoras met the strong resistance of the kings of Kition, Amathus and Soloi, the others having submitted to him either voluntarily or by force. These allied cities successfully applied to the Great King to intervene in 391 BC. Although Evagoras captured Amathus in the same year, he had to give up his efforts. Thus, Soloi went over to the pro-Persian camp after a whole century of pro-Greek policy, no doubt the result of Evagoras' ambitious policy. It must have been during this period that the Palace of Vouni, built to watch over the rebellious city of Soloi, was destroyed.

There was a final attempt by the Athenians to help their ally realize his aims: they sent Chabrias, with ten triremes and eight hundred peltasts, to assist Evagoras in dethroning Melekiathon, the Phoenician king of Kition, and to enthrone the Athenian, Demonikos, in his place.

123 Marble head of
Aphrodite, or Hygeia,
discovered in the Roman
gymnasium at Salamis where
it had been built into a wall.
The facial expression and the
treatment of the hair recall the
style of Greek sculpture of the
beginning of the 4th century
BC. This was the time of the
reign of Evagoras at Salamis,
who is known to have
favoured Greek culture.
Ht 31.2 cm. Cyprus Museum,
Nicosia (excavated by the
Cyprus Department of
Antiquities, 1952), Salamis
Sculptures, no. 2.245.

Evagoras also managed to control a large part of the island, but fate
once again was against him; in 386 BC the Peace of Antalkidas decreed
that all cities of Asia and Cyprus should belong to the Great King and
Chabrias accordingly had to leave Cyprus, thereby depriving Evagoras
of a last chance to fulfil his dreams. He nonetheless decided to continue
his efforts without the Athenians, and employed cunning diplomacy to
create an army of various Near Eastern powers hostile to the Persians,
but without success. The Great King sent two generals against him,
Orontes and Tyribazos, who commanded a great land and naval force.
Evagoras was defeated in a naval battle off Kition in 381 BC, but he still
resisted on land at Salamis. Fate favoured him for once: while Orontes
and Tyribazos were engaged in a personal conflict, he signed a treaty

with Orontes in 381 BC on relatively mild terms, as an equal to the Great King. But he still had to pay tribute and was forced to renounce all his ambitious plans for hegemony over Cyprus. He confined himself to Salamis and died in 374/3 BC; it is even said that he was murdered along with his son, Pnytagoras.

Whatever the weaknesses in the character of Evagoras and the folly of his ambition, there is no doubting his diplomatic capabilities and political courage. He was not deterred by the smallness and weakness of his kingdom when he decided to play an intermediary role between the Persians and the Greeks. If he failed in accomplishing his vision of the unification of all the Greeks, it was due as much to his mistakes as to the adversity of fate and the eternal divisions and conflicts among the Greeks of Greece on the one hand, and the Greek kingdoms of Cyprus on the other. This great political figure wished to make Salamis the Athens of the East Mediterranean. Although an Oriental at heart he was imbued with the ideals of Hellenism, and was not only a dreamer, but also a great leader such as the Greek world rarely nourished. His political career made a deep impression: he transplanted Greek culture into the East Mediterranean, with far-reaching effects on the historical development of Cyprus.

It is always difficult to follow such a leader, and even more so when the successor is a person of inferior quality, as was Nicocles, the son of Evagoras, who succeeded to the throne of Salamis in 374 BC.[18] The ten years of his reign were difficult. Not only was he unable to restore Salamis to its former role after the disastrous economic effects of the long wars of his father, but he could not depend on help from the Athenians, who were faced with their own internal problems. Nicocles died in prison in 361 BC, during the great Revolt of the Satraps, and was succeeded by his son (or brother) Evagoras II (361–351 BC).

In 351 BC, following the revolt of the Egyptians and Phoenicians against the Persians, nine kingdoms of Cyprus formed an alliance and also rebelled. The only king who refused to join the alliance was Evagoras II of Salamis, who was accordingly dethroned and expelled. He was succeeded by Pnytagoras, but although he bears the same name as the son of Evagoras I, it is not certain whether he was even a member of the royal family. The Persians sent an army against the rebellious kings under the leadership, ironically enough, of the Athenian General Phokion. With them was Evagoras II who took advantage of this opportunity to regain his throne. The mercenaries of Phokion pillaged the countryside of Cyprus and subdued all the kingdoms except Salamis. Evagoras II lost the confidence of the Persian King Artaxerxes as a result of false accusations against him by Pnytagoras; he was thus obliged to leave the island and was given the kingdom of Sidon instead. Pnytagoras was left as king of Salamis on condition that he remained loyal to the Persians and paid tribute. He maintained the cultural policies of his ancestors, for his coins represent Athena and Artemis and he went as a *proxenos* to Delos, where his gifts are recorded on the bronze stele commemorating his visit – two gold wreaths, one of myrtle and the other of laurel leaves.

The Hellenistic period

Exhaustion from wars and political intrigues did not interrupt the cultural development of Cyprus, now firmly based on Greek culture. Greek goods were imported to all the major cities, including Kition where they have recently been excavated in large numbers. We also know that in 333/2 BC Kitian merchants requested permission to build a temple of Aphrodite in Piraeus, which indicates that commercial relations between Greeks and Phoenicians were good.

The reign of Pnytagoras coincides with the expedition of Alexander the Great to the East. When Alexander was besieging Tyre the kings of Cyprus were anxious to help him, firstly in order to win his favour and secondly because they regarded him as a fellow Greek who was crushing Persian tyranny. When the Persian empire was in decay they were able to send one hundred and twenty ships to help Alexander. Even Poumyathon, the Phoenician king of Kition, sent him a special sword described by Plutarch, no doubt in order to gain his goodwill. Indeed, the Greek kings of Cyprus took part in the battle of Tyre and their contribution was not negligible. When Alexander organized Greek contests in Phoenicia to celebrate his victory in Egypt, Pnytagoras and Pasikrates were anxious to patronize these games as *choregoi* (financial supporters of dramatic performances). Alexander rewarded the Cypriot kings for their assistance: Pnytagoras received Tamassos and her rich copper mines, Stasanor of Soloi became satrap of several provinces in Alexander's empire, while the remainder were granted other high posts or previous gifts.

With Alexander's victory the Cypriot kings freed themselves from the Persian yoke, but it was clear that Alexander considered the island part of his empire and was not prepared to recognize the absolute authority of the individual kings. He issued coins for the whole of Cyprus, abolishing the coinage of the city states, though for a while Salamis was allowed to cast her own bronze coinage in the name of the Salaminians themselves, but not in that of the king.

Alexander's death in 323 BC and the subsequent turmoil among his successors affected Cyprus directly, for the island became a bone of contention between Ptolemy and Antigonus, the main antagonists. Her strategic position almost in the heart of the area, and her economic resources, particularly timber and copper, made her important to the future masters of the East Mediterranean. The kingdoms of Salamis, Paphos, Soloi and Amathus sided with Ptolemy, while Kition, Lapethos, Marion and Kyrenia supported Antigonus. Ptolemy sent a strong force under his brother Menelaos to subdue the four kings who were hostile to him, and he partly succeeded. Only Poumyathon of Kition resisted, and Ptolemy killed him and burnt down the Phoenician temples there in 312 BC, putting an end to the Phoenician dynasty. Ptolemy's policy was ruthless: the rebellious cities were punished and were offered to King Nicocreon of Salamis. Marion was razed to the ground and the inhabitants transferred to Paphos. Nicocreon became a *strategos* (military governor), but Menelaos also retained the same title, producing considerable friction.

Nicocreon, the last king of Salamis, proved a worthy successor to Evagoras I whose policy he adopted. His relations with Greek culture and the Greek world in general are mentioned by Greek authors and recorded in inscriptions. He maintained special relations with Argos, where an epigram was found mentioning a prize which he offered at the Heraean games there. In a recently discovered inscription from Nemea he is mentioned as one of the *theorodokoi* for the Nemean Games, i.e. those who played host to the heralds who went out to the various parts of the Greek world to announce the games and the truce.[1] Two such hosts are mentioned at Salamis: Nicocreon son of Pnytagoras, and Teukros son of Aristocreon, probably another Aeakid. Nicocreon portrayed Apollo and Aphrodite on his coins and sent gifts to the temples of Apollo at Delphi and Delos.

Diodoros narrates the dramatic events which led to the death of Nicocreon, though in his text he refers to a King Nicocles of Paphos. Most philologists, however, are of the opinion that the name is an error and that the events recorded do refer to Nicocreon of Salamis.[2] According to this account, Ptolemy was informed that Nicocreon was plotting with Antigonus to overthrow him. Ptolemy believed the accusation, and in 311 BC he sent his two generals, Argaios and Kallicrates, to kill Nicocreon. The generals besieged Salamis, assisted by Menelaos, and asked Nicocreon to commit suicide. When he could not prove his innocence he did end his own life. When his wife, Axiothea, was told of the king's fate she killed all her unmarried daughters, so that they would not fall into the hands of the enemy, and persuaded her sisters-in-law to do the same. Nicocreon's brothers closed the palace gates and set it on fire. Thus the whole royal family of Salamis suffered a tragic death under the debris of the palace.

Recent excavations at Salamis have revealed a funerary monument which may be connected with Diodoros' story.[3] Under a tumulus of earth a stepped platform of mudbrick was found. It is rectangular, measuring 17 × 11.5 m; its height is 1.1 m. It has a narrow ramp on the western side, and a staircase of four steps on all sides. The platform resembles a Classical Greek altar. Its plastered steps give the impression of a marble edifice. On top of the platform there are obvious traces of a pyre: charcoal, ashes and carbonized seeds recall the funerary custom of *panspermia* or *pankarpia*, mentioned previously in relation with the Archaic necropolis of Salamis. In the debris of the pyre, which was covered with a mound of stones, lay gilded and painted clay perfume bottles (alabastra), the metal mountings from shields, iron spearheads of a Macedonian type, fragments of gold wreaths (in many cases the gold had melted on the pyre and solidified into gold drops) and five heads of unbaked clay, approximately life-size, two of which

124 (*Opposite*) Clay head of a woman with idealized facial characteristics, found on the funerary pyre discovered under a tumulus on the outskirts of the necropolis of Salamis. The tumulus and pyre are believed to have been offered in honour of the last king of Salamis, Nicocreon, and the members of the royal family who committed suicide in 311 BC after having decided not to surrender to King Ptolemy I. This head and several others were erected around the funerary pyre. The male heads betray influences of the style of the Greek sculptor Lysippos. Ht 26 cm. Cyprus Museum, Nicosia (excavated by the Cyprus Department of Antiquities), Tomb 77, no. 870.

124 are portraits of men. Of the other three, all idealized, one is the head of a woman. There are impressions of wood at the back of the heads. Numerous other fragments of heads and bodies of statues have been found, as well as the head of a horse. These statues, which were all erected around the pyre, may have been moulded around wooden poles; some of them wore crowns or wreaths; their bodies were draped with garments. A suggestion has recently been made that there was a wooden structure on top of the platform resembling a small temple, but the only archaeological evidence for this is a number of inconclusive depressions on the platform. The funerary pyre caused the collapse of the wooden poles which supported the clay statues. The latter were baked or hardened by the high temperature of the pyre; some were flattened when they fell. The wooden structure, if it existed, would also have collapsed. At the end of the ceremony the debris was piled up on top of the platform. It is interesting to note that the circular tumulus covering these remains was erected so the platform lay off-centre – a common ploy in such funerary monuments, that was intended to mislead looters. No human skeletal remains were found either on top or underneath the platform. This structure may have been a cenotaph associated with a pyre to purify those who suffered a violent death. The pyre can be dated by the heads, whose style recalls that of the Greek sculptor Lysippos (end of the 4th century BC), as well as by the rest of the material. There is no doubt that such a funerary monument would have been erected in honour of important citizens of Salamis, and Diodoros' account provides a reasonable explanation for it.[4]

It is not certain who erected the cenotaph. The discovery at the very top of the tumulus of a number of stone catapults suggests, when seen in the context of references in Plutarch (*Demetrios*, 17.1–5), that this monument may have been erected at the time of Demetrios Poliorketes in 306 BC. He, having become ruler of Cyprus, ordered the burial of all the war-dead. According to Plutarch this burial was 'splendid'. There is also evidence for burials of ordinary people in simple shaft graves without any gifts, over a large area of the Salamis necropolis and dating from the same period as the cenotaph.[5]

If the interpretation of the archaeological material is correct, then there is a tangible link with the last great king of Salamis, whose valour and virtues were appreciated and honoured even by his enemies.

Another important political personality in Cyprus at this time was King Nicocles of Paphos, a member of the Kinyrad family.[6] They were not favoured by Alexander because they were too preoccupied with their religious functions as high priests of Aphrodite, but after Alexander's death they rose to power again. At the beginning of his reign Nicocles followed a conservative policy. He retained the Cypriot syllabary for inscriptions and coins, whereas at Salamis and elsewhere it was replaced by the Greek alphabet. Later, however, he adopted the Greek alphabet side by side with the syllabary; he introduced the cult of Hera to Paphos, on a par with that of Aphrodite, perhaps purposely: Hera is the goddess of family life, with qualities opposite to those of Aphrodite. It was he who transferred the throne from Palaepaphos to Nea Paphos where he built a temple to Artemis Agrotera.

There is also information concerning King Androcles of Amathus.

He was among those who helped Alexander the Great at Tyre. His cultural policy must have been similar to that of Nicocreon of Salamis. He is reported to have dedicated a gold wreath at Delos between 315 and 310 BC. He is also mentioned in an inscription recently found at Amathus in honour of Aphrodite, who is referred to as Kypria, the goddess of Cyprus.[7]

With the death of Nicocreon and Nicocles, c. 310 BC, the last protagonists of the ancient regime had disappeared and Menelaos remained the sole ruler of Cyprus. This, however, troubled Antigonus who could not bear this strategically important and rich island being in the hands of his rival. Thus, in 306 BC, he instructed his son Demetrios to occupy Cyprus. Demetrios sailed with a considerable force to Cilicia and, having obtained more reinforcements there, disembarked on the northern coast of Cyprus, occupying the towns of Ourania and Karpasia and marching across the Kyrenia mountains to Salamis. Menelaos met Demetrios in battle seven miles outside Salamis, but was defeated and suffered heavy losses: one thousand of his troops were killed and three thousand taken prisoner and deported to Antioch in Syria. Menelaos now prepared to resist a siege, having previously reinforced the walls and asked for help from Ptolemy. Demetrios besieged Salamis, employing his famous machine the 'helepolis' and various other devices which he had invented, such as catapults. The beleaguered Salaminians resisted successfully and even managed to burn Demetrios' machines and kill their users. Demetrios then decided to attack Salamis from the seaward side.

But Ptolemy had responded to Menelaos' appeal for help and had brought a naval force which went first to Paphos, where it was joined by others from cities still loyal to him. He next sailed to Kition where he prepared to face the forces of Demetrios, having sent a message to Menelaos to attack Demetrios' ships from the rear. But Demetrios took all the necessary measures to neutralize the sixty ships of the Salaminians. Thus Ptolemy had to fight this battle alone, with the result that his fleet was annihilated. He set sail for Egypt with its remnants. Demetrios showed his magnanimity towards the prisoners by freeing them, and towards the dead by burying them with honours. It was perhaps then that he erected the cenotaph in memory of Nicocreon, wishing to honour a valiant king who suffered death at the hands of Ptolemy.

For the next twelve years (306–294 BC) Demetrios ruled throughout Cyprus without any difficulty. Indeed Salamis was so loyal to him that he brought the royal treasure of Antigonus there and even settled his mother Stratonice in the city. Ptolemy seems to have recognized the rule of Demetrios, and in 299/8 BC he offered to give him his daughter, Ptolemaïs, in marriage.

The situation changed, however, when Demetrios began neglecting Cyprus and becoming involved in Macedonian affairs. When Ephesos and Miletos were taken away from Demetrios by Lysimachos, and Seleucos invaded Cilicia, it was an opportune moment in 294 BC for Ptolemy to enter an undefended Cyprus; her ships were employed by Demetrios elsewhere and Ptolemy was able to capture Salamis after only a short siege. Demetrios' mother and children were in the city, but were well treated by Ptolemy who sent them to Demetrios laden with gifts.

Thus Ptolemy I Soter, of the dynasty of the Lagids, took possession of Cyprus, and for the next two hundred and fifty years or so it remained part of the Egyptian kingdom, until it became a Roman province in 58 BC. The island was of extreme importance to them. Her proximity to Syria and Anatolia gave her strategic value as an outpost for the protection of Egypt and the East Mediterranean.

During the reign of Ptolemy I Soter and his successor Ptolemy II Philadelphos (285–246 BC) there was peace and prosperity in Cyprus. Philadelphos built new towns there in honour of his wife and sister Arsinoe, whose cult had been established after her death and was identified with the cult of Aphrodite. He first rebuilt the town of ancient Marion, which had been destroyed c. 312 BC, and renamed it Arsinoe. Two other cities were established bearing the same name: one on the east coast between Salamis and Lefkolla, and the other between Palaepaphos and Nea Paphos. Soon, however, Cyprus was involved in all the intrigues and the tumultuous history of the Lagids in Egypt, who were ultimately so weakened as to be unable to face the rising power of Rome. The Romans controlled the fate of the Ptolemaic empire during its final decades, and the Ptolemies sought the favour and approval of Rome for all their actions. The last Ptolemaic ruler in Cyprus was the illegitimate son of Ptolemy Soter II, known simply as King Ptolemy of Cyprus. It was during his reign that the Romans found a pretext to annex Cyprus in 58 BC.

In the Ptolemaic period Cyprus was ruled by a *strategos* who resided at Salamis, at least to the beginning of the first century BC. He governed in the name of the king and was, therefore, always in his confidence and usually a 'relative' of his (the highest rank in the royal court) or a member of the royal family. We have already noted that the first two *strategoi* were Nicocreon, former king of Salamis, and Menelaos. In later years two other titles were added to that of *strategos*: he also became high priest of all the island (*archiereus*) as well as naval commander (*nauarchos*). There must have been a complicated and well-defined administration for financial, economic and other matters. An *antistrategos*, for example, was responsible for the working of the copper mines; two *grammateis* assisted the *strategos* in matters concerning the infantry and naval forces. Almost all high officials were non-Cypriots and were appointed by the king, who held the political, economic and military authority.

The internal governmental structure of certain cities under Ptolemaic rule is known from inscriptions on statue bases erected in honour of kings or high officials, or from decrees.[8] Salamis, for instance, the largest of the Cypriot cities, had a governor (*o epi tis poleos*), archivists (*chreophylakes*) and a director of the gymnasium (*gymnasiarchos*). The latter office was usually held by rich citizens who could provide funds for the maintenance of the gymnasium. Sometimes they were appointed for life. The *agonothetes* organized various contests. Salamis was also the headquarters for the secretariat of the guild of theatrical actors for the whole island.

Paphos, which became the capital of Cyprus in the 1st century BC, had a *boule* (council). There was also a gymnasium in the city and a guild of theatrical actors. Similar institutions existed in other cities. Economic affairs were looked after by an *economos*. Cyprus produced corn, oil, wine and timber. We know that in 238 BC, during a period of famine in Egypt, Ptolemy III Evergetes imported corn from Syria, Phoenicia and Cyprus.

The monetary system for the whole island was unified under the Ptolemies. Between 323 and 306 BC each city minted its own coins according to the system instituted by Alexander the Great, but after 294 BC this prerogative fell to the Ptolemies. During the period 306–294 BC, Antigonos and Demetrios issued their own coinage.

There were mints at Paphos, Salamis and Kition where copper, gold and silver coins were issued. Moulds from the Paphos mint have been discovered in recent years,[9] as well as a hoard of 2484 silver tetradrachms including coins from all three mints and ranging chronologically from 204 to 88 BC.[10]

Two institutions which supported Hellenic culture in Cyprus were the gymnasium and the various theatrical, musical and athletic contests (*agones*). The gymnasia, which existed in all the main cities, trained the minds and the bodies of the young people. Philosophers, poets, historians and medical doctors propagated Greek education and culture. One of the most famous was Zeno of Kition, a philosopher of Panhellenic fame (336–264 BC) and founder of the Stoic philosophy. He was born at Kition but settled in Athens in 315 BC where he developed his philosophy at the *Poekile Stoa* in the Agora of Athens.

Culturally Cyprus was considered part of the Hellenic world, so her cities were included in the lists of those to be visited by the *theoroi*, the heralds of the various Panhellenic Games who were received by the *theorodokoi* in each city, the names of many of whom are known. Cypriots took part in the Panathenaic and Olympic Games. Two Salaminian sculptors, Kallicles and Histiaios, worked at Delphi, and others, also from Salamis, were employed at Lindos on Rhodes.[11]

Despite these connections with the Greek mainland, it should be stressed that the new cultural capital of the Ptolemaic kingdom was no longer Athens but Alexandria. The influence of Alexandrine art is to be seen in the development of Cypriot art during the Hellenistic period, but the main influences are religious. Though the old cults continued – Apollo at Kourion, Aphrodite at Palaepaphos, Zeus at Salamis – two new elements were now introduced: the cult of Egyptian gods, and that of the Ptolemaic rulers. All religious matters were under state control, as the *strategos* was also high priest for all cults.

The Egyptian gods whose cults are attested on the island are Sarapis, Osiris and Isis.[12] By the end of the 4th century BC there was already a temple of Osiris at Paphos, but on the whole the Egyptian gods did not find favour among the Cypriots. The cult of the Ptolemaic rulers was more firmly established, and for its better organization a society known as the *Koinon Kyprion* (Confederation of the Cypriots) was formed.[13]

Although cultural life was centred round the gymnasia, theatres and stadia, very few remnants of these survive, though there is abundant epigraphic evidence for their existence. At Salamis there are traces of the Hellenistic gymnasium below the remains of the Roman one.[14] But

in general, Roman restoration work carried out after repeated earthquakes resulted in the complete destruction of many Hellenistic buildings. The same may be said of the temples, of which only a few remains are visible today: at Nea Paphos there is the rock-cut Temple of Apollo Hylates consisting of two subterranean chambers,[15] and at Salamis there is the peripteral hexastylos Temple of Zeus in the Corinthian order.[16]

The cult of a nymph discovered on top of the Kafizin hill near Nicosia may represent a continuation of a primitive rural cult.[17] Large numbers of inscribed vases were dedicated to her in a rock-cut 'cave', particularly by a certain taxcollector. The inscriptions are engraved in both the Cypriot syllabary and the Greek alphabet. These constitute the latest use of the Cypriot syllabary (3rd century BC) and are further proof of the conservative character of Cypriot culture.

The arts

It has already been noted that sculpture flourished in Cyprus and that Cypriot sculptors were active even outside the island. Though the *koene* Hellenistic styles prevailed, the influence of the Alexandrine and Pergamine schools of sculpture was strong. Two of the most famous Cypriot works produced during this period are the marble statue of Artemis of the 2nd century BC found at Kition,[18] and the limestone head of a woman from Arsos perhaps influenced by portraits of Ptolemaic queens of the 3rd century BC.[19] A marble frieze from Soloi, representing an Amazonomachy and dated to the end of the 4th century BC, attests the existence of Greek temples in this city.[20] The limestone altar from Vitsadha, dated to *c.* 200–150 BC, is decorated with figures in high relief representing the myth of Persephone.[21] The gods are shown in the traditional Greek style as, for example, Athena Promachos.[22] The young man of Mersinaki with a passionate facial expression is characteristic of Pergamene sculpture style,[23] whereas funerary stelae and portrait heads display Alexandrine influences. There must also have been large numbers of bronze, marble and limestone statues of gods and rulers of the Ptolemaic period, of which only the bases with dedicatory inscriptions have survived in public buildings, as in the gymnasium at Salamis and the Temple of Aphrodite at Palaepaphos.[24]

The minor arts and crafts (jewelry, pottery, terracottas) no longer follow local traditions but rather the trends of *koene* Hellenistic art, and Alexandrine styles in particular.

Tomb architecture

In funerary architecture there are several excellent examples of built tombs with large chambers in Larnaca.[25] Tomb 9 has a chamber 4.5 × 3.5 m and 2.5 m high. It is constructed of well-dressed stone blocks with a moulded frieze all around near the ceiling. Along the north side of the chamber is a vaulted recess. Another tomb, known as 'Evangelis Tomb', has a stepped dromos, a vaulted chamber and a vaulted antechamber. Even more elaborate is the so-called 'Copham's Tomb', which consists of a long stepped dromos, a main chamber and a smaller one at the far end.

125

125 (*Opposite*) Limestone head of a female figure from Arsos wearing a veil which leaves the front part of the hair uncovered. The facial expression recalls the style of Hellenistic sculpture of the 3rd century BC. Ht 27 cm. Cyprus Museum, Nicosia, Cyprus Museum Excavations at Arsos, no. 282.

126 Rock-cut tomb with a peristyle around a rectangular courtyard, from the necropolis known as 'The Tombs of the Kings' at Nea Paphos. The architecture of these tombs recalls that of Hellenistic Alexandria. At this time Nea Paphos was the capital of Cyprus and these tombs may have been the burial ground for officials or nobles.

A new type of rock-cut tomb appears at Nea Paphos in this period, with a large rectangular peristyle court; its Doric columns support an entablature with triglyphs and metopes also carved out of the rock; behind the colonnaded porticos there are accesses to rock-cut chambers with numerous burial cavities, or *loculi*.[26] These tombs, known as 'Tombs of the Kings' owing to their extraordinary architecture, must have belonged to high officials or rich Paphians, since they imitate Alexandrian funerary monuments. Of special interest too are the rock-cut tombs of Paphos which are decorated with abstract and floral wall-paintings on their plastered interiors. An elaborate rock-cut tomb with numerous loculi was excavated in the necropolis of Salamis, near the village of Ayios Serghios.[27] Like most monumental Hellenistic tombs this was also used during the Roman period.

The Roman period

After about two hundred and fifty years of Ptolemaic rule in Egypt and Cyprus, the Lagid dynasty was undermined by jealousies, internal strife and intrigue. On several occasions the rising power of Rome had challenged the authority of the Ptolemies over the island. P. Clodius, brother of Appius Claudius Pulcher, was taken prisoner by pirates off the coast of Cyprus in 67 B C.[1] King Ptolemy (who reigned 80 B C–58 B C) was asked to pay the ransom demanded by the pirates, but handed over only two talents. The pirates refused to accept this sum, but nevertheless freed P. Clodius without the ransom. When he went back to Rome, however, he passed a law, known as *Lex Clodia de Cypro*, by which Cyprus became a Roman province. M. Porcius Cato implemented this law in 58 B C and Cyprus accordingly became part of the province of Cilicia. To Ptolemy, the last Lagid king of Cyprus, he offered honours and gifts as a consolation, but Ptolemy preferred to commit suicide, having first refused to surrender the island. The royal treasure was confiscated and part of it was sold for 7000 talents, the rest being transported to Rome. Among the treasures taken home by Cato the proconsul was the statue of the Stoic philosopher Zeno whose philosophy he had studied. Plutarch relates that he took more treasures to Rome from Cyprus than Pompey brought back from his wars.

There is no doubt that the occupation of the island had been planned by the Romans, since she was a valuable possession not only because she could aid their plans for expansion in the East Mediterranean, but also because of her wealth. Cato, as the first proconsul, was accepted by the Cypriots with friendliness. Dio Cassius, the historian, remarks that the Cypriots characteristically preferred to become the friends of the Romans than their slaves. The Romans, on the other hand, ruled remorselessly. When Cicero was proconsul of Cilicia, and therefore responsible for Cyprus, an incident in 51/50 B C gave him the opportunity to show his favour towards the Cypriots. Two Romans, at the instigation of Brutus himself, lent money to the Salaminians at an interest rate of 48 per cent. One of them, who was appointed by Cicero's predecessor as cavalry officer to Cyprus so as to apply pressure on the Salaminians to pay off their debt, shut the members of the Senate into the Senate House and left them there until they agreed to pay. It is said that five of them starved to death. When Cicero took office, a delegation from Salamis visited him in Tarsus and sought his intervention for the reduction of the interest rate to 12 per cent, but this was without success. When Cicero returned to Rome, however, he showed his sympathy towards the Cypriots in a letter written to Sextius

127 Bronze coin of the Roman Emperor Caracalla. On the reverse the Temple of Aphrodite at Palaepaphos is depicted as a tripartite building with a fenced courtyard in front. The central part of the building (which may be the holy-of-holies) shelters a conical object, perhaps a baetyl; on either side there are free-standing pillars topped by horns of consecration. Such coins were issued by the 'Confederation of the Cypriots' which had its headquarters at Palaepaphos.

Rufus, governor of Cyprus between 50 and 48 BC, in which he praises the Cypriots, particularly the Paphians.

For about thirty years after the Roman annexation the island continued to be involved in the interminable bargaining between the remnants of Ptolemaic rule in Egypt on the one hand and Rome on the other, and was temporarily restored to this dynasty in 47 BC. After the battle of Aktion, Anthony and Cleopatra were finally defeated, and in 30 BC Cyprus once more became a Roman province. In 22 BC the island was proclaimed an imperial province and was governed by an ex-praetor with the title of proconsul. It was divided into four districts, namely Paphos, Salamis, Amathus and Lapethos. This division may already have existed at an earlier period. Some of the cities known in the Classical and Hellenistic periods now disappeared, or were absorbed by larger neighbouring centres. The geographer Ptolemy records the following cities of the 2nd century AD: Paphos, Salamis, Amathus, Arsinoe, Chytroi, Karpasia, Kyrenia, Kition, Kourion, Lapethos, Soloi, Tamassos and Tremithus. There were, however, also smaller townships, such as Limenia, Aphrodision, Ourania, Lefkolla, Drepanon, Melabron and others.

Salamis was no longer the capital, having been succeeded by Paphos which was named *metropolis* and found favour with the emperors. After its destruction in the earthquake of 15 BC Paphos was rebuilt by means of a generous grant from Augustus who referred to the city as Sebaste Augusta. Claudius referred to it as Sebaste Claudia Flavia. No doubt the Temple of Aphrodite, that had been founded in Cypro-Archaic times, gave the city prestige and importance not only as a religious centre but also as a source of considerable wealth. When Titus visited Paphos in AD 69 he seized the temple treasures but did not, however, refrain from consulting it about the outcome of his journey to Syria and Palestine.

The establishment of the *Koinon Kyprion* (Confederation of the Cypriots) towards the end of Ptolemaic rule in Cyprus has already been mentioned. Its functions were centred mainly around the cult of the

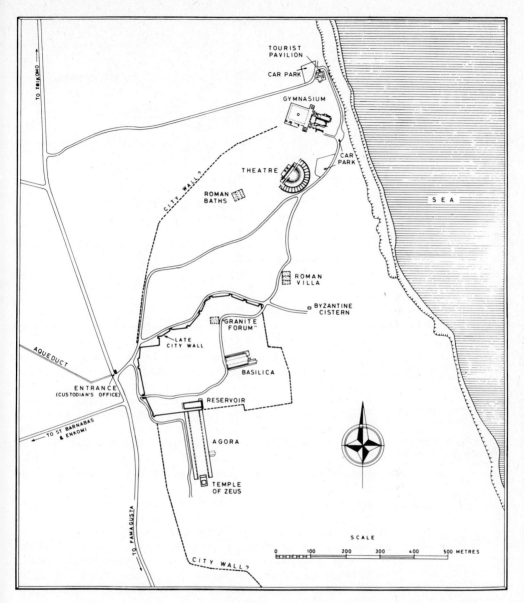

128 The city of Salamis on the east coast was the most prominent city of the island throughout the historical period. Even during the Roman period, when the capital of Cyprus was Paphos, Salamis retained its importance, being the 'emporium of the East'. Excavations carried out by the Cyprus Department of Antiquities from 1952 to 1974 revealed a number of public buildings at the northernmost end of the city, including a gymnasium, theatre, stadium, amphitheatre and public baths. Among other public buildings excavated in the centre of the city were the Temple of Zeus and the Roman forum.

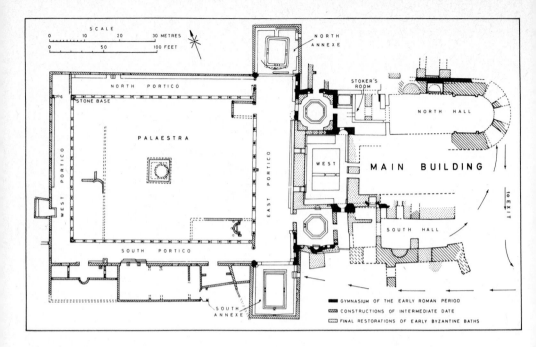

GYMNASIUM OF THE EARLY ROMAN PERIOD
CONSTRUCTIONS OF INTERMEDIATE DATE
FINAL RESTORATIONS OF EARLY BYZANTINE BATHS

129 Plan of the gymnasium at Salamis. It was built during the Augustan period, but was enlarged during the reign of Hadrian and Trajan to include a spacious palaestra and baths, decorated with wall mosaics and frescoes. Its porticoes were adorned with marble statues of Greek gods and heroes. The gymnasium was destroyed during the 4th-century-AD earthquakes, but was rebuilt as baths for the Christian city of Constantia.

Ptolemaic rulers. The Romans retained the *Koinon* but its activities changed radically. Although one of its functions was to attend to the imperial cult, to which was added the members of the imperial family as well as Rome itself, it was now also responsible for religious matters throughout the island and for the control of bronze coinage. The cult of Aphrodite was the most important annual festival in Cyprus and the *Koinon* organized all the festivities and contests on the island. For these festivities the *Koinon* issues special coins with the words *Koinon Kyprion* within a circular laurel wreath. The coins of Vespasian, Titus and Domitian also mention the date of issue. Other members of the confederation, such as Salamis and Kition, celebrated their own festivals.

127 The mint of Paphos issued coins for the whole island, but there were now two types of coins in Cyprus, with representations of both the Temple of Aphrodite and the statue of Zeus Salaminios, suggesting that there was also a mint at Salamis. It is significant that the legends on the coins are in Greek, which was the official language of the *Koinon*.

Salamis

Although Salamis had lost the administrative privileges of the capital, she was nonetheless the richest city on the island, as recent excavations have indicated. This was mainly due to the harbour and the fertile hinterland. Her population was vast and included Greeks, Romans and Orientals, most of them Jews. The latter had begun to settle there since the reign of Ptolemy I and were occupied mainly in the copper trade. They had several synagogues, none of which has yet been excavated. The number of Jewish inhabitants must have increased considerably with the dispersion of the Jews after the destruction of Jerusalem in

AD 70. Although it is difficult to estimate the population of Salamis, an indication is given by the 240,000 who died during the Jewish revolt of AD 116. Even if this figure is considered a gross exaggeration, it is not improbable that the total population of Salamis was around 350,000.

The harbour of Salamis was the emporium of the East. Most of the products of Cyprus, especially copper, timber and corn, were exported from there. The harbour was connected with that of Soloi by an inland route. As is attested from inscriptions, Salamis was connected with all other harbour towns by a coastal route which went completely round the island with the exception of the west coast. There were also properly maintained routes from the north to the south and from the east to the west coasts, as for example from Soloi to Kition.

The basis of cultural life in Salamis was Greek, mainly owing to activities in the gymnasium, the theatre which was built at the time of the Emperor Augustus (27 BC–AD 14) and the other contests.[2] But Romanization is also apparent. The city had spacious baths and an amphitheatre for gladiatorial games. The theatre was adapted in the 3rd century AD to accommodate other contests such as 'naval battles' (*naumachiae*). The statuary which adorned the stoas of the spacious gymnasium and theatre represent Greek gods and heroes, like the Muses and Apollo Musagetes in the theatre, and Heracles, Hera, Demeter and Persephone in the gymnasium. There were, however, also statues of the Roman emperors and numerous decrees in their honour.[3]

128

130 Plan of the theatre at Salamis. It was constructed during the period of Augustus and survived to the end of the Roman period. It was reconstructed for mime productions during the Early Christian period. It was a very large theatre, holding some 15,000 spectators; its orchestra had a diameter of 27 m. The stage building was decorated with marble statues of the Muses and their leader, Apollo. A number of these statues were found in the debris of the stage building during the excavations by the Cyprus Department of Antiquities.

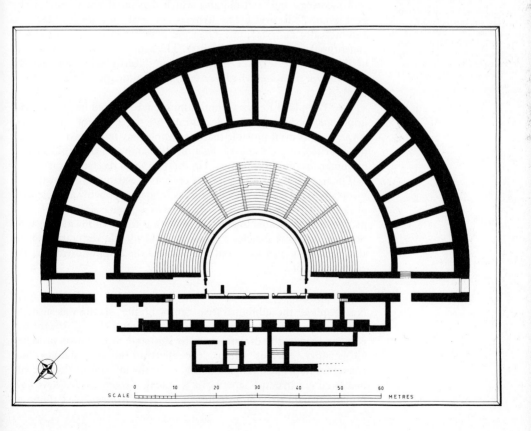

SCALE 0 10 20 30 40 50 60 METRES

Aerial view of the
northernmost part of Salamis
showing the gymnasium on
the left and the theatre on the
right. Between them there are
the remains of an
amphitheatre and stadium.
The site lies under a forest of
mimosas and is covered with
sand. It was abandoned after
the final destruction of the
ancient city by the Arab
invaders in the 7th century
AD.

In one such decree Hadrian is hailed as benefactor of Salamis and
saviour of the world. Trajan also favoured Salamis with various
constructions and reconstructions of public buildings, and particularly
after the earthquakes of AD 77 Greek mythological themes dominate the
wall-paintings and wall-mosaics which decorated the rooms of the
gymnasium.[4] Between the gymnasium and the theatre lay the
amphitheatre and stadium. Thus the northernmost part of the city
constituted a kind of cultural centre. The agora was in the central part
of the town, near the Temple of Zeus. Nearby there was a large
reservoir for the water which was brought by aqueduct all the way from
Chytroi.

The Temple of Zeus Salaminios must have retained its prestige and
importance, since his statue appears on the coins of the *Koinon
Kyprion*; it is even possible that the temple may have played a role in
the activities of the *Koinon* at Salamis. It is known that the old custom
of human sacrifice was practised in this temple to the 1st century AD.

The names of several important citizens of Salamis are known from
inscriptions.[5] Teukros son of Diagoras, who was probably a descendant
of the ancient Teukrid family, is named as a gymnasiarch for life on a
marble altar dedicated to Hermes which was found in the gymnasium.
Servius Sulpicius Pancles Veranianus paid for the restoration of the
statues in the gymnasium and also restored the amphitheatre after the
earthquakes of AD 77.

Nea Paphos

Nea Paphos, the administrative centre of the island, was also the
headquarters of the Roman garrison. In the *Acts of the Apostles* the city
is mentioned as the capital where St Paul and St Barnabas preached
Christianity. Sergius Paulus, the governor of Nea Paphos, was
converted to the new religion in AD 45. Strabo informs us that the city
had 'well constructed sanctuaries' (14.6.3). Recent excavations have
brought to light some of the public buildings of Roman Nea Paphos: an

odeon with an agora in front of it, and next to the odeon what may be an Asklepeion (a temple dedicated to Asklepios).[6] There was also a theatre. Something of the city's importance in Roman times may be seen from the remains of two villas which have been excavated in Nea Paphos.[7] The floors of their rooms and corridors are decorated with polychrome mosaics depicting mostly mythological scenes. The 'House of Dionysos' comprises twenty spacious rooms round two open peristyle courts. There are numerous panels with pictorial compositions on the mosaic floors, including a procession of Dionysos, Hippolytos and Phaedra, hunting scenes, and so on. The second villa is known as the 'House of Theseus' after the best preserved of its mosaic floors which depicts the story of Theseus, the Minotaur and Ariadne, all represented within a circle around which lies the Labyrinth. It was decorated with fine marble sculptures. On account of its size and the quality of its mosaic floors this villa has been identified with the palace of the Roman Governor. It dates to the 3rd century AD, as does the 'House of Dionysos', but it continued in use until the 5th century AD.

132 Floor mosaic in the 'House of Dionysos' at Kato Paphos (excavated by the Cyprus Department of Antiquities). Within a long rectangular panel is illustrated the myth of Dionysos who was entertained by King Ikarios of Attica. The god, in order to thank Ikarios for his hospitality, taught him the art of making wine. Ikarios is shown carrying wine-skins in his cart. While he was passing through the countryside he gave some wine to shepherds to drink. They are shown falling down on the right part of the panel, intoxicated by this new product. The inscription above them says: 'those who drank wine for the first time'. 3rd century AD.

133 Floor mosaic in the 'House of Theseus' at Kato Paphos (excavated by a Polish Mission). The pictorial composition within a circle represents Theseus in the centre with Ariadne, the Minotaur, a personified labyrinth and a personified Crete, with their names written above their heads in Greek. Surrounding the composition is a labyrinth. The mosaic dates to the 3rd century AD.

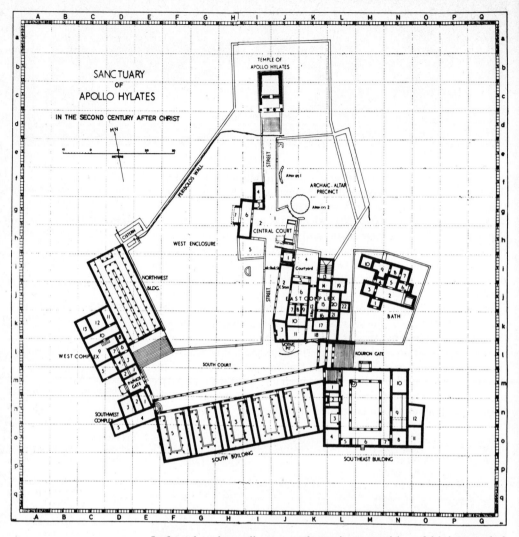

SANCTUARY
OF
APOLLO HYLATES

IN THE SECOND CENTURY AFTER CHRIST

In fact, there is a well-preserved mosaic composition of this later period in one room of the villa, illustrating the first bath of the baby Achilles, with his parents and the Three Fates in attendance.

Kourion

Remains of public buildings and villas are also visible at Kourion. The theatre, which was originally built in the 2nd century BC, was extended and remodelled in the 2nd century AD.[8] About AD 200 it was adapted to accommodate gladiatorial games, an echo of which is seen in the mosaics of the gladiators found in a late-3rd-century-AD peristyle villa within the city limits.[9] A large building complex probably of the 2nd century AD which is currently being excavated may prove to be a gymnasium.[10] The remains of a house of the late 4th or early 5th century AD known as the 'House of Eustolios' has spacious rooms and bathrooms, the floors of which are decorated with mosaics. This is indicative of the continuation of a luxurious life-style at Kourion even towards the end of the Roman period.[11] One room is decorated with a bust of 'Ktisis' (the personification of construction), holding a measuring rod. The mosaic floors of other rooms bear inscriptions, one of which mentions Christ and the advent of the Christian faith.

The most important buildings of Roman Kourion, however, are located outside the limits of the city. The Sanctuary of Apollo Hylates, built originally in the 8th century BC, was considered in the Roman period one of the three chief sanctuaries of Cyprus, and had the privilege of offering *asylum*; the other two were the Temple of Aphrodite at Paphos and the Temple of Zeus at Salamis. The Sanctuary of Apollo Hylates is situated about 2 km west of the ancient city of Kourion;[12] it was enclosed by a wall with two monumental gates, one facing Paphos to the southwest and the other Kourion in the southeast. It was destroyed in the earthquakes of AD 77 but was rebuilt by Trajan (AD 98–117), according to epigraphical evidence. There was a small podium temple, access to which was provided by a paved sacred street with marble-covered platforms on either side and statues, of which only the bases are preserved. Other buildings within the peribolos wall include a small palaestra, baths, dormitories and storerooms. Of particular importance is a recently discovered ring-shaped walkway, which was probably for dancing or processions during ritual performances around a sacred grove. Four pits cut into the bedrock encircled by the walkway may have contained trees such as laurels and myrtles sacred to Apollo.

The stadium of Kourion is 233 m long and situated between the city and the Sanctuary of Apollo. It was built in the 2nd century AD and remained in use until about AD 400. There were seven rows of seats giving a capacity of about 6000 spectators.[13]

Soloi

Soloi was given important monuments, of which several have been uncovered.[14] These include a theatre and a colonnaded paved street which leads to an agora adorned with a marble nymphaeum – a shrine dedicated to a fountain or spring, often richly decorated with sculptures. Among the works of art found in recent years is a life-size bronze head of the time of the Antonines (see ills 135, 136).[15]

The arts

Individual works of art – mainly statues in the gymnasium and theatre at Salamis and in the public and private buildings at Kourion and Nea Paphos – usually imitate Classical Greek prototypes and show influence from the great schools of sculpture of Asia Minor. The 2nd century AD witnessed considerable building activity following the earthquakes of AD 77, and the emperors Trajan and Hadrian aided the cities of Cyprus in the reconstruction and redecoration of public buildings. Of exceptional importance is the more than life-size bronze statue of Septimius Severus (2.08 m high) found near ancient Chytroi.[16] There must have been a great demand for the production of statues of emperors and other high officials, to judge by the number of

134

134 (*Opposite*) Sanctuary of Apollo outside the Kourion city site. The sanctuary was encircled by a wall with two gates connected by roads leading to Paphos and Kourion respectively. At the northernmost part of the site was the Temple of Apollo. The rest was occupied by storerooms, dormitories, a palaestra, baths, etc. The sanctuary, dedicated to Apollo of the Woods (Hylates), was first built in the 8th century BC. Together with the Sanctuaries of Zeus Salaminios and Aphrodite of Paphos, it was considered one of the most important sacred places in Cyprus. Numerous remains (including deposits of votive offerings) of the early periods have been discovered. Most, however, as shown on this plan, date to the 2nd century AD (After Robert Scranton, 'The Architecture of the Sanctuary of Apollo Hylates at Kourion', in *Transactions of the American Philosophical Society* 57 (1967), 76, plan I).

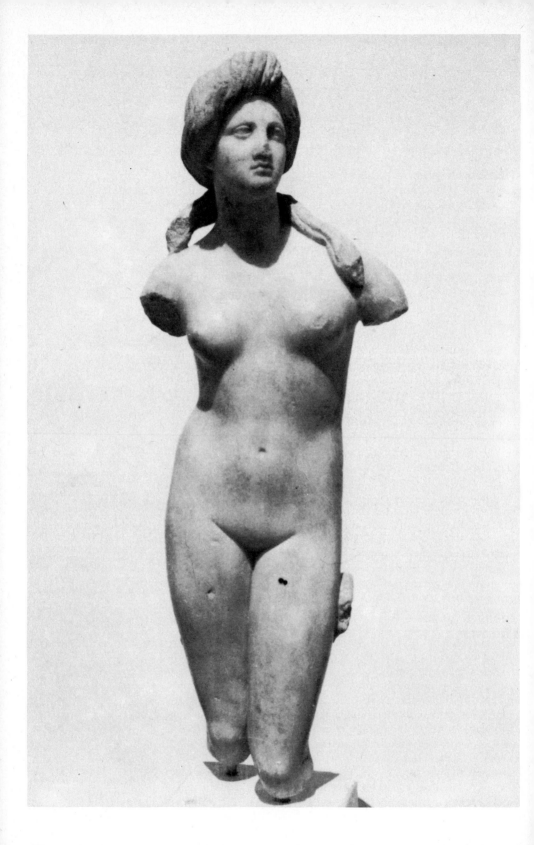

136 Bronze head of a youth from Soloi (excavated by the Canadian Mission). More than life-size, with stylistic characteristics of the Antonine period. Ht 25.5 cm. Cyprus Museum, Nicosia, *c* Canadian Excavations, no. A13.

inscribed statue bases found in sites such as the Sanctuary of Aphrodite at Paphos and the public buildings at Salamis and Kourion. The unfinished limestone statues found near a quarry at Xylophagou in the Larnaca District are indicative of this activity.[17]

As regards other artistic crafts such as jewelry, glass and the ceramic industry, Cyprus shows no divergence from Roman *koene* styles. Large quantities of such objects have been found in tombs throughout the island. These are rock-cut, with long, stepped dromoi and multiple chambers, with *loculi* for clay or stone sarcophagi. Chamber tombs of the Hellenistic and even earlier periods were frequently reused.

The decline of Rome

The very end of the Roman period is represented by buildings constructed after the earthquakes of the 4th century AD. The 'House of

135 (*Opposite*) Marble statue of a nude Aphrodite from Soloi, of the type known as Aphrodite of Cyrene. 1st century AD. Ht 81 cm. Cyprus Museum, Nicosia, no. E510.

Eustolios' at Kourion and the large Roman villas at Paphos are cases in point. The Emperor Constantius II (AD 337–61) did not request the payment of taxes by the inhabitants of Salamis for four years so they could rebuild the city, but they did this on a much smaller scale. The new Christian city was called Constantia after the emperor. Some public buildings outside the walled city of Constantia[18] were also rebuilt by the Christian citizens, as for example the baths of the Roman gymnasium. Marble statues of pagan gods, after being mutilated, were retained to decorate the stoas and the rooms of the baths. This would suggest that Christianity was already firmly established. The palaestra of the gymnasium was paved and used as a meeting place, and the adjacent latrines were screened off by a wall so that their users could not be seen from the palaestra as before, in conformity with the new moral code of the Christian era. There are indications that the theatre was also rebuilt for mime productions as at Constantinople. Salamis demonstrates an interesting transition from paganism to Christianity, with the comfortable life of the pagan period resisting the growth of asceticism.

At Phasoula, a remote site north of Limassol, the message of Christianity was not acceptable so early;[19] on top of a hill, Zeus Labranios ('of the double-axes'?) was still worshipped as late as the 5th century AD and his statues betray stylistic tendencies which are apparent in Coptic art. The main towns, however, are mainly Christian by the beginning of the 5th century AD and were experiencing an arduous recovery after the disastrous earthquakes which marked the end of the ancient world as well as the pagan spirit. St Jerome's account of Paphos may be characteristic of all the ancient cities of Cyprus: 'The city, so celebrated by poets, destroyed by frequent earthquakes, has now only its ruins to show what it once was'.[20] But the fact that the island was included in the Eastern Roman Empire had a profound effect on the course of her historical development. Through contacts with Byzantium, Cyprus was able to retain the Greek language and Greek culture along with her own special cultural traditions.

With the above survey of more than seven thousand years of Cypriot archaeology and history we intended to illustrate some of the most characteristic aspects of the culture of Cyprus. It has always been subject to influences from more powerful neighbours, but never failed in originality and liveliness. Situated at the crossroads between the Aegean and the Near East, the island developed a distinctive culture, the study of which helps us to understand the interrelations of both these great regions of the ancient world. The Cyprus soil always served as a meeting place for cultural ideas. At the same time the island exercised an influence on both the East and the West to a surprising extent, thus contributing substantially to the development of Mediterranean culture.

137 (*Opposite*) Bronze statue of the Roman Emperor Septimius Severus (AD 193–211) standing on its original base. The emperor is represented nude, with an athletic body. The portrait is one of the finest known of Severus. It was found at Kythrea (ancient Chytroi). Ht 208 cm. Cyprus Museum, Nicosia, no. E 549.

Notes

Abbreviations

AA	Archäologischer Anzeiger
AJA	American Journal of Archaeology
BASOR	Bulletin of the American Schools of Oriental Research
BCH	Bulletin de Correspondence Hellénique
BSA	Annual of the British School at Athens
CAH³	Cambridge Ancient History, Third Edition
CRAI	Comptes Rendus de l'Académie des Inscriptions et Belles-Lettres
IEJ	Israel Exploration Journal
JAOS	Journal of the American Oriental Society
JdI	Jahrbuch des Deutschen Archäologischen Instituts
JHS	Journal of Hellenic Studies
Op. Arch.	Opuscula Archaeologica
Op. Ath.	Opuscula Atheniensia
PPS	Proceedings of the Prehistoric Society
RDAC	Report of the Department of Antiquities of Cyprus
SCE	The Swedish Cyprus Expedition Vols I–IV, Lund 1934–72

Chapter I

There follows a selected reading list.

H. W. Catling, 'Patterns of settlement in Bronze Age Cyprus', *Opuscula Atheniensia*, IV(1963), 133ff.

— 'Cyprus in the Neolithic and Chalcolithic periods', *CAH³*, I1, chap. IX(c), 539ff.

E. Gjerstad, *Studies on Prehistoric Cyprus*, 15ff.

J. B. Hennessy, 'Cyprus in the Early Bronze Age', *The Cypriot Bronze Age, some recent Australian contributions to the Prehistory of Cyprus* (Australian Studies in Archaeology, no. 1) 1973, 1f.

G. F. Hill, *A History of Cyprus*, 1ff.

R. S. Merrillees, *Introduction to the Bronze Age Archaeology of Cyprus* (1978), 1ff.

Chapter II

1 E. Stockton, in *RDAC* 1968, 16–19; Vita-Finzi, in *PPS* 39 (1973), 453–4; N. P. Stanley Price, in *Levant* IX (1977), 69.

2 T. F. Watkins, in *RDAC* 1973, 37, 48f.; *idem*, in *Studies presented in memory of Porphyrios Dikaios* (1979), 12–20.

3 P. Dikaios, *Khirokitia*; *idem*, in *SCE* IV:1A, 5–62; N. P. Stanley Price and D. Christou, in *RDAC* 1973, 1–33; N. P. Stanley Price, *Levant* IX (1977), 66–89.

4 E. J. Peltenburg, in *Levant* X (1978), 55ff.; *idem*, in V. Tatton-Brown (ed.) *Cyprus BC*, 15–17.

5 A. Le Brun, yearly reports in V. Karageorghis, 'Chronique des fouilles', *BCH* since 1977.

6 I. A. Todd, in *RDAC* 1979, 13–68; *idem*, in *Journal of Field Archaeology* 6 (1979), 265–300; also annual reports, in V. Karageorghis, 'Chronique des fouilles', *BCH* since 1977; in *Antiquity* no. 213 (1981), 47–51.

7 N. P. Stanley Price, in *Levant* IX (1977), 83f.

8 A. Le Brun, in *RDAC* 1974, 1–23; yearly reports in V. Karageorghis, 'Chronique des fouilles', *BCH* 1971–4; see also Le Brun, *Un site néolithique précéramique en Chypre*.

9 N. P. Stanley Price, in *Levant* IX (1977), 79f.

10 See Watson *et al.*, in *RDAC* 1977, 248.

11 N. P. Stanley Price, in *Levant* IX (1977), 70ff.

12 I. A. Todd, in *RDAC* 1979, pl. II.3.

13 N. P. Stanley Price, in *Levant* IX (1977), 83.

14 For Khirokitia, see J. A. Angel, in Dikaios, *Khirokitia*, 416. For the LBA see J. A. Angel, in Benson, *Bamboula*, 149ff.; J. H. Schwartz, in Karageorghis, *Excavations at Kition I. The Tombs* (Nicosia 1974), 153, fig. 1.

15 P. Dikaios, in *SCE* IV:1A, 63–72; E. J. Peltenburg, in *Studies presented in memory of Porphyrios Dikaios* (1979), 21–45.

16 Y. M. Lehavy, in E. L. Stager *et al.*, *American Expedition to Idalion, First Preliminary Report: Seasons of 1971 and 1972* (1974), 85–102.

17 E. J. Peltenburg, in *PPS* 41 (1975), 17–45.

18 T. F. Watkins, in *RDAC* 1970, 1–10; *idem*, in V. Karageorghis, 'Chronique des fouilles', *BCH* 1966–71; *idem*, in *RDAC* 1973, 34–61.

19 P. Dikaios, *Sotira*; *idem*, in *SCE* IV:1A, 73–105; E. J. Peltenburg, in *Levant* X (1978), 55–74; N. P. Stanley Price, in *Levant* XI (1979), 46–83.

20 P. Dikaios, in *SCE* IV:1A, 106–12.

21 H. W. Catling, in *CAH* I, chap. IX(c); T. F. Watkins, in *RDAC* 1973, 34–61; E. J. Peltenburg, in *RDAC* 1979, 69–99; *Chalcolithic Cyprus and Western Asia* (British Museum Occasional Paper 26, 1981, edited by Julian Reade).

22 P. Dikaios, in *SCE* IV:1A, 113–32.

23 E. J. Peltenburg, in *RDAC* 1979, 69–99, with references to previous literature; *idem*, in *Levant* XIII (1981), 28–50.

24 V. Karageorghis, in *Studi Micenei ed Egeo-Anatolici* XXI (1980), 18–20.

25 E. J. Peltenburg, in *Antiquity* 51 (1977), 140–143.

26 L. Vagnetti, in *Studi Micenei ed Egeo-Anatolici* XXI (1980), 22–72; J. Crouwel, *RDAC* 1978, 33–8.

27 V. Karageorghis, *Prehistoric Cyprus*, pl. 25.

28 See Th. M. Pantazis, in *Studi Micenei ed Egeo-Anatolici* XXI (1980), 68ff.

29 A. Caubet, in *RDAC* 1974, 35–7.

30 V. Karageorghis and L. Vagnetti, in J. Reade, *Chalcolithic Cyprus and Western Asia* (1981), 52–5.

31 V. Karageorghis, *Prehistoric Cyprus*, pl. 27.

32 For a recent study on the transition from the Chalcolithic to the Early Bronze Age, see E. Gjerstad, in *RDAC* 1980, 1–16, with references to previous literature.

Chapter III

1 Gjerstad, *Studies*, 293ff.
2 *Idem*, in *RDAC* 1980, 1–16.
3 See Merrillees, in P. Åström, *Excavations at Kalopsidha and Ayios Iakovos* (*SIMA* II, 1966), 33–4; Merrillees, *Introduction to the Bronze Age Archaeology of Cyprus* (*SIMA* Pocket Book 9, 1978), 29–36.
4 R. S. Merrillees (*SIMA* II 1966), 33–4; Swiny in *Levant* XIII (1981), 84.
5 P. Dikaios, in *SCE* IV:1A, 190f.
6 Hetty Goldman, *Excavations at Gözlü Kule, Tarsus II* (1956), 130, fig. 263, nos 371–78.
7 See note 2 above. For a preliminary report by Dikaios, see *JHS* 65 (1945), 104.
8 All the metal objects are pure copper, tin bronze having yet to be introduced to Cyprus.
9 Recently discussed by Swiny in *Levant* XIII (1981). The sites are Evdhimou-*Trapezi* and Sotira-*Kaminoudhia*. The first season of excavations carried out by Stuart Swiny in 1981 at Sotira-*Kaminoudhia* revealed part of a settlement dated to the 'Philia Culture'. Among the architectural remains there was a sub-rectangular multi-roomed structure built of stone. The pottery associated with it was Chalcolithic Red-on-White and good quality Red Polished ware.
  In the cemetery, where P. Dikaios carried out a limited excavation in 1947, Swiny excavated two tombs (partly disturbed in antiquity), which contained a number of Red-and-Black Polished vessels, dating also to the 'Philia Culture'.
10 E. J. Peltenburg, in *Levant* XI (1979), 9ff.
11 S. Swiny, in *AJA* 84 (1980), 235 and *Levant* XIII (1981), 81.
12 See Dikaios, in *Archaeologia* LXXXVIII (1940), pl. XXXVII:b, right-hand corner of a probable 'Philia Culture' bowl from Arpera, 10 km south-west of Larnaca. See also in connection with 'Philia Culture' and early Cypriot I material in the southeast: R. S. Merrillees, 'Finds from Kalopsidha Tomb 34', in 'Excavations at Kalopsidha and Ayios Iakovos in Cyprus' (*SIMA* II 1966), 31ff.
13 P. Åström, *Excavations at Kalopsidha and Ayios Iakovos* (*SIMA* II, 1966), 14f., 31ff.
14 The controversy is apparent in the *SCE* IV:1A, where both Dikaios (first part) and Stewart (second part) explain their views. For further literature on this problem see H. W. Catling, in *CAH*³ vol. I2, 808ff; J. B. Hennessy and R. S. Merrillees, in *The Cypriot Bronze Age* (Australian Studies in Archaeology no. 1, 1973); R. S. Merrillees, in *RDAC* 1974, 38–41.
15 Cf. Merrillees in *The Cypriot Bronze Age* (Australian Studies in Archaeology no. I, 1973), 58.

16 Cf. Merrillees, in *RDAC* 1974, 38–41.
17 *Idem, Introduction to the Bronze Age Archaeology of Cyprus* (*SIMA* pocket book 9), 36.
18 R. S. Merrillees, in *RDAC* 1977, 44–5.
19 J. B. Hennessy, in J. Birmingham, *The Cypriot Bronze Age*, 8–9; E. J. Peltenburg, in *Levant* XI (1979), 36.
20 J. R. Stewart, 'The Melbourne Cyprus Expedition, 1955', *University of Melbourne Gazette* vol. XIII, no. 1 – April 1957.
21 J. B. Hennessy, 'The Cypriot Bronze Age', (Australian Studies in Archaeology, no. 1, 1973).
22 P. Dikaios, in *Archaeologia* 88 (1940); C. F. A. Schaeffer, *Missions en Chypre 1932–5* (1936); E. and J. Stewart, *Vounous 1937–38* (1950).
23 Recent excavations at Alambra would suggest, however, that the site was mainly occupied in the Middle Cypriot. Cf. Coleman, in *RDAC* 1979, 159–67.
24 See in this connection, T. S. Wheeler, J. D. Muhly, R. Maddin, 'Mediterranean Trade in Copper and Tin in the Late Bronze Age', *Annali* 1979, 139ff.
25 J. D. Muhly, *Copper and tin* (1973).
26 V. Karageorghis, in *RDAC* 1970, 10ff.
27 *Idem, Prehistoric Cyprus* (1976), pl. 74; Veronica Tatton-Brown (ed.), *Cyprus BC*, nos 62–4; J. Karageorghis, *La grande déesse de Chypre*, 33 ff.; Des Gagniers and Karageorghis, *Vases et Figurines*, pl. 60.
28 Des Gagniers and Karageorghis, *op. cit.*, 8, pls 56–8.

Chapter IV

1 For a general survey, see P. Åström, in *SCE* IV:1B, with references to previous literature; D. Frankel, in *The Cypriote Bronze Age* (Australian Studies in Archaeology, no. 1, 1973), 23–43.
2 J. R. Stewart, in *Op.Ath.*4 (1962), 197ff.
3 Cf. R. S. Merrillees, in *RDAC* 1977, 33–50; Diane Lynn Saltz, *ibid.*, 51–70.
4 H. W. Catling, in *Op.Ath.*4 (1963), 139ff.
5 S. Swiny, in *Levant* XIII (1981), 51–87.
6 Ellen Herscher, in *RDAC* 1980, 17–21.
7 E. J. Coleman, in *RDAC* 1977, 71–9; John E. Coleman and Jane A. Barlow, in *RDAC* 1979, 159–67 and yearly reports, in V. Karageorghis, 'Chronique des fouilles', *BCH* since 1977.
8 K. Nicolaou, *Ancient Monuments of Cyprus* (1968), pl. V.
9 David Frankel, *Middle Cypriote White Painted Pottery* (1974).
10 V. Karageorghis, in *RDAC* 1970, 10–13; David Frankel and Angela Tamvaki, in *Australian Journal of Biblical Archaeology* Vol. II no. 2 (1973), 39–44.
11 V. Karageorghis, *Prehistoric Cyprus*, pl. 98.
12 *Ibid.*, pl. 83.
13 *BCH* 99 (1975), 812, fig. 21.
14 V. Karageorghis, *Prehistoric Cyprus*, pl. 99.
15 H. W. Catling, in *Op.Ath.*4 (1963), 139–41.

Chapter V

1 R. S. Merrillees, in *Op.Ath*.6 (1965), 139–48; *idem*, in *Levant* III (1971), 56–79; P. Åström, in *SCE* IV:1C; Merrillees, in *RDAC* 1977, 33–50.

2 Karageorghis and Masson, in *Studi Ciprioti e rapporti di scavo* I (Biblioteca di antichità cipriote, 1971), 237–47.

3 H. W. Catling, in *Op.Ath*.4 (1963), 142–6.

4 H. W. Catling, in *Archaeologia Viva* I (1969), 81–8; P. Åström, in the same volume, 73–80; J. D. Muhly, *Copper and Tin* (1973), 192–9; *idem*, in *The Coming of the Age of Iron* (ed. T. Wertime and J. D. Muhly, 1980), 40–6; H. W. Catling, *CAH* II³, part 2, 213–15.

5 Trude Dothan and A. Ben-Tor, in *IEJ* 22 (1972), 201–8.

6 For two recent studies, with references to previous literature, see E. Masson, in *Acts of Symposium Cyprus–Crete*, 134–8 and, in the same volume, L. Godart and Anna Sacconi, 128–33.

7 Sir Arthur Evans, *Palace of Minos* IV.2 (1935), 758–63.

8 E. Masson, in *AA* 1976, 139–65.

9 V. E. G. Kenna, in *Acts of the Mycenaean Symposium*, 290–4; in the same volume E. Porada, 260–73; more recently E. Porada, in *Acts of Symposium Cyprus–Crete*, 111–20; in the same volume, I. Pini, 121–7; *idem*, in *JdI* 95 (1980), 77ff.

10 Y. Lynn Holmes, in *The Archaeology of Cyprus, Recent Developments*, 90–120.

11 See recently H. Georghiou, in *Levant* XI (1979), 85–100; L. Hellbing, *Alasia Problems* (1979). R. S. Merrillees opposes the identification of Alashiya with Cyprus in *Praktika tou Protou Diethous Kyprologikou Synedriou* I (1972), 201–19; see also H. W. Catling, in *CAH* II³, part 2, 201–5.

12 O. Masson, in *Kadmos* 12 (1973), 98f.

13 P. Åström, in *Studies presented in memory of Porphyrios Dikaios* (1979), 46–8.

14 Found in 1980, deciphered by M. J. Leclant.

15 J.-C. Courtois, in *Florilegium Anatolicum, Mélanges offerts à Emmanuel Laroche* (1979), 89–95.

16 Andreas Müller-Karpe, in *AA* 1980, 303f.

17 H.-G. Buchholz, in *AA* 1973, 301f., fig. 4a–b, with references in n. 20.

18 P. Åström and E. Masson in *RDAC* 1981, 98f.

19 V. Karageorghis, *Excavations at Kition* I, 60; *idem*, in Åström *et al.*, *Hala Sultan Tekké* I (1976), 87.

20 V. Karageorghis, *Kition, Mycenaean and Phoenician discoveries in Cyprus* and yearly reports, in V. Karageorghis, 'Chronique des fouilles', *BCH* since 1976.

21 P. Åström, in *SCE* IV:1C, 1–11; Sarantis Symeonoglou, in *The Archaeology of Cyprus, Recent Developments*, (ed. Noel Robertson, 1975), 61–75.

22 P. Åström, in *SCE* IV:1C, 11–30.

23 William Johnstone, in *Alasia* I (1971), 51–122; O. Pelon, *Tholoi, Tumuli et Cercles Funéraires* (1976), 427–32.

24 O. Pelon, *op. cit.*, 432.

25 P. Åström, in *SCE* IV:1C, 44–51; J.-C. Courtois, in V. Karageorghis, 'Chronique des fouilles', *BCH* 90 (1966), 344–5; O. Pelon, *op. cit.*, 430, n. 7.

26 Emily T. Vermeule, *Toumba tou Skourou*.

27 *Idem*, in *Acts of the Mycenaean Symposium*, 25–33. In a recently published article H. Catling has suggested that the appearance of Late Minoan I pottery at Morphou-*Toumba tou Skourou* may be due to the settlement at this site of some Theran refugees who evacuated their island after the eruption of the volcano at the end of the 16th century BC (H. W. Catling, *Cyprus and the West 1600–1050 B.C.*, Ian Sanders Memorial Lecture, 1980, 12).

28 P. E. Pecorella, in *Acts of the Mycenaean Symposium*, 19–24; *idem*, *Le tombe dell età del Bronzo Tardo della Necropoli a mare di Ayia Irini* (1977).

29 R. S. Merrillees, *Trade and Transcendence*, 5–8. For a recent account of objects found in the Aegean, particularly Thera, in the 16th and 15th centuries BC, see H.-G. Buchholz, in *Thera and the Aegean World* II (ed. C. Doumas, 1980), 227–40.

30 R. S. Merrillees, *Trade and Transcendence*, 32ff. For White Slip ware, see Mervyn R. Popham, in P. Åström, in *SCE* IV:1C, 431–71.

31 Emily T. Vermeule, *Toumba tou Skourou*.

32 Michal Artzy, F. Asaro and I. Perlman, in *JAOS* 93 (1973), 446–61; *idem*, in *IEJ* 25 (1975), 129–35.

33 R. S. Merrillees, *Trade and Transcendence*, 43ff.; M. Artzy and F. Asaro, in *RDAC* 1979, 135–50.

34 Cf. P. Åström, in *Acts of the Mycenaean Symposium*, 122–7. Catling has recently suggested that some of the Mycenaean pottery found in Cyprus reached the island indirectly from certain major Near Eastern clearing houses, such as Ras Shamra (Catling, *Cyprus and the West 1600–1050*, 17–19). This suggestion, apart from being based on a hypothetical argument that Levantine merchants acted as middlemen in the trade of Cypriot copper, disregards the fact that wherever we find Mycenaean pottery in the Near East, this is usually found together with large quantities of Cypriot pottery. The natural explanation would be that the Mycenaean pottery from the Aegean harbours reached Cyprus first and was then distributed to the Near Eastern centres, together with the Cypriot pottery.

35 Emily Vermeule and V. Karageorghis, *Mycenaean Pictorial Vase-painting* (1981).

36 H. W. Catling and others, in *RDAC* 1978, 70–90.

37 V. Karageorghis, *Mycenaean Art from Cyprus* (1968); H.-G. Buchholz and V. Karageorghis, *Altägäis und Altkypros*, 148–73; see also V. Tatton-Brown (ed.) *Cyprus BC*, 37–60, with bibliographical references.

38 V. Karageorghis, in *RDAC* 1979, 209.

39 V. Desborough, *Acts of the Mycenaean Symposium*, 79; for a general historical survey of the Late Cypriot III period, see P. Åström, in *SCE* IV:1D, 775–81.

40 For a recent account, see Nancy K. Sanders, *The*

Sea Peoples (1978).

41 E. Porada, in Dikaios, *Enkomi*, 801f.

42 For the historical interpretation of the stratigraphical phenomena at Enkomi, see Dikaios, *Enkomi*, 514ff.

43 *Ibid.*, 841ff.

44 V. Karageorghis, *Excavations at Kition* I, 87, no. 339; cf. also F. Schachermeyr, *Die Mykenische Zeit und die Gesittung von Thera (Die ägäische Frühzeit*, 2, 1976), 291f.

45 V. Karageorghis, in P. Åström *et al.*, *Hala Sultan Tekké* I, 76, Tomb 1 no. 16.

46 V. Karageorghis, *Nouveaux Documents* (1965), 176.

47 *SCE* I, pl. 88.

48 H. W. Catling, in *Op.Ath.* 2 (1955), 21–36.

49 Emily Vermeule and V. Karageorghis, *op. cit.*; D. Anson, in *RDAC* 1980, 109–27.

50 H.-G. Buchholz, in *Bronze Age Migrations in the Aegean* (ed. R. A. Crossland and Ann Birchall, 1974), 179–87; J.-C. Courtois, in C. F. A. Schaeffer, *Ugaritica* VII (1978), 364, with bibliographical references.

51 V. Karageorghis, in *BCH* 104 (1980), 786–8; and *BCH* 105 (1981).

52 For a short report on excavations conducted by P. Dikaios, see his *Enkomi*, 907–11.

53 F.-G. Maier, in *Acts of the Mycenaean Symposium*, 69–78. A suggestion has been made recently by Catling that the Achaean refugees, before reaching Cyprus after the turmoil of Mainland Greece at the end of the 13th century BC, went to the Levantine coast and established themselves for a while, before turning to Cyprus (Catling, *Cyprus and the West 1600–1050 B.C.*, 24). We find this suggestion rather hazardous and undocumented. The fact that the culture of Cyprus in the 12th century BC is still a mixed culture, the result of amalgamation, is due to the slow process of colonization. The Achaean refugees found a flourishing local culture in the island which could not be obliterated overnight.

54 Only a summary report has been published by A. Furumark, in *Op.Ath.* 6 (1965), 99–116.

55 *Ibid.*, 101.

56 Dikaios, *Enkomi*, 911f.

57 Cf. *Acts of the Mycenaean Symposium*, 79.

58 *Ibid.*

59 *Op. cit.*, 81f.

60 For short accounts, see H. W. Catling, in *CAH* II³, part 2, 209–13; Desborough, *The Last Mycenaeans*, 196–205; Dikaios, *Enkomi*, 523ff.

61 L. Hellbing, *op. cit.*, 67–9, 73–6; Dikaios, *op. cit.*, 533f.

62 Dikaios, *op. cit.*, 514ff.; various articles in *Alasia* I (1971); yearly reports in V. Karageorghis, 'Chronique des fouilles', *BCH*, 1958–74.

63 H. W. Catling, in *RDAC* 1975, 50–3.

64 C. F. A. Schaeffer, in *Alasia* I, 567–73 and dépliant IV.

65 Dikaios, *op. cit.*, 514ff.; see recently, Nancy K. Sanders, *The Sea Peoples* (1978), 145–6, 151–2.

66 V. Karageorghis, in *Athens Annals of Archaeology* 4 (1971), 106; F.-G. Maier, in *RDAC* 1979, 170.

67 J.-C. Courtois, in *Alasia* I, 151–362.

68 J. du Plat Taylor *et al.*, *Myrtou-Pigadhes*, 103ff.; Jennifer Webb, in *RDAC* 1977, 113–32.

69 F.-G. Maier, in *Neue Forschungen in Griechischen Heiligtümern* (1976), 234.

70 Cf. R. D. Barnett, in *Temples and High Places in Biblical Times* (1981), 10–20.

71 *Ibid.*, 219–38.

72 See note 5 above.

73 V. Karageorghis, in *Harvard Theological Review* 64 (1971), 261–70; A. Hermary, in *BCH* 103 (1979), 734ff.

74 M. Loulloupis, in *Acts of Mycenaean Symposium*, 225–44.

75 Colin Renfrew, in *Antiquity* 52 (1978), 7ff.

76 Dikaios, *op. cit.*, 527–30; K. Hadjiioannou, in *Alasia* I, 32–42.

77 C. F. A. Schaeffer, in *Alasia* I, 505ff.

78 H. W. Catling, in *Alasia* I, 15–32.

79 See note 10 above. See also Amihai Mazar, *Excavations at Tell Qasile* I (*Qedem* 12, 1980), 78–86.

80 Jennifer Webb, in V. Karageorghis, *Two Cypriote sanctuaries of the end of the Cypro-Archaic period* (1977), 74–80.

81 V. Karageorghis, in *Antiquity* 50 (1976), 125–9.

82 *Idem*, in *CRAI* 1976, 229–45.

83 A. Caubet and J.-C. Courtois, in *RDAC* 1975, 43–9.

84 C. F. A Schaeffer, *Enkomi-Alasia*, 97–9.

85 *BCH* 102 (1978), 885, fig. 10.

86 V. Karageorghis, *Prehistoric Cyprus*, pl. 182.

87 H. W. Catling, *Cypriote Bronzework*, 157ff., pls 23–4.

88 *Ibid.*, 150f., pl. 19, f-h.

89 V. Karageorghis, *Excavations at Kition* I, 90, pls 85, 163, no. 283, 286.

90 P. Åström, in V. Karageorghis, 'Chronique des fouilles', *BCH* 104 (1980), 783, fig. 61.

91 V. Karageorghis, in *RDAC* 1979, 203–8, with references to relevant literature.

92 In the Royal Ontario Museum, Canada, illustrated in an exhibition catalogue, *Ladders to Heaven*, by Suzanne M. Heim (1979), 16f., pl. 14 and cover.

93 V. Karageorghis, in *RDAC* 1972, 72–4.

94 P. Åström, in V. Karageorghis, 'Chronique des fouilles', *BCH* 104 (1980), 783, fig. 62.

95 J.-C. Poursat, *Les ivoires mycéniens* (1977), 159–65.

96 *Ibid.*, 201, 240.

97 *Ibid.*, 161f.

98 V. Karageorghis, *Excavations at Kition* I, 91, pls 87, 170, no. 354.

99 Marguerite Yon, in *Studies presented in memory of Porphyrios Dikaios* (1979), 63–75; cf. Claude Baurain, in *BCH* 104 (1980), 571–80.

100 H.-G. Buchholz and V. Karageorghis, *Altägäis und Altkypros*, nos 1785–7.

101 E. Porada, in Dikaios, *Enkomi*, 801–10, pls 183–4, 322–3.

102 F. Schachermeyr, *Die Mykenische Zeit und die Gestittung von Thera*, 286–96; Dikaios, *Enkomi*, 324–6.

103 F. Schachermeyr, *op. cit.*, 296ff.; *idem*, *Acts of Symposium Cyprus-Crete*, 204–14.

104 V. Karageorghis, *Nouveaux Documents* (1965), 250, pl. 28.2.

105 F. Schachermeyr, *op. cit.*, 301–3.

106 Marguerite Yon, in *Acts of Symposium Cyprus-Crete*, 241–8, with relevant literature; V. R. d'A. Desborough, *The Greek Dark Ages*, 49–57.

107 V. Karageorghis, in *Scripta Minora 1977–1978 in honorem Einari Gjerstad* (1977), 5–31.

108 V. Karageorghis, in *BCH* 94 (1970), 27–33.

109 J.-C. Courtois, in *Alasia* I, 287–308.

110 Angeliki Pieridou, *O protogeometrikos rythmos en Kypro*; V. Karageorghis, *Alaas, a protogeometric cemetery in Cyprus* (1975), 46ff.

111 V. Karageorghis, in *RDAC* 1967, 17f., no. 7, pl. I.

112 V. Karageorghis and des Gagniers, *La céramique chypriote de style figuré*, Supplément (1979), 1–2.

113 J.-C. Courtois, in *Alasia* I, 268–72.

114 See note 110 above.

115 V. Desborough, *op. cit.*, 49–63, 141f., 316f.; *idem*, in *Acts of the Mycenaean Symposium*, 79–87.

116 For a 12th-century BC iron dagger from Kition, see *BCH* 102 (1978), 917, fig. 84; for a general survey, see James D. Muhly, in Wertime and Muhly, *The Coming of the Age of Iron* (1980), 47–53; *ibid.*, section on Cyprus by A. Snodgrass, 335–74; Desborough, *op. cit.*, 314ff.

117 See note 115 above; also Jane C. Waldbaum, *From Bronze to Iron* (1978), with references to previous literature.

118 See J. D. Muhly and A. Snodgrass, in Wertime and Muhly, *The Coming of the Age of Iron* (1980), chaps 2 and 10 respectively.

Chapter VI

1 For an admirable account on the Early Iron Age, see Gjerstad, in *SCE* IV:2, 428ff.

2 V. Desborough, in M. Popham *et al.* (eds) *Lefkandi* I, 357ff.

3 M. Popham and L. H. Sackett, *ibid.*

4 Marie-José Chavane, in '*Testimonia Salaminia*' (*Salamine de Chypre* X, 1978), 31ff. with references to previous literature. For other foundation legends, see also Michel Fortin, in *Mélanges d'Etudes Anciennes offerts à Maurice Lebel* (1980), 25–44.

5 T. B. Mitford and I. K. Nicolaou, *Inscriptions from Salamis*, 11f.; see recent reference to a Teukros of the 4th century BC by Stephen G. Miller, in *Hesperia* 48 (1979), 78f.

6 Gjerstad, in *Op.Arch.* 3 (1944), 107–23.

7 Marguerite Yon, in *Salamine de Chypre, Histoire et Archéologie* (Colloques Internationaux du CNRS, no. 578, 1980), 71–80.

8 J. Pouilloux, in *CRAI* 1966, 232–56.

9 Marguerite Yon, *La tombe T. I.*

10 V. Desborough, in *Salamine de Chypre, Histoire et Archéologie*, 111–14.

11 Gjerstad, in *SCE* IV:2, 431ff.

12 George McFadden, in *AJA* 58 (1954), 131–42.

13 J. L. Benson, *The Necropolis of Kaloriziki*, 23f.

14 V. Karageorghis, in *CRAI* 1980, 122–36, for the 1979 campaign. There was a second campaign in 1980 (see *idem*, 'Chronique des fouilles', *BCH* 105 (1981), 991f.

15 H. W. Catling, in Popham *et al.*, *Lefkandi* I, 237.

16 W. F. Albright and E. Gjerstad, in *BASOR* 130 (1953), 22–6; Judy Birmingham, in *AJA* 67 (1963), 32–6.

17 Gjerstad, in *SCE* IV:2, 431–5.

18 V. Desborough, in *JHS* 77 (1957), 212–19; see also M. Popham *et al.*, *Lefkandi* I, 358.

19 *Ibid.*

20 Coldstream, *Geometric Greece*, 33.

21 *Idem*, in *Praktika tou Protou Diethnous Kyprologikou Synedriou* I (1972), 15–22; *idem*, *Geometric Greece*, 45–52.

22 Desborough, *The Greek Dark Ages*, 225ff., 306ff.; Coldstream, *Geometric Greece*, 99–102; Boardman, *The Greeks Overseas*, 35–8.

23 F. Canciani, in *Acts of Symposium Cyprus-Crete*, 269–78; Boardman, *op. cit.*, 56ff.

24 V. Karageorghis, *Kition, Mycenaean and Phoenician*, 95ff.; Coldstream, *Geometric Greece*, 65–8; Boardman, *op. cit.*, 35–8.

25 *RDAC* 1979, 234–54.

26 Marguerite Yon, in V. Karageorghis, 'Chronique des fouilles', *BCH* since 1978.

27 See bibliography and discussion, in V. Karageorghis and M. G. Guzzo-Amadasi, *Fouilles de Kition III. Les inscriptions phéniciennes* (1977), 149ff.

28 V. Karageorghis, in *Rivista di Studi Fenici* 3 (1975), 161–7.

29 V. Karageorghis, in E. Gjerstad, *Greek Geometric and Archaic Pottery found in Cyprus* (1977), 61f., pl. I.1,4.

30 Coldstream, *Geometric Greece*, 68.

Chapter VII

1 Cf. N. Coldstream, *Greek Geometric Pottery* (1968), 318–20; E. Gjerstad, in *Acta Archaeologica* 45 (1974), 107–23.

2 Coldstream, *Geometric Greece*, 59f.

3 V. Karageorghis, in *RDAC* 1980, 132–5.

4 Karageorghis and des Gagniers, *La céramique Chypriote de style figuré* I, 6–11.

5 Hill, *A History of Cyprus*, 103f.

6 For a recent synthesis, see J. M. ªBlazquez, *Tartessos y los origines de la colonizacion fenicie en Occidente* (1975).

7 Juan Pedro Garrido Roiz and Elena M. Orta Garcia, *Excavaciones en la Necropolis de 'La Joya' Huelva* II (1978), supplemented by personal information from Prof. Garrido Roiz.

8 Gjerstad, in *SCE* IV:2, 449ff.

9 Cf. recently Claude Baurain, in *BCH* 105 (1981).

10 V. Karageorghis, in *BCH* 91 (1967), 202–45.

11 V. Karageorghis, *Excavations in the Necropolis of Salamis* IV, 11ff., T.50A.

12 E. Gjerstad, in *Studies presented in memory of Porphyrios Dikaios*, 89–93; V. Desborough, *ibid.*, 119–22, who favours a gift-exchange idea.

13 Excavations of 1979–80, unpublished.

14 Peter P. Kahane, in Noel Robertson, *The Archaeology of Cyprus, Recent Developments* (1975), 151–210.

15 Boardman, *The Greeks Overseas*, 44.

16 V. Karageorghis, in *The Proceedings of the Xth International Congress of Classical Archaeology* I (1978), 361–8.

17 V. Karageorghis, *Excavations in the Necropolis of Salamis* I and III; *idem*, *Salamis* (New Aspects of Antiquity, 1969).

18 V. Karageorghis, *Excavations in the Necropolis of Salamis* II.

19 O. Masson, in *BCH* 95 (1971), 295–304.

20 Gerhard Schmidt, *Kyprische Bildwerke aus dem Heraion von Samos* (Samos VII, 1968).

21 Ulf Jantzen, *Ägyptische und Orientalische Bronzen aus dem Heraion von Samos* (Samos VIII, 1972), 43–6.

22 Boardman, *op. cit.*, 74.

23 Karageorghis and des Gagniers, *La céramique chypriote de style figuré* I.

24 V. Karageorghis, in *Studies presented in memory of Porphyrios Dikaios* (1979), 124–8.

25 Gjerstad, in *SCE* IV:2, 466ff.

26 Gjerstad, in *SCE* IV:2, 467.

27 V. Karageorghis, in *Athens Annals of Archaeology* 6 (1973), 145–9.

28 V. Karageorghis, *Excavations in the Necropolis of Salamis* III, 123–7.

29 O. Masson, *Inscriptions Chypriotes Syllabiques*, 199, no. 188.

30 Gjerstad, in *SCE* IV:2, 356f.

31 *Ibid.*, 361ff.

32 E. Gjerstad *et al.*, *Greek Geometric and Archaic pottery found in Cyprus*, passim.

33 L. Lerat, in *BCH* 104 (1980), 102.

34 J. H. and S. H. Young, *Terracotta figurines from Kourion in Cyprus* (1955).

35 See Diana Buitron, in *The Walters Art Gallery Bulletin*, Dec. 1980, vol. 33, no. 3.

36 Gjerstad, in *SCE* II, 671ff.; *idem*, in *SCE* IV:2, 1, 3f.

37 V. Karageorghis *et al.*, *Cypriote Antiquities in the Medelhavsmuseet, Stockholm* (1977), pl. XXVIII.1.

38 Gjerstad, in *SCE* IV:2, 467.

39 *Ibid.*, 5ff.

40 O. Masson, in *Eléments orientaux dans la réligion grecque ancienne* (1960), 129–42; K. Hadjiioannou, *I archaia Kypros eis tas ellinikas pigas* vol. 4 (i) and (ii) (1980), 27ff.

41 V. Karageorghis, in *RDAC* 1977, 178–201.

42 K. Hadjiioannou, in *Alasia* I, 33–42.

43 Veronica Wilson, in *Levant* VII (1975), 77–103.

44 V. Karageorghis, *Two Cypriote sanctuaries of the end of the Cypro-Archaic period*, 17–45.

45 *Ibid.*, 49–65.

46 V. Karageorghis, in *RDAC* 1978, 156–96.

47 *Idem*, in *RDAC* 1979, 289–315.

48 Marguerite Yon, *Un depôt de sculptures archaïques*.

49 H.-G. Buchholz, yearly reports, in V. Karageorghis, 'Chronique des fouilles', *BCH* 1971–80; *idem*, in *AA* 1973, 295–387, in *AA* 1974, 554–614, and in *AA* 1978, 155–230.

50 For preliminary reports on recent excavations, see *BCH* 1978–80.

51 A. Caubet, in *Studies presented in memory of Porphyrios Dikaios* (1979), 94–118; Philip P. Betancourt, in *AJA* 75 (1971), 427f., pls 91–2.

52 V. Karageorghis, in *Proceedings of the Xth International Congress of Classical Archaeology* I (1978), 367; H.-G. Buchholz, in *AA* 1973, 322ff., and *AA* 1974, 578ff.

53 *BCH* 103 (1979), 723, figs 100, 101.

54 V. Karageorghis, *Kition, Mycenaean and Phoenician*, 142–4.

55 Gjerstad, in *SCE* IV:2, 471ff.

56 J. L. Myres, *Handbook of the Cesnola Collection of Antiquities from Cyprus* (1914), 203, no. 1285. For a study of a limestone kouros head from Salamis dated to *c.* 490 BC, see Nicole Weil, in *Anthologie Salaminienne* (*Salamine de Chypre* IV, 1973), 57–79.

57 *Ibid.*, 226ff., no. 1364.

58 A. Pierides, *Jewellery in the Cyprus Museum* (1971), 27f., pl. XV.

59 Karageorghis and des Gagniers, *La céramique chypriote*, vol. II, 91–3.

60 Gjerstad, in *SCE* IV:2, 472f.

61 *Ibid.*, 473.

62 *Ibid.*, 460f.

63 *Ibid.*, 475ff. For a historical account of this and the subsequent periods, see also G. F. Hill, *A History of Cyprus* I, 111ff.

64 For a short account, see F.-G. Maier, *Archäologie und Geschichte: Ausgrabungen in Alt-Paphos* (1973).

Chapter VIII

1 Kyriakos Nicolaou, *The Historical Topography of Kition*, pl. XXI.1.

2 Gjerstad, in *SCE* IV:2, 488; C. C. Vermeule, *Greek and Roman Cyprus* (1976), 15f., fig. 1.

3 C. C. Vermeule, *op. cit.*, 16f., fig. 2.

4 V. Wilson, in *RDAC* 1969, 56–63.

5 E.g. C. C. Vermeule, *op. cit.*, figs 20, 23.

6 E.g. Gjerstad, in *SCE* IV:2, fig. 54, 10–12.

7 J. Boardman, in E. Porada (ed.), *Ancient Art in Seals* (1980), 111.

8 G. F. Hill, *Catalogue of the Greek Coins of Cyprus* (1904).

9 O. Masson, *Inscriptions Chypriotes Syllabiques*, 235 ff.

10 V. Karageorghis, in L. Kahil and C. Augé, *Mythologie Gréco-Romaine, Mythologies Périphériques, Etudes d'Iconographie* (Colloques Internationaux du CNRS, no. 593, 1981), 79ff.

11 Gjerstad, in *SCE* IV:2, 485.

12 C. C. Vermeule, *op. cit.*, 35f., fig. 26.
13 Gjerstad, in *SCE* IV: 2, pl. XVI.1.
14 V. Karageorghis, in *RDAC* 1977, 178–201.
15 Anita Walker and L. Stager, in V. Karageorghis, 'Chronique des fouilles', *BCH* 103 (1979), 708–10.
16 D. M. Lewis and Ronald S. Stroud, in *Hesperia* 48 (1979), 180–93.
17 V. Karageorghis and C. C. Vermeule, *Sculptures from Salamis* I (1964), 8–10, pls VIII–IX; E. Vermeule, *op. cit.*, 48, 60 n. 6.
18 For a historical account of the period after the death of Evagoras, see C. Spyridakis, *Kyprioi vasileis tou 4ou ai. p. x (411–311/10 p. x.)*; also Hill, *A History of Cyprus* I, 156ff.

Chapter IX

1 See chapter VIII, note 16, above. Diodorus XX.21. V. Karageorghis, *Excavations in the Necropolis of Salamis* III, 201ff.
2 See opposing view by I. Michaelidou-Nicolaou, in *Kypriakai Spoudai* 1976, 24f.
3 V. Karageorghis, *Excavations in the Necropolis of Salamis* III, 128ff.
4 For suggestions about a hypothetical monument above the funerary platform, see Catheryn Leda Cheal, *Early Hellenistic architecture and sculpture in Cyprus: Tumulus 77 at Salamis* (Brown University PhD 1978).
5 V. Karageorghis, *Excavations in the Necropolis of Salamis* IV, 27.
6 I. Michaelidou-Nicolaou, in *Kypriakai Spoudai* 1976, 15–28.
7 M.-C. Hellmann and A. Hermary, in *BCH* 104 (1980), 259–66; A. Hermary, in *RDAC* 1980, 231f.
8 For the various officials of Salamis mentioned in inscriptions, see Mitford and Nicolaou, *Inscriptions from Salamis*; see also references in K. Hadjiioannou, *I archaia Kypros eis tas ellini kas pigas* vol. 4 (i) and (ii) (1980); T. B. Mitford, in *Aegyptus* 33 (1953–4), 80–90; *idem*, in *BSA* 56 (1961), 1–41.
9 K. Nicolaou, in I. Nicolaou and O. Mørkholm, *A Ptolemaic Coin Hoard* (Paphos I, 1976), 9f.; *idem*, *Praktika tou Protou Diethnous Kyprologikou Synedriou* I, 121–4.
10 *Ibid.*
11 Hadjiioannou, *op. cit.*, *passim*; J. Pouilloux, in *RDAC* 1975, 111–21; *idem*, in *RDAC* 1976, 158–67; *Etudes Déliennes* (*BCH*, Suppl. I, 1973), 399, 413; I. Michaelidou-Nicolaou, in *Kypriakai Spoudai* 1961, 63–72.
12 K. Nicolaou, *ibid.*, 849–53; Alfred Westholm, *The Temples of Soloi* (1936); I. Michaelidou-Nicolaou, in *Hommages à Maarten J. Vermaseren* II (1978), 891–6.
13 Hadjiioannou, *op. cit.*, *passim*; Hill, *A History of Cyprus* I, 178, 185, 233f.
14 V. Karageorghis, *Salamis in Cyprus*, 167f.
15 Jolanta Mlynarczyk, in *RDAC* 1980, 239–52.
16 G. Argout, O. Callot, B. Helly, in *RDAC* 1975, 122–41.
17 T. B. Mitford, *The Nymphaeum of Kafizin. The Inscriptions of a Hellenistic Cult site in Central*

Cyprus (1979).
18 K. Nicolaou, *The Historical Topography of Kition*, 220, with references.
19 C. L. Cheal, *Early Hellenistic Architecture and Sculpture in Cyprus: Tumulus 77 at Salamis* (Brown University PhD 1978), 78–98; C. C. Vermeule, *Greek and Roman Cyprus*, 53, pl. II. 14.
20 O. Vessberg, in *SCE* IV:3, 95, pl. XIII. 1; C. C. Vermeule, *op. cit.*, 47, pl. II. 3.
21 H. Cassimatis, in *RDAC* 1976, 178–84.
22 V. Karageorghis, in *RDAC* 1977, pl. 64, no. 125.
23 Vessberg, *op. cit.*, 87, pl. VIII.
24 Mitford and Nicolaou, *op. cit.*; T. B. Mitford, in *BSA* 56 (1961), 1–41.
25 V. Karageorghis, *Kition, Mycenaean and Phoenician*, 144ff.
26 S. Hadjisavvas, in V. Karageorghis, 'Chronique des fouilles', *BCH* since 1978.
27 V. Karageorghis, *Excavations in the Necropolis of Salamis* IV, 27ff.

Chapter X

1 Hill, *A History of Cyprus*, 226ff.
2 V. Karageorghis, *Salamis in Cyprus*, 185ff.
3 V. Karageorghis and C. C. Vermeule, *Sculptures from Salamis* I (1964) and II (1966).
4 V. Karageorghis, *Salamis in Cyprus*, pls XVII, 123, 124; *Idem*, *Cyprus* (Archaeologia Mundi, 1968), pls 173–6.
5 Mitford and Nicolaou, *Inscriptions from Salamis*.
6 K. Nicolaou, in *Mélanges offerts à Kazimierz Michalowski* (Warsaw, 1966), 561–602; also yearly reports in V. Karageorghis, 'Chronique des fouilles', *BCH* 1963–78; *idem*, in *RDAC* 1963, 56–72; *idem*, *Ancient Monuments of Cyprus* (1968), 28ff.
7 K. Nicolaou, *ibid.*; A. W. Daszewski, annual reports, in V. Karageorghis, 'Chronique des fouilles', *BCH* since 1966; *idem*, in *RDAC* 1968, 1970, 1972, 1976; *idem*, *La mosaïque de Thesée* (Nea Paphos II, 1977).
8 R. Stillwell, in *Proceedings of the American Philosophical Society* 105 (1951), 37–78.
9 M. Loulloupis, in *RDAC* 1971, 86–116.
10 D. Christou, in V. Karageorghis, 'Chronique des fouilles', *BCH* since 1979.
11 J. F. Daniel, in *The University Museum Bulletin* 7 (1938), 30ff.
12 R. L. Scranton, in *Transactions of the American Philosophical Society* 57,5 (1967), 3–85; Diana Buitron, David Soren, in *Muse* 13 (1979), 22–31.
13 V. Karageorghis, in *BCH* 84 (1964), 369–71.
14 J. des Gagniers, Annual reports, in V. Karageorghis, 'Chronique des fouilles', *BCH* 1965–75; *idem et al.*, in *RDAC* 1967, 50–8.
15 L. Kahil, in *Antike Kunst* 19 (1976), 41–50; C. C. Vermeule, *Greek and Roman Cyprus*, 84.
16 C. C. Vermeule, *op. cit.*, 86, fig. 21.
17 C. C. Vermeule, in *Studies presented in memory of Porphyrios Dikaios* (1979), 189–93.
18 V. Karageorghis, *Salamis in Cyprus*, 197f.
19 V. Karageorghis, in *BCH* 83 (1959), 343.
20 Hieronymus, *Vita S. Hilarionis eremitae*, 42.

Select bibliography

Acts of the International Archaeological Symposium 'The Mycenaeans in the Eastern Mediterranean'. Nicosia 1973.

Acts of the International Archaeological Symposium 'The relations between Cyprus and Crete ca. 2000–500 BC'. Nicosia 1979.

ÅSTRÖM, P. *The Middle Cypriote Bronze Age. The Late Cypriote Bronze Age. The Swedish Cyprus Expedition*, vol. IV(IB–ID). Lund 1972.

BENSON, J. L. *The Necropolis of Kaloriziki* (*SIMA* XXXVI). Göteborg 1976.

BENSON, J. L. *Bamboula at Kourion.* Pennsylvania, Philadelphia 1972.

BOARDMAN, J. *The Greeks Overseas* (revised ed.). London 1980.

BUCHHOLZ, H.-G. and KARAGEORGHIS, V. *Altägäis und Altkypros.* Tübingen 1971.

CATLING, H. W. *Cypriot Bronzework in the Mycenaean World.* Oxford 1974.

CATLING, H. W. 'Cyprus in the Neolithic and Bronze Age Periods', *Cambridge Ancient History* (3rd revised ed. vols I–II pts 1–2). Cambridge 1970–71.

COLDSTREAM, J. N. *Geometric Greece.* London 1977.

DESBOROUGH, V. R. d'A. *The Last Mycenaeans and their Successors.* Oxford 1964.

DESBOROUGH, V. R. d'A. *The Greek Dark Ages.* London 1972.

DES GAGNIERS, J. and KARAGEORGHIS, V. *Vases et figurines de l'Age du Bronze à Chypre.* Quebec 1976.

DIKAIOS, P. 'The Excavations at Vounous-Bellapais in Cyprus, 1931–32', *Archaeologia* 88 (1938), 1ff.

DIKAIOS, P. *Khirokitia.* Oxford 1953.

DIKAIOS, P. *Sotira.* Philadelphia 1961.

DIKAIOS, P. *A guide to the Cyprus Museum* (3rd ed.). Nicosia 1961.

DIKAIOS, P. *Enkomi.* Excavations 1948–1958. Vols I–III. Mainz 1969 and 1971.

DIKAIOS, P. and STEWART, J. R. *The Stone Age and the Early Bronze Age in Cyprus. The Swedish Cyprus Expedition*, vol. IV(IA). Lund 1962.

FURUMARK, A. *The Mycenaean Pottery. Analysis and Classification.* Stockholm 1941.

GJERSTAD, E. *Studies on Prehistoric Cyprus.* Uppsala 1926.

GJERSTAD, E. *The Swedish Cyprus Expedition. Finds and Results of the Excavations in Cyprus 1927–1931.* Vols I–III. Stockholm 1934–1937.

GJERSTAD, E. *The Cypro-Geometric, Cypro-Archaic and Cypro-Classical Periods. The Swedish Cyprus Expedition*, vol. IV(2). Stockholm 1948.

GJERSTAD, E. 'The phoenician colonization and expansion in Cyprus', *Report of the Department of Antiquities Cyprus*, 1979, 230ff.

GJERSTAD, E. 'The origin and chronology of the Early Bronze Age in Cyprus', *Report of the Department of Antiquities Cyprus*, 1980, 1ff.

HADJIIOANNOU, K. *I archaia Kypros eis tas Ellinikas pigas.* Vols 1–3. Nicosia 1971–7. Vol. 4 was published in 1980.

HILL, G. F. *A Catalogue of the Greek Coins of Cyprus in the British Museum.* London 1904.

HILL, G. F. *A History of Cyprus.* Cambridge 1940.

KARAGEORGHIS, J. *La grande déesse de Chypre et son culte.* Lyon 1977.

KARAGEORGHIS, V. *Nouveaux documents pour l'étude du Bronze Récent à Chypre* (Etudes Chypriotes III). Paris 1965.

KARAGEORGHIS, V. *Excavations in the Necropolis of Salamis*, I–IV. Nicosia 1967, 1970, 1973 and 1978.

KARAGEORGHIS, V. *Salamis in Cyprus. Homeric, Hellenistic and Roman* (New Aspects of Antiquity). London 1969.

KARAGEORGHIS, V. *The civilization of Prehistoric Cyprus.* Athens 1976.

KARAGEORGHIS, V. *Kition. Mycenaean and Phoenician discoveries in Cyprus* (New Aspects of Antiquity). London 1976.

KARAGEORGHIS, V. *Two Cypriote sanctuaries of the end of the Cypro-Archaic period.* Rome 1977.

KARAGEORGHIS, V. *The goddess with uplifted arms in Cyprus* (Scripta Minora 1977–8). Lund 1977.

KARAGEORGHIS, V. and others *Excavations at Kition*, I–III. Nicosia, 1974, 1976, 1977.

KARAGEORGHIS, V. and DES GAGNIERS, J. *La céramique chypriote de style figuré* (Biblioteca di Antichita Cipriote 2). Roma 1974.

LE BRUN, A. *Un site néolithique précéramique en Chypre: Cap Andreas-Kastros.* Paris 1981.

MAIER, F. G. 'Excavations at Kouklia, Palaepaphos', *Report of the Department of Antiquities Cyprus* (since 1967).

MASSON, E. *Cyprominoica. Répertoires, documents de Ras Shamra. Essais d'interprétation* (*SIMA* XXXI:2). Göteborg 1974.

MASSON, O. *Les Inscriptions Chypriotes Syllabiques* (Etudes Chypriotes I). Paris 1961.

MERRILLEES, R. S. *Trade and Transcendence in the Bronze Age Levant* (*SIMA* XXXIX). Göteborg 1974.

MITFORD, T. B. and NICOLAOU, I. *The Greek and Latin Inscriptions from Salamis* (Salamis vol. 6). Nicosia 1974.

NICOLAOU, K. *The Historical Topography of Kition.* Göteborg 1976.

PELTENBURG, E. J. 'Ayios Epiktitos Vrysi, Cyprus', *Proceedings of the Prehistoric Society* 41 (1975), 17ff.

PELTENBURG, E. J. 'The Sotira culture', *Levant* X (1978), 55ff.

PELTENBURG, E. J. 'Lemba Archaeological project, Cyprus, 1976–77', *Levant* XI (1979), 9ff.

PELTENBURG, E. J. 'The Prehistory of West Cyprus: Ktima Lowlands. Investigations 1976–1978', *Report of the Department of Antiquities Cyprus*, 1979, 69–99.

PELTENBURG, E. J. 'Lemba, Archaeological project, Cyprus, 1978', *Levant* XII (1980), 1ff.

PELTENBURG, E. J. 'Lemba Archaeological project, Cyprus, 1979', *Levant* XIII (1981), 28ff.

PIERIDOU, A. *O protogeometrikos rythmos en Kypro*. Athens 1973.

POPHAM, M. R. and others (ed.) *Lefkandi I. The Iron Age*. London 1979–80.

SALAMINE DE CHYPRE. Histoire et Archéologie. Colloque du CNRS no. 578, Lyon 1317 mars 1978. Paris 1980.

SCHACHERMEYR, F. *Die ägäische Frühzeit*. Band 2: *Die Mykenische Zeit*. Wien 1976.

SCHAEFFER, C. F. A. *Enkomi-Alasia* I. Paris 1952.

SCHAEFFER, C. F. A. and others *Alasia* I. Paris 1971.

SJÖQVIST, E. *Problems of the Late Cypriote Bronze Age*. Stockholm 1940.

SPYRIDAKIS, C. *Kyprioi vasileis tou 4ou ai. p. x* (411–311/10 p. x.). Nicosia 1963.

STANLEY PRICE, N. P. 'Khirokitia and the initial settlement of Cyprus', *Levant* IX (1977), 66ff.

TATTON-BROWN, V. (ed.) *Cyprus BC. 7000 years of history*. London 1979.

TAYLOR, J. DU PLAT, *et al.*, *Myrtou-Pighades*. Oxford 1957.

TODD, I. A. 'Vasilikos valley project, 1977–1978: an interim report', *Report of the Department of Antiquities Cyprus*, 1979, 13ff.

VERMEULE, E. *Toumba tou Skourou. The mound of darkness*. Boston 1974.

VERMEULE, E. and KARAGEORGHIS, V. *Mycenaean Pictorial vase-painting*. 1981.

VESSBERG, O. and WESTHOLM, A. *The Hellenistic and Roman periods in Cyprus. The Swedish Cyprus Expedition*, vol. IV(3). Stockholm 1956.

WATKINS, T. 'Some problems of the Neolithic and Chalcolithic period in Cyprus', *Report of the Department of Antiquities Cyprus*, 1973, 34ff.

YON, M. *La Tombe T.I du XIe s. av. J.-C. (Salamine de Chypre II)*. Paris 1971.

YON, M. *Un dépôt de sculpture archaïques (Salamine de Chypre V)*. Paris 1974.

Sources of the illustrations

Illustrations are reproduced by courtesy of the Department of Antiquities, Cyprus, unless otherwise credited below or acknowledged in the captions:
Dr A. Le Brun 4, 7, 10; Professor Ian Todd 5, 6; Dr E. Peltenburg 14, 18, 25; Professor J. Carpenter 37, 38; Professor J. Coleman 39; Professor E. Vermeule 49, 50; Medelhavsmuseet, Stockholm 108, 121.

Index